AF556236

UNDERSTANDING EVOLUTIONARY BIOLOGY

UNDERSTANDING EVOLUTIONARY BIOLOGY

By

Dr. Rajeev Tyagi

Deptt. of Chemistry

M.M.H. Post Graduate College

Ghaziabad (U.P.)

(India)

DISCOVERY PUBLISHING HOUSE PVT. LTD.

NEW DELHI-110 002

Published by:
Tilak Wasan
DISCOVERY PUBLISHING HOUSE PVT. LTD.
4831/24, Ansari Road, Prahlad Street
Darya Ganj, New Delhi-110002 (India)
Phone: +91-11-23279245, 43764432
Fax: +91-11-23253475
E-mail: parul.wasan@gmail.com
info@discoverypublishinggroup.com
discoverypublishinghouse@gmail.com
web: www.discoverypublishinggroup.com

First Edition: 2011
ISBN: 978-81-8356-857-9

Printed at:
Mehra Offset Press
Delhi

PREFACE

The present title "*Understanding Evolutionary Biology*" provides a structured approach to learning by covering all the important topics in a uniform, systematic format. The book has been comprehensively designed incorporating recent advances in this fast moving field. It is written to provide accessible information on evolutionary biology in compact form for undergraduate students in biology and related life sciences. It will be useful for both beginning students and those who are more advanced. In addition, busy lecturers who require a quick reference compendium will find it useful, particularly for tutional planning. Simple, yet hopefully clear figures and tables are provided throughout the book.

The over-riding goal of this book, and indeed of the whole *Understanding series,* is to present the essential information concering microbiology in a compact, readily accessible form which leads itself to student learning and revision. The convergence of various approaches has generated a rich panorama of detail, the significance of which we are still attempting to unraval. The present text has been written as an introduction to this rapidly growing field.

To make the work more comprehensive and informative, the author has consulted many authoritative books, research journals, abstracts, monographs etc., so there can be no claim to originality except in the manner of treatment.

The author expresses his thanks to his friends and colleagues whose continue inspirations have initiated him to bring out this book.

The author expresses his gratitude to Mr. Wasan and staff of M/s Discovery Publishing House Pvt. Ltd. for their whole hearted co-operation in the publication of this book.

In the mean time, the author will remain sincerely responsible for any shortcomings of the book and be grateful to the readers for their suggestions and constructive criticism for the continuous betterment of the book. He takes this opportunity to appeal to the readers to send their suggestions straightaway to his Publisher.

Author

CONTENTS

Chapter 1: CELLS AND TISSUES

The biological world is made up of a great variety of shapes and sizes of organisms, and all of them operate according to the principle of molecular economy discussed in other chapter of this book. Furthermore, the use of biomolecules is done in a most orderly way. This should immediately suggest that the physical organization of living things also is orderly, and it is.

When molecular processes are carried out in small volumes, the surface-to-volume ratio is low and favours an easy exchange between the surface and the interior. Large volumes have relatively small surfaces proportionately unless the volumes are spread out in very thin films. But a man, or a whale, has a seemingly large surface-to-volume ratio.

Thus we look to see how life can be organized so that there is orderly biomolecular activity, so that there is an adequately low surface-to-volume ratio, and so that large size can be accounted for.

We find that the universal unit which accommodates to these three points is the cell. The cell is the structural and functional unit of life. The cell concept was stated over 135 years ago.

It was not possible to determine that all organisms are composed of cells and cell products until the development of the microscope because of the small size of most plant and animal cells, which vary in size from 10 to 100 μm. [1 μm = 0.001 millimeter (mm), or approximately 1/25,000 inch.]

THE IMPORTANCE OF THE CELL CONCEPT

In addition to being the unit of structure and function of living matter, the cell is the unit of heredity, pathology, and reproduction. While there is no such thing as a typical cell, there are two basic cell types. One type, the *prokaryotic* cell, is represented by bacteria and blue-green algae; it lacks a well-defined nucleus.

The other is the *eukaryotic* cell, which has a well-defined nucleus. The following discussion concentrates on eukaryotic cells found in all animals. In relating cellular structure and function, four common kinds of

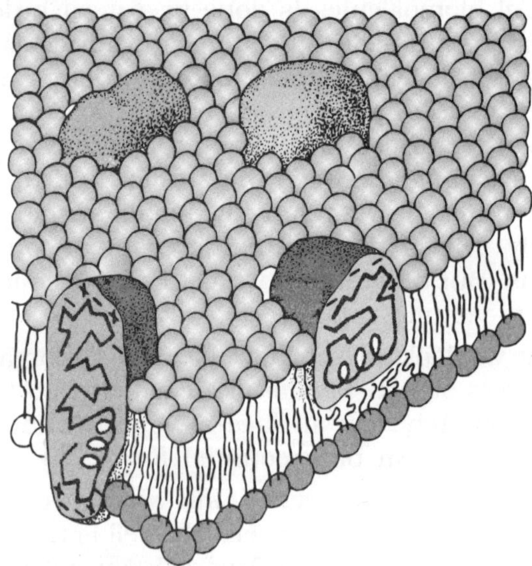

Figure 1.1: Fluid mosaic model of cell membrane. Globular proteins bearing various charges are viewed as distributed throughout the plane of the membrane. They are partially or cross-sectionally embedded in a matrix of two layers of phospholipids.

functions are discussed to give a broad description of cells.

1. Cells regulate the orderly movement of materials into and out of themselves, and involve the limiting boundary to the cell, the *plasma membrane.*
2. Cells use energy in doing work, synthesizing and degrading molecules, and exporting products. This is accomplished chiefly in the *cytoplasm.* The cytoplasm consists of many parts and, with a few exceptions, makes up most of the mass of the cell.
3. Cells operate under the control of the hereditary material, DNA (deoxyribonucleic acid), which is localized in the *nucleus.* The details of the chemistry of the genetic material are discussed in other chapters of this book.
4. Related to DNA is the function of cell duplication. Usually two cells arise from one cell by cell division. In eukaryotic cells, especially, a complex set of structures is involved in cell division.

PHYSICAL AND FUNCTIONAL PARTS OF A CELL

Historically, the *cell wall,* which is actually a nonliving product of the plant cell, was the first structure to be identified. However, cell walls will be omitted in this discussion for they do not exist with animal cells.

A typical cell has three major parts. The outer, limiting *cell* or *plasma membrane* regulates the traffic of materials into and out of the cell. Inside the plasma membrane is the *cytoplasm,* composing the bulk of most cells and being the site where energy is used and substances are produced.

The *nucleus* is usually centrally placed and contains the genetic material that is transmitted from one cell generation to the next; it instructs and regulates the activities of the cytoplasm.

The Membranes

Plasma Membrane

This important membrane bounds the living substance of the cell, although it is invisible with the light microscope. Its capacity to regulate selectively the movement of materials between the cell and the surroundings helps determine whether a cell is living or dead.

There have been numerous models of membrane structure. Presently receiving strong support is the *fluid mosaic* hypothesis. This hypothesis assumes that there are two layers of phospholipids. Attached to, embedded in, or crossing the phospholipids are highly folded globular proteins. This model is especially attractive because of the growing recognition of specific receptor sites on membranes.

For example, in animal cells, membranes are known to have specific receptor sites for the pancreatic hormone, insulin, or the dendritic ends of neurons have specific receptor sites for transmitter substances produced by the axon of an adjacent neuron.

Also, this model permits greater flexibility of form and function of the membrane than some of the other models of membrane structure. Some cells secrete materials that lie between cells. These materials are sometimes called cementing substances. However, the precise conditions that lead to cellular adhesion are not fully understood and are actively being investigated.

Movements of Materials

Two physical processes involved in the movement of materials are *diffusion* and osmosis, which provide methods for examining the role of the plasma membrane. Diffusion is the movement of molecules, atoms, and ions from regions of their high concentration to regions of their low concentration. For instance, the odor of an open container of pungent chemical or perfume will spread through the surroundings.

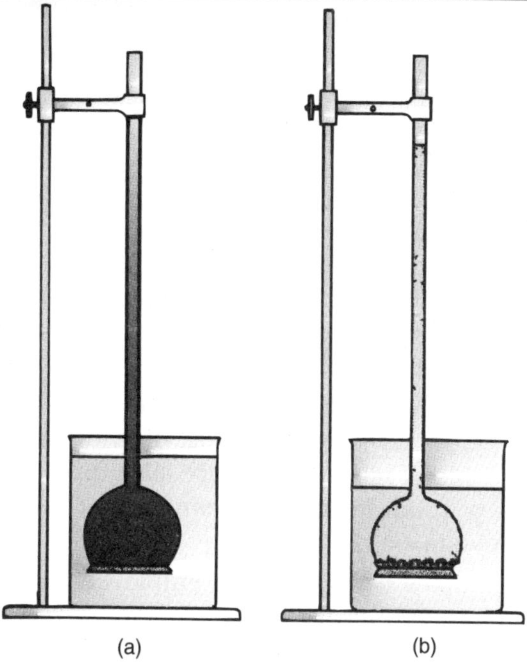

(a) (b)

Figure 1.2: Osmometer (a) Beginning of the experiment. (b) After two hours.

Because of the kinetic energy of the ions and molecules this is accomplished by their tendency to distribute equally in space. Diffusion is an important phenomenon to living cells and organisms because they are composed primarily of water and most cells are surrounded by a watery medium of some proportions.

Nearly every student at some time has seen the classical demonstration of diffusion where coloured crystals are carefully placed in the bottom of a stationary test tube or glass cylinder and observed over a span of time.

The water adjacent to the crystals first becomes coloured and the colour spreads until it is equally distributed throughout the container. The principle of diffusion can be related to membranes and their roles. A membrane that allows all molecules to move across it is freely permeable.

Living cell membranes are differentially permeable and allow some molecules to diffuse across the membrane but retard or prevent others from moving across. Some nonliving membranes can serve as models of semipermeability.

For instance, an artificial system consisting of two solutions of different concentrations separated by a membrane impermeable or semipermeable to the substances in solution, but freely permeable to water, results in a diffusion of water to the solution of lower concentration of water.

This net movement of water that tends to equalize the concentrations on each side of the membrane is called osmosis. Figure anywhere else in this chapter illustrates a reliable kind of osmometer for demonstrating osmosis.

The principles of osmosis are employed in the kitchen

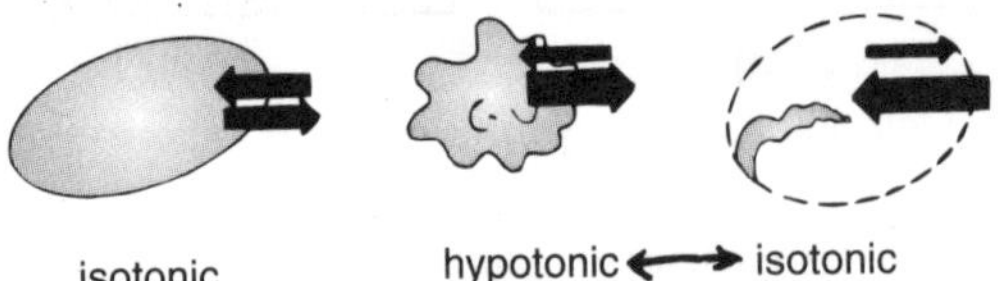

Figure 1.3: Behavior of red blood cells in isotonic, hypertonic, and hypotonic selections.

in soaking vegetables in water to make them crisp, or in wilting lettuce with vinegar. The following laboratory experimentation illustrates the role of the plasma membrane or identifies its existence.

Osmosis

Red blood cells are excellent osmometers. To maintain their normal shape outside the blood stream, they must be kept in an *isotonic* solution, one where the concentration of water and solutes is the same as that of the cytoplasm with water leaving and entering the cell at the same rate.

A solution of 0.9 percent NaCl is isotonic for mammalian red blood cells. (An isotonic salt solution is not necessarily a *balanced salt solution;* the latter contains proper proportions of the salts found in the cytoplasm, for instance, sodium, potassium, magnesium, and calcium.)

If red blood cells are placed in distilled water, they will tend to swell and burst because distilled water is *a hypotonic* solution (lesser solute concentration) with the concentration of water greater than that within the cell.

In contrast to this, if red blood cells are placed, for example, in a 10 percent salt solution, they very quickly lose water, shrink, and appear wrinkled. This salt solution is *hypertonic* (greater solute concentration) for the red cells as the concentration of water is less than that in the cytoplasm.

The term applied to the shrinking of animal cells is *crenation.* It is obvious from the foregoing statement that cells, such as red blood cells, may be killed by being surrounded by hypotonic or hypertonic solutions.

It should also be obvious that in handling living tissues, such as blood in blood banks, during surgery, and so forth, it is important to maintain isotonic conditions. More dynamic controls on the movement of materials across membranes exist, however, and are referred to as transport mechanisms.

Another role of membranes is associated with the second messenger concept. These are briefly discussed here to relate them to the activities of membranes that will be discussed in numerous places.

Active Transport

This is a process acting across membranes such as plasma membranes, mitochondria, and the endoplasmic reticulum. Molecules move across the membrane against a diffusion gradient, from the lower to the higher concentration, and employ the energy of ATP as a "pump."

This sometimes concentrates materials to over 1000 times that of its surroundings. It is believed that molecules are moved in active transport by forming loose combinations with proteins that release the molecules at the other surface of the membrane.

A number of experiments demonstrate the need for ATP, one being that the lowering of oxygen concentration halts active transport because ATP production is reduced.

THE ROLE OF CYCLIC AMP

Cell membranes have specific receptor sites for hormones on their surfaces. Many hormones function through their action on receptor sites. The major differences in the actions of these hormones is in the presence or absence of receptor sites specific for each specific hormone. When these sites are activated by

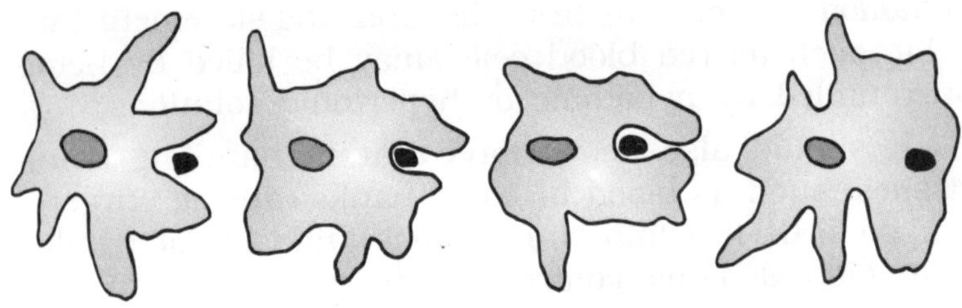

Figure 1.4: Diagram of phagocytosis by an amoeba.

specific hormones, an inactive enzyme in the membrane, adenylate cyclase, is activated and released toward the interior of the cell.

There it catalyzes the hydrolysis of ATP to a monophosphate having the peculiarity that its persisting phosphate is bonded to the pentose sugar at two points, thus cyclic 3', 5'-adenosine monophosphate *(cyclic AMP* or cAMP). Cyclic AMP then activates a series of intracellular enzymes that produce specific cellular activities.

Thus when epinephrine (adrenalin) reacts with an epinephrine receptor site on the outside of the cell membrane, adenylate cyclase is activated. This causes the ATP to produce cyclic AMP that, in turn, activates a series of enzymatic activities that release glucose from glycogen for delivery into the blood stream.

Or, if a thyroidstimulating hormone is received on the surface of the cells of the thyroid gland, the cAMP activates the secretion of thyroxin. The Nobel Prize for physiology and medicine was given in 1971 to Earl W. Sutherland, Jr., for the work that led to the generalization that primary chemical messengers, hormones located extracellularly, can activate a second messenger, CAMP, located intracellularly, to produce specific reactions in accordance with the stimulus of the primary messenger.

Until this generalization was formulated, most inquiries had labored with the question of how some hormone molecules could enter the cell and control the direction of the cell's activities. Recently, other cyclic monophosphates have been shown to be important at the cell surface.

For instance, cyclic guanosine monophosphate *(cGMP)* has been shown to function in an antagonistic way to cAMP. The roles of these second messengers will be discussed elsewhere.

Cell Surface Configurations

While appearing to be smooth under the light microscope, three aspects of the free surfaces of cells are noteworthy. Cells specialized for absorption such as those lining the intestine and composing kidney tubules show thousands of minute cylindrical processes, *microvilli.*

Also, active movement of the surface of the cell, energy-expending processes, enclose substances from the surroundings into vesicles or vacuoles; such enclosing activity is called en*docytosis* and is of two forms.

The first, *pinocy*tosis, involves the formation of fluid-filled vacuoles at the surface of the cell; the second, *phagocytosis,* as seen in amoebae and in scavenging white blood cells, involves the engulfing of solid materials into vacuoles. In both forms of endocytosis the vacuoles usually move away from the surface to another site in the cell for further processing.

The Cytoplasm

The cytoplasm is not a simple homogeneous material. In addition to water, salts, and biomolecules, it contains numerous complex organelles. Cytoplasmic organelles are organized structures with particular functions. They partition the cytoplasm into smaller, organized units in which biochemical reactions can take place in a well-ordered way.

They function to process food, to extract the chemical energy from it, to transfer the energy to special molecules in the cell, to assist in building cell parts, and to produce compounds either for use by the cell or for export.

In some cells the total number of organelles clearly distinguishable in the cytoplasm may be small. The cytoplasmic matrix of such cells is called the *ground substance.* On the other hand some cells are so laden with organelles and membranous structures that the ground substance is not observed.

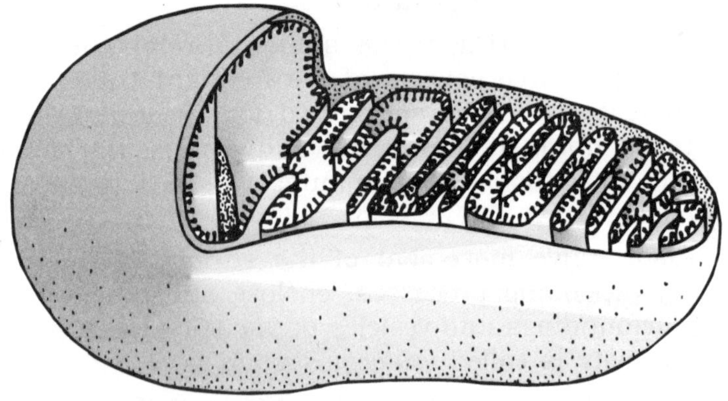

Figure 1.5: Figure 4.9 Diagram of a mitochondrion showing a few of the elementary particles at the cut edges of the folded inner membrane (crista).

Energy-Associated Organelles

Living organisms have two major organelles that deal especially with the conversion of light energy to usable chemical energy or to the orderly release of the chemical energy.

Conversion of light energy to usable chemical energy is a function of plant organelles, the *chloroplasts.* Interested students will find these organelles discussed in biology or botany textbooks. As they are only rarely found in animal cells and are not produced there, they will not be discussed here.

However, it should be noted that they have a highly organized internal membrane structure. The other organelle actively associated with energy utilization is a universal one, found in both plants and animals; this is the *mitochondrion.*

Mitochondria

Mitochondria have a double membrane. The outer one is about 7.5 nanometers (nm) thick and conforms to the shape of the organelle. The inner one, 5-5.5 nm thick, is characteristically thrown into shelflike folds called *cristae,* that can vary among tissues and among species.

In some organisms, such as protozoans, or in mammalian kidney tissue, the inner membrane may form tubules. Mitochondria are heavily laden with enzymes, some in the central fluid matrix, others embedded in the inner membrane.

When seen under the electron microscope, the inner membrane has particles on 4-5 nm-stalks topped by 7.5-10 nm spheres. Each mitochondrion may have from 100,000 to 1,000,000 of these elementary particles which possess many enzymes, including those of the hydrogen transport system that synthesize adenosine triphosphate (ATP).

Because the enzymes of mitochondria control an orderly series of reactions that hydrolyze fats and organic acids while transferring their energy to energy-rich phosphorus-containing molecules, they have been appropriately called the "powerhouses" of the cell.

There are four steps in the hydrolysis of molecules whose energy ends up in such molecules as ATP: glycolysis that produces two three-carbon compounds from a six-carbon sugar; a decarboxylation step that converts the three-carbon compound to a two-carbon one; the Krebs citric acid cycle that incorporates the two-carbon compound and proceeds through many steps that liberate hydrogen atoms; and the hydrogen transport system that cascades the electrons associated with the hydrogen atoms in a series of steps that convert adenosine diphosphate (ADP) to high-energy ATP.

The details of these steps are discussed in other chapter of this book. The point to be made here is that glycolysis and decarboxylation occur outside the mitochondria and the actual production of ATP is small.

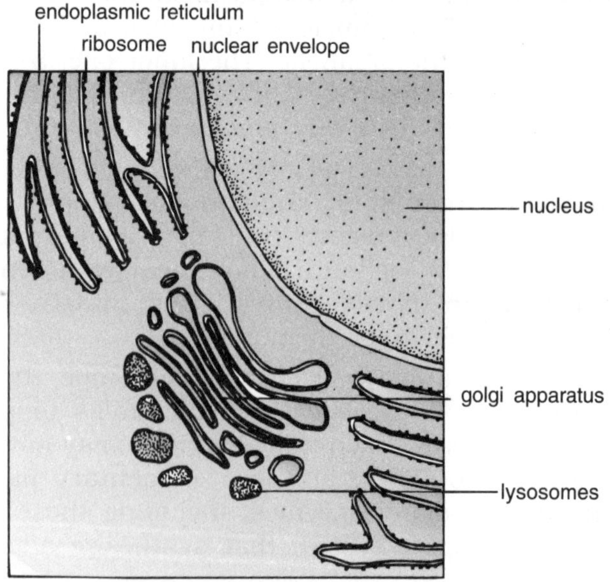

Figure 1.6: Interrelationships among the endoplasmic reticulum, Golgi apparatus, and lysosomes.

The last two steps, the Krebs citric acid cycle and hydrogen transport, are closely coupled inside the mitochondrion. These occur in association with the inner membrane and the attached elementary particles and result in production of large amounts of ATP.

In addition to having DNA and RNA that differ from that of the cell's nucleus, both mitochondria and chloroplasts have ribosomes, and those organelles control most, but not all, of their own reproduction. In most cells mitochondria appear to be randomly placed.

However, some cells have specific associations for mitochondria. For instance, mitochondria are located among the contractile elements in muscles and they lie near the junctions of nerve cells.

These relationships place them in a position to provide a ready supply of ATP for muscle contraction or nerve impulse transmission. Actively secreting cells have especially numerous mitochondria.

Golgi Apparatus (Dictyosome)

Another cytoplasmic organelle common to all eukaryote cells is the *Golgi apparatus.* The Golgi apparatus requires special staining for identification with the light microscope. It is composed of flattened smooth vessels whose membranes are tightly packed into layers.

Its position in the cell is usually near the nucleus, often as a cap over a pair of centrioles. The Golgi apparatus is prominent in secretory cells. It is polarized, with one edge of the complex usually near the rough endoplasmic reticulum.

At this edge it takes up the products of synthesis from the endoplasmic reticulum by accepting these products into small vesicles. It moves and concentrates the products to the opposite face, called the "secretion or maturation face."

Here larger vesicles are produced to move the secretions to other parts of the cell or to the surface to be released from the cell. Another important function of the Golgi apparatus is to add carbohydrates to the proteins as they progress through the apparatus.

The Endoplasmic Reticulum and Ribosomes

The endoplasmic reticulum may be either smooth or rough, depending on the absence or presence of *ribosomes.* The ribosomes are composed of a small and a large subribosomal particle.

Those that are attached to the endoplasmic reticulum synthesize proteins, including enzymes, that are generally exported to other cells, tissues, or the surroundings. The ribosomes that are free in the cytoplasm function to produce enzymes used by the cell. The ribosomes themselves are synthesized underthecontrol of the RNA messengers (mRNA) that are constructed under the direction of DNA.

When ribosomes are linked together by RNA in the process of assembling amino acids into proteins, they are called polyribosomes. It is interesting to note that the proteins that make up part of ribosome structure are synthesized on cytoplasmic polyribosomes and migrate rapidly into the nucleus to participate in ribosome assembly in the nucleolus.

This is an excellent example of the dynamic movements that occur in cells at the molecular level. Differences in the relationships of ribosomes to the endoplasmic reticulum are illustrated by cells of the pancreas and of striated muscle.

The pancreatic cells that export digestive enzymes such as trypsin and lipase have a rough endoplasmic reticulum. Muscle cells, principally composed of contractile proteins that are not secreted, have a smooth endoplasmic reticulum called the sarcoplasmic reticulum.

Lysosomes and Secretory Vesicles

Lysosomes are membrane-bound packages of enzymes. Usually they are formed on the secreting face of the Golgi apparatus. Sometimes the lysosomes simply store the enzymes. Sometimes they join vacuoles that have formed on the surface of the cell and moved inward; here they can digest ingested material.

Sometimes they contribute to the enzymatic breakdown of the cells that produce them. This is an important function in animals undergoing rapid change, such as in amphibian metamorphosis where a tadpole's tail is rapidly destroyed as it becomes a frog.

Secretory vesicles also are produced on the secreting face of the Golgi apparatus but move to the surface to discharge their contents and to add to the plasma membrane.

Nuclear Envelope

A better appreciation of membrane structures will be obtained from viewing the role of the nucleus in controlling membrane synthesis. The nuclear envelope is composed of two distinct membranes. The inner smooth one, facing the nucleus, is associated with chromatin (nucleic acids and proteins) and bioinformation is transferred to the outer membrane that possesses ribosomes.

Here a new membrane is formed that moves outward and makes up an *endomembrane* system consisting of endoplasmic reticulum, Golgi apparatus, secretory vesicles, endocytotic vesicles (those that are formed at the edge of the cell) and vacuoles, and the plasma membrane itself.

Thus except for the mitochondria and plastids and fibrillarstructures in the cytoplasm, all membranous structures are related in their origin near the nucleus, can have continuity, and may be transformed from one membranous structure to another.

Other Membrane-Bound Structures

The remaining structures of the cytoplasm that can be seen in cells are the *vacuoles.* These are membrane-bound cavities within the cytoplasm filled with water and dissolved salts. In animal cells they are. usually small and often numerous. Vacuoles in some lower animals are utilized to move food through the cytoplasm where it is digested.

Some protozoa have contractile vacuoles with associated radiating canals that deliver fluid to the vacuoles; the vacuoles rhythmically discharge the fluid to the exterior. Movement of these organelles is accomplished with the aid of microtubules attached to their membranes.

The contractile vacuoles function as a mechanism for maintaining fluid balance in the protozoa. In addition to the principal structures just described, both plants and animals may have nonliving materials, or inclusions, present such as starch grains, crystals, pigment granules, and secretory granules in the cytoplasm, many of which are not membrane bound.

It is important to understand that individual organelles do not operate independently. For instance, mitochondria convert energy and make it more useful to the cell, Golgi bodies package products resulting from the energy provided by the mitochondria, and some vacuoles containing these products may transport them to other parts of the cell or to the exterior.

Filamentous Organelles

Three major kinds of cellular structures exist in filamentous form. The ones studied longest are the *myofibrils* that form the contractile elements in muscle cells. They consist of parallel and interdigitating arrays of two kinds of proteins, actin and myosin. *Microtubules* form the second kind of filamentous structure.

They are formed from a protein, *tubulin.* They are long straight structures that, in cross section, appear as a circle of about 24 nm in outside diameter. The protein in these microtubules is arranged in parallel, slightly pitched subunits that probably have cross-

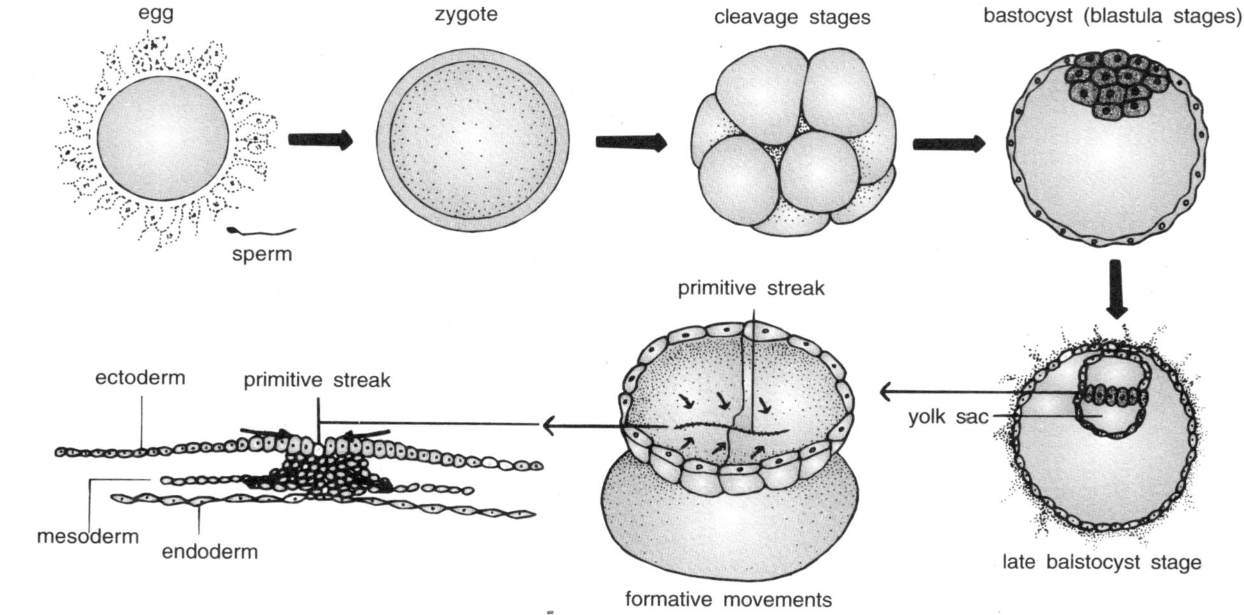

Figure 1.7: Some steps in development from an egg illustrating the appearance of organization and pattern.

bridges between the molecules. Also there are often lateral projections between tubules.

Organelles constructed of microtubules are cilia, flagella, basal bodies, sperm tails, centrioles, and spindle fibers. A characteristic organization of such structures is a "9 + 2" microtubular arrangement. Centrioles and spindle fibers illustrate two forms of microtubular organization.

A centriole is a self-replicating organelle whose progeny centriole lies at right angles to the parent organelle; each centriole is approximately 330 nm long and 150 nm in diameter. Each cylinder is composed of 9 sets of triple tubules running in the long axis.

Spindle fibers in animals are synthesized in association with centrioles as the nuclear envelope disappears and the two centrioles move toward opposite poles in karyokinesis. The spindle fibers are assembled from shorter preexisting segments rather than by being synthesized on ribosomes at the time.

Some spindle microtubules are continuous between the centrioles and some terminate on the chromos-omes. *Microfilaments* form the third kind of filamentous organelle. As with microtubules, they seem to be universal among eukaryote cells. These structures are not hollow and range between 5 and 8 nm in diameter.

Both actin and myosin are found. The microfilaments function in several ways. Noteworthy is their involvement in creating the constriction of the plasma membrane during the cytokinesis process when one cell becomes two.

They have been implicated in streaming motions of the cytoplasm of such cells as amoebae, migrating fibroblasts, and glial cells of the nervous system. In some cells it can be seen that the microfilaments are of two kinds or distributions.

Some microfilaments lie in parallel distributions in cells while others form a loose network. There are two

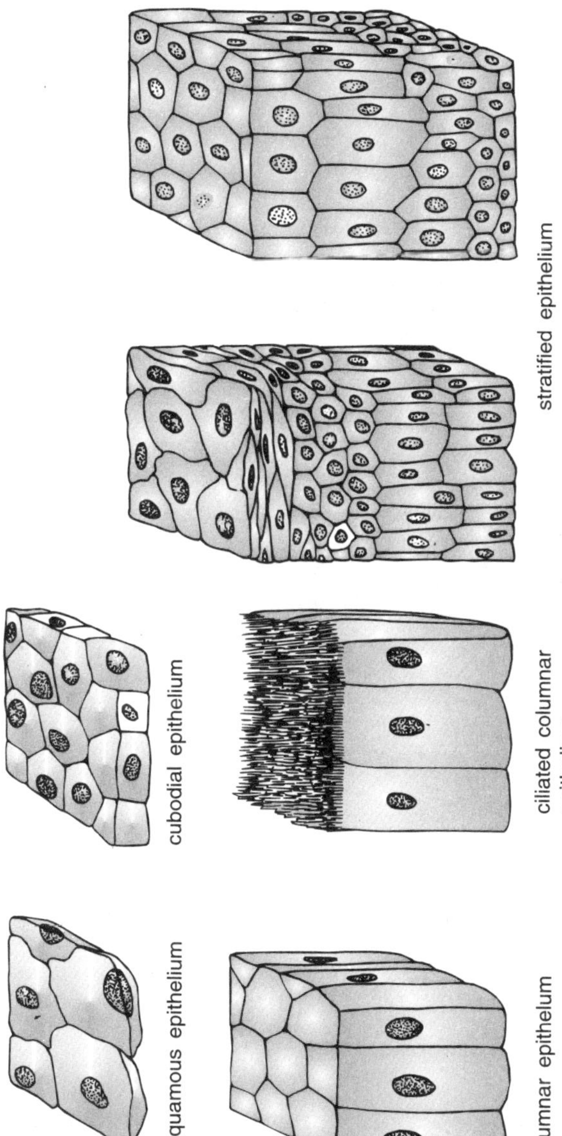

Figure 1.8: Epithelial tissues.

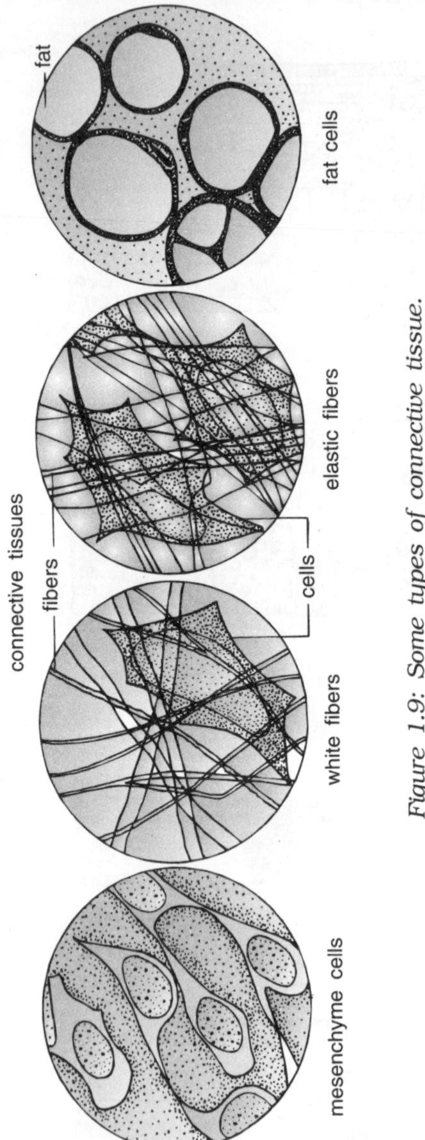

Figure 1.9: Some types of connective tissue.

inhibitors of the assembly of microtubules and microfilaments, both of which interfere with cell division. One inhibitor, colchicine, specifically prevents the assembly of subunits of microtubules.

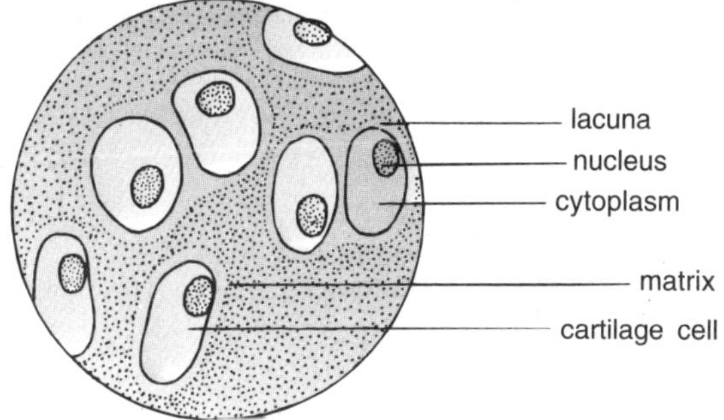

Figure 1.10: Hyaline cartilage showing cartilage cells, lacunae, and matrix.

The other inhibitor, cytochalasin B, interferes with the functioning of microfilaments. These two inhibitors have been selectively used to study the functions of microtubules and microfilaments.

The Nucleus

The nucleus receives expanded treatment in other chapter of this booki and, therefore, is only briefly discussed here. In the interphase stage, when the nucleus is organized to control cellular functions, electron micrographs show a granular background in which lie a few large, round, dark nucleoli, and areas of dense irregular chromatin masses are associated with the inner membrane of the nuclear envelope.

There are no discernible membranes or microtubules within the nucleus, except in protozoa that produce a mitotic spindle within the nuclear membrane. There are pores in the nuclear envelope that are not simply holes, but have a complex structure and regulate exchange between the nucleoplasm and the cytoplasm.

JUNCTIONS BETWEEN CELLS

There is usually an identifiable intercellular space of about 20 nm between the plasma membranes of adjacent cells. However, there are three major kinds of junctions between cells. *Tight junctions* are places where the intercellular spaces are absent. They usually exist between unlike kinds of cells or tissue layers.

They seem to prevent easy access of materials from one population of cells to the other. *Gap junctions*, on the other hand, are places where membranes of two adjacent cells create passageways between the cytoplasms of the cells, enhancing the molecular traffic between cells. They can be found between smooth muscle cells, for instance.

The third junction type, desmosomes, can be visua-

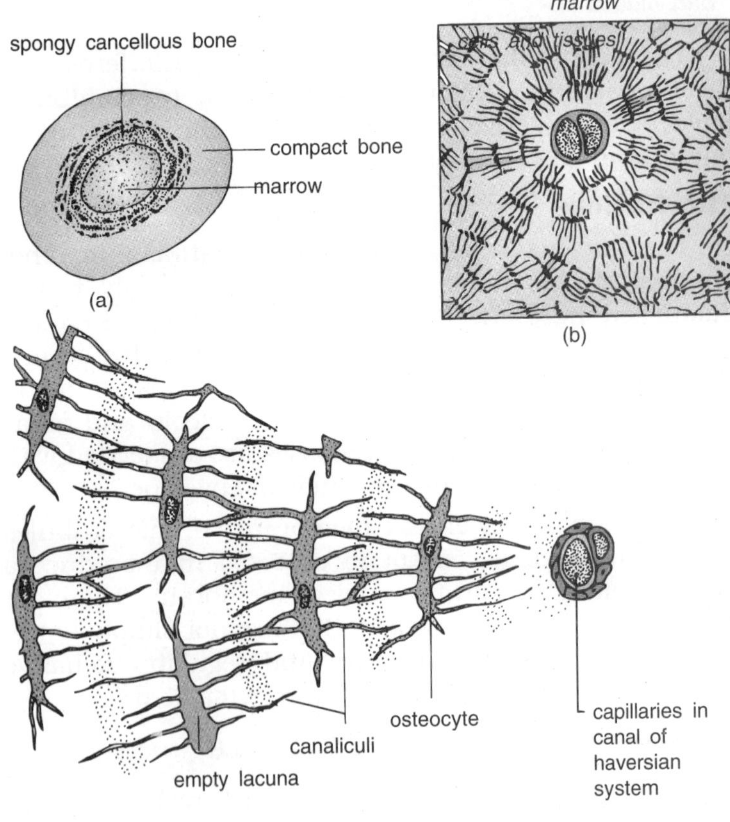

Figure 1.11: Bone. (a) Cross section of a long bone. (b) A small section of bone. (c) Enlargement of (b).

lized as localized "spot welds." Locally the intercellular space is filled with a dense, fibrous material, and internally microfilaments, *tonofibrils*, extend into the cytoplasmic matrix.

The function of desmosomes seems to be purely mechanical, reenforcing contacts between, for example, epithelial cells where considerable strength is advantageous; a special and large desmosome association exists in the form of intercalated discs of heart muscle, another place where intercellular strength is important.

CELL DIVISION

Although cell division is considered in more detail in other chapter of this book, the main features of the process are outlined here because of its importance to the survival of cells. Cell division involves two processes: nuclear division, called *mitosis;* and a division of the cytoplasm, called *cytokinesis.*

During the intervals between the stages of mitosis, the chromosomes are extended and not easily recognized. A condensation of chromosomes so that they become visible signals the onset of mitosis. By this time, replication has occurred in each of the chromosomes.

In most cells, when the chromosomes have stopped contracting, the nuclear envelope disappears. This is accompanied by the formation of *a spindle* composed of microtubules, called spindle fibers, that converge at the two poles.

The chromosomes move into position on the equatorial region of the spindle and the replicated, but still joined, chromosomes become attached to the fibers, which converge on centrioles. The two strands of each chromosome then separate and move toward the centrioles at opposite poles where they aggregate, and a new nuclear envelope forms around them.

This creates two nuclei, each with identical complements of chromosomes. The process of mitosis is usually followed by cytokinesis. There are a number of instances

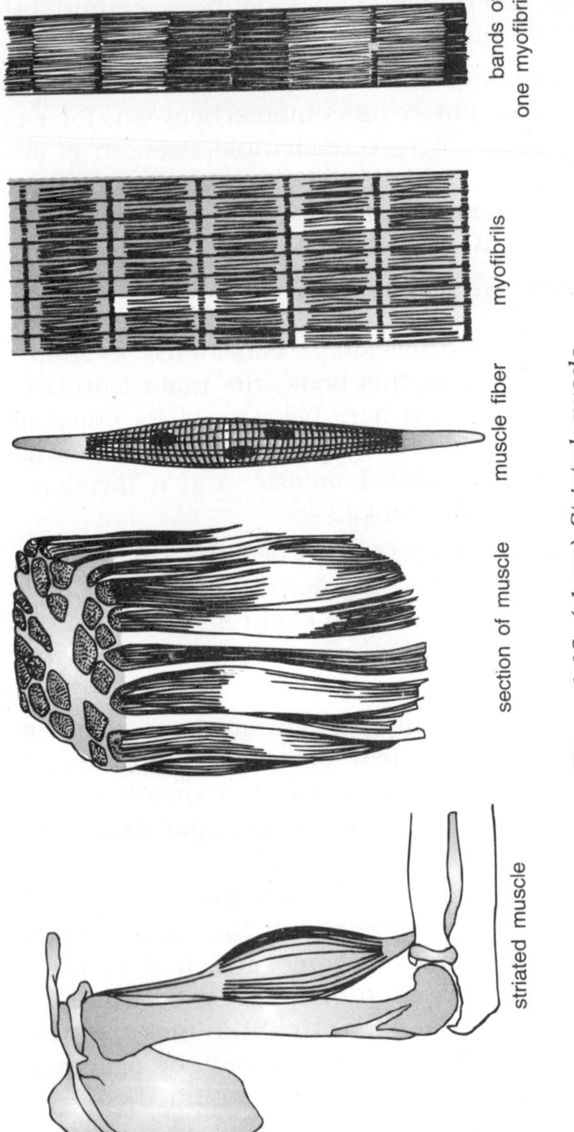

Figure 1.12: (above) Striated muscle.

in plants and animals where nuclei divide but the cytoplasm does not.

In animals, the multinucleate condition is called a *syncytium*. Syncytia can occur in two ways. One is for the nuclei to divide without the cytoplasm dividing. Some embryonic tissues associated with the placenta illustrate this.

The other way of creating a syncytium is for originally separate cells to fuse. This occurs in the development of striated muscle in vertebrates.

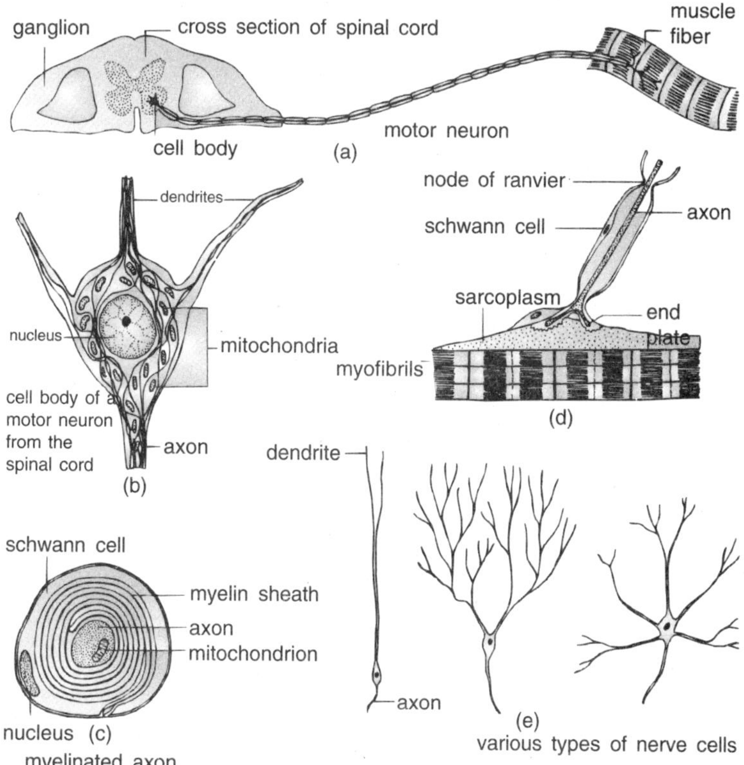

Figure 1.13: Neuron, structural unit of the nervous system. (a) Complete motor neuron. (b) Organization of cell body. (c) Cross section of axon showing myelin sheath. (d) Neuromotor junction. (e) Variations in the shapes of neurons.

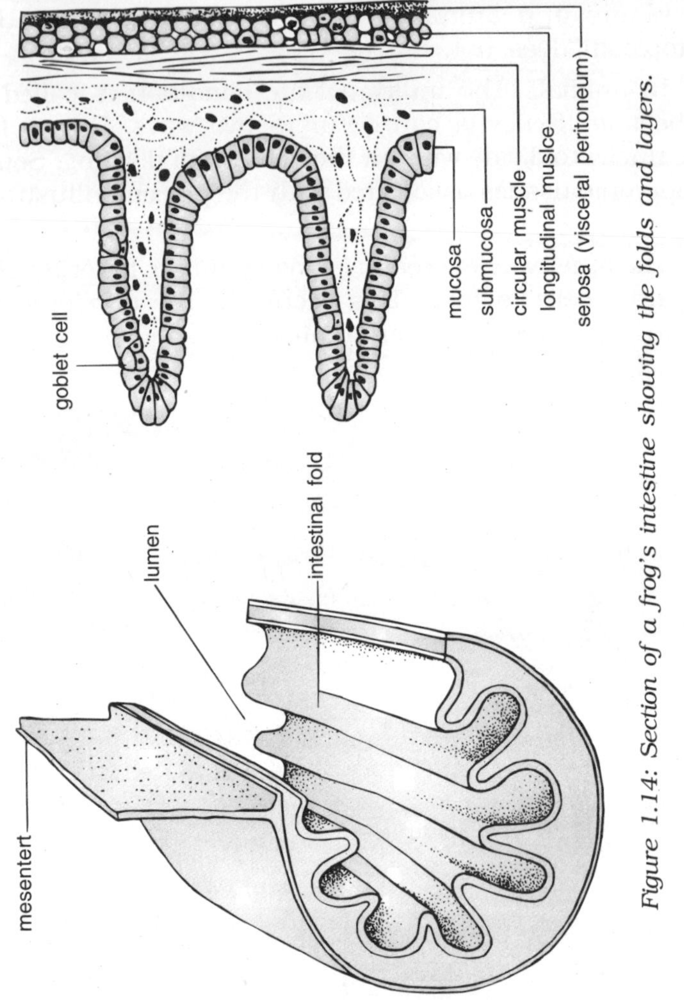

Figure 1.14: Section of a frog's intestine showing the folds and layers.

COMMUNITIES OF CELLS

When cells remain together, forming multicellular organisms, most of the cells become specialized. This provides for a division of functions among cells that usually does not occur in unicellular forms of life such as bacteria, some fungi, protozoa, and some algae.

While singlecelled organisms are capable of immortality in that their cell division is capable of continuing their kind indefinitely, the multicellular condition is accompanied by a restriction of potential immortality to special *primordial germ* cells.

These cells are the progenitors of eggs and sperm. The remaining animal cells are called *somatic* cells.

Multicellular Organization

The fertilized egg of an animal divides a large number of times. Its cells remain adherent to each other. In time, a stage is reached when adherent groups of cells move as sheets or clusters of cells. Beginning certainly with flatworms and all higher phyla, this produces three kinds of cell layers called the *germ layers.*

They are an outer layer, *ectoderm, a* middle meso*derm,* and an inner *endoderm.* From these three embryonic layers, cells differentiate and become unlike in structure and function. Those groups of similar cells that remain together constitute *tis*sues.

In a complex animal such as humans, five basic kinds of tissues are recognized: epithelial, supporting, muscle, nervous, and vascular.

As will be seen in other chapters of this book, invertebrate developments can be of several kinds. In these animals movement of cells in layers or sheets is not as usual as it is in the vertebrates used here.

Epithelial Tissue

The cells of epithelial tissues are closely connected, with little intercellular material between them. They cover the body and line the various cavities, ducts, and vessels as continuous layers. The various glands, such as the salivary glands, the pancreas, and the sweat glands, are derived from specialized epithelial cells.

The most important general function of epithelial tissue is in connection with the movement of materials. All substances that normally enter and leave the body tissues must pass through an epithelium.

The several shapes and arrangements of epithelial cells assist in classifying them. *Squamous* epithelium has thin, flat, tilelike cells.

Such an epithelium lines the body cavity, covers many of the internal organs, and composes the mesenteries that form the thin sheets of tissue that support the internal organs of vertebrate animals.

Cuboidal epithelium may be found in the cells of kidney tubules. Co*lumnar* epithelium is generally found lining the alimentary tracts of animals, and there the elongated cells are fitted together in sheets, with the long axes of the cells at right angles to the cavity. Squamous, cuboidal, and columnar are the basic shapes of epithelial cells.

Each type may exist as several layers forming *a stratified epithelium.* The outer part of human skin is *a stratified squamous epithelium,* for instance. Also, each type may have cilia, vibratile hairlike extensions of the cytoplasm, on the free surface.

The epithelium lining the air passages (the trachea) is a *ciliated epithelium.* While epithelium can be formed from all three germ layers, it is interesting from a functional standpoint that ectodermally derived epithelia generally serve a protective function, and that one of the common molecules produced by these cells is the protein *keratin* that can be found in skin, nails, claws, hooves, and hair.

Epithelia produced by the endoderm tend to be mucous cells providing lubrication and secretions, as well as allowing absorption and transport across the cells.

A common product of these cells is *mucin.* Epithelia derived from mesoderm primarily function in the movement of materials in from one side of the cell and out on the other side and do not have prominent special secretions.

Supporting Tissue

The supporting tissues are made up of *fibrous connective tissue, cartilage,* and *bone.* These tissues support and bind the different parts of the body together.

They differ from other tissues in that they all produce a very large amount of intercellular material. This intercellular material, the *matrix,* is different in the three types mentioned.

The mature cells are distributed in the matrix, which is secreted by the cells during growth and development. Fibrous connective tissue is found in many places in the body; it binds the skin to the muscles, attaches muscles to bones, covers the blood vessels, and so on.

The matrix of such tissue may contain white fibers, yellow elastic fibers, or both. The white fibers, composed of *collagen* (a source of gelatin), are the most characteristic elements of this type of tissue.

In hyaline cartilage the cells are scattered through a matrix of uniform appearance. This cartilage is a tough, somewhat elastic material found at the ends of bones, in the nose, and in the ear.

In the early embryo most of the skeleton is composed of cartilage, which is later converted into bone. Other types of cartilage have fibers in the matrix. Bone is the characteristic vertebrate supporting, or skeletal, tissue.

Due to the calcium salts deposited in the bone matrix, it forms a very hard, rigid tissue. The bone cells are scattered in this matrix, usually in a definite pattern and with numerous fine processes extending in all directions.

As Figure anywhere else in this chapter shows, the cells are arranged in concentric circles around canals through which the blood vessels and nerves pass.

These are called Haversian systems. *Adipose* tissue, or fat tissue, is considered to be a modified form of fibrous connective tissue.

Here the cells have enlarged through the deposition of fat in large vacuoles. Adipose tissue is found in many parts of the body. The degree to which these cells are laden with fat determines the obesity of the person, not the number of fat cells, which is determined early in life.

A person who early develops a relatively large number of fat cells will later have greater difficulty in coping with the control of body weight than one who has fewer fat cells.

Muscle Tissue

Muscle tissue functions in contraction. Muscle cells have thin threads, *myofibrils*, in their cytoplasm which are responsible for the contractile qualities of muscle tissues. Three kinds of muscle tissues are recognized in vertebrates:

1. *Smooth* or *involuntary* muscle found in the various internal organs, the blood vessels, and the ducts of glands
2. *Striated* or *voluntary* muscle associated with the skeleton and constituting the bulk of the body tissues—the "meat" we eat
3. *Cardiac* muscle found in the heart

Smooth muscle cells are long and spindle shaped. The oval nucleus lies near the widest part of the spindle. With proper staining, the myofibrils in the cytoplasm can be seen. Smooth muscle cells are found in the form of sheets in 'the various internal organs, especially around fluid-filled sacs.

As a rule, these sheets are double, with the axes of the cells in one sheet at right angles to the axes of the cells in the other sheet. Striated muscle tissue, found attached to the skeleton, is a syncytium composed of long multinucleate structures called *fibers*. Each fiber is bounded by a thin membrane, the *sarcolemma*.

The sarcolemma bounds the cytoplasm, called *sarco-*

plasm, and the long cross*striated myofibrils.* Muscle fibers are organized into bundles that compose whole muscles. Cardiac muscle has myofibrils that are cross-striated, but the tissues give the appearance of typical uninucleate, not multinucleate, cells.

Each cell, however, is connected with adjacent cells by specializations of the membrane. From a functional standpoint, cardiac muscle differs from both the involuntary and voluntary muscles. It contracts automatically and rhythmically.

For instance, the heart muscle of a chick embryo starts contracting during the second day of development, before there are any nerve connections to the heart.

Nervous Tissue

The *nervous tissue* is composed of very specialized cells, called neurons, that are involved in the coordination of the organism and in its conscious experiences. Neurons function in *irritability* and *conductivity* and are of several kinds; however, they all possess some basic features that can be illustrated in *a motor neu*ron, one that transmits impulses from the brain or spinal cord to skeletal muscle.

Each neuron is composed of a cell *body* containing the nucleus and two kinds of cytoplasmic processes, numerous short *dendrites,* and a single long axon. From a functional point of view a dendrite carries an impulse toward the cell body, and the axon carries the impulse away from the cell body.

Neurons do not exist singly but in aggregations. What one commonly calls *nerves* are bundles composed of nerve processes, axons and dendrites. When the cell bodies of neurons are in aggregates outside of the brain and spinal cord, these aggregates are called *ganglia* (singular, *ganglion).*

Neuron processes may exist as unmyelinated fibers (naked), or they may be surrounded by an insulating sheath, the *myelin* or *medullary sheath,* as shown in

Figure elsewhere in this chapter. This sheath is composed of fatty material and tends to give the nerves and other parts of the nervous system, where it is present, a white appearance.

Vascular Tissue

The *vascular tissue* is the blood, a liquid tissue whose matrix is the *blood plasma.* Suspended in the fluid matrix are three general types of cells or cell fragments:

1. Red blood cells, or *erythrocytes,* containing the compound hemoglobin which greatly increases the oxygen-carrying capacities of the blood
2. White blood cells, or leucocytes, some of which are amoeboid and capable of engulfing bacteria and foreign substances that may be present in the body while others produce antibodies
3. Blood platelets, or *thrombocytes,* small colourless structures that function in the formation of blood clots

The blood vessels do not qualify as part of the vascular tissue but are organs composed of several tissues, such as epithelial, connective, and muscular. Further details of the blood are presented in other chapter of this book.

Organs of an Animal

The different types of tissues described above are combined to form the various organs, such as the heart, lungs, stomach, kidneys, bladder, small intestine, and large intestine.

In each of the various organs the kinds of tissues are arranged in a characteristic way, making it possible for the organ to perform its particular functions.

An examination of the small intestine of a frog shows how tissues are combined into organs. Five rather well-defined regions will be described in order, beginning with the cavity, or *lumen,* of the gut and working out.

The lining layer, or mucosa, is composed mainly of

columnar epithelium. The cells of the mucosa perform at least three functions. Distributed among the main kinds of columnar cells are *goblet cells,* so-called due to the gobletlike cavity filled with *mucin.*

This secretion serves as a lubricant. The majority of the epithelial cells perform the other two major functions: they secrete enzymes into the lumen of the intestine and they absorb digested material from the lumen.

Next to the mucosa is a layer that is somewhat irregular in appearance. This is the *submucosa,* composed primarily of fibrous connective tissue. Pockets of epithelial cells from the mucosa form *intestinal glands* that project into the submucosa.

The submucosa is also richly penetrated by small blood and lymph vessels and by nervous tissue. Adjoining the submucous layer is the *circular muscle layer* whose smooth muscle cells have their long axes arranged around the lumen.

Just external to the circular muscle layer is the *longitudinal muscle layer* whose smooth muscle cells are at right angles to the circular muscle cells. The contraction of the cells in the longitudinal layer ca-uses the intestine to shorten, while the contraction of the circular muscle layer constricts the lumen and elongates the intestine.

The very thin, outermost layer of the intestine is the serosa, or the *visceral peritoneum.* It is composed of a sheet of flat squamous epithelium. The segment of intestine just described does not function as five separate parts.

Instead, the individual cells of each layer operate as members of a community of similar cells, or as a tissue, and the tissues operate in a coordinated fashion as an organ. Cells in the mucosa are primarily involved in the absorption of digested food material.

Cells in the submucosa support the blood and lymph

vessels into which the absorbed food materials are passed to other parts of the body; the two layers of muscle tissue churn the contents of the lumen and move it along; and the serosa acts to encase and support the other tissues.

Organ Systems

The small intestine is an organ forming a part of a larger *organ system*, the digestive system. In addition to the small intestine, the digestive system includes the mouth, salivary glands, esophagus, stomach, large intestine, pancreas, and liver.

Throughout the body, tissues are organized into organs and organs function together as organ systems. There is a definite hierarchy in the organization of most organisms. The *cells* are the basic units of structure and form the different tissues. The tissues are combined into *organs*, and a number of organs functioning together constitute an *organ system*. The following organ systems are found in the vertebrates:

1. Digestive system
2. Respiratory system
3. Circulatory system
4. Excretory system
5. Reproductive system
6. Nervous system
7. Muscular system
8. Skeletal system
9. Integumentary system
10. Endocrine system

Chapter 2 BIOENERGETICS

The thousands of compounds found in living organisms are related to each other through *metabolism.* This ability to capture, transform, and store various forms of energy according to the instructions of their genetic material is an essential feature of living organisms.

A cell's cytoplasm is not a random suspension of enzymes, substrates, and products, but it possesses an intricate organization that is not completely understood. The specificity of enzymes operates at the molecular level; above the molecular level there is an intricate organization of macromolecu lar complexes, membranes, particles, fibrils, and organelles.

This highly organized state of living material is difficult to maintain from the energetic standpoint; the structural framework of the cell must have a continuous supply of energy provided for it.

Energy is the capacity to do work. Energy may be subdivided into two broad categories: *potential energy* (the energy of position) and *kinetic energy* (the energy of motion). Positional, radiant, electrical, chemical, and atomic energies are forms of potential energy.

MASS AS A FORM OF ENERGY

In 1905 Albert Einstein formulated a statement that

mass and energy are interconvertible:

$$E = mc^2$$

where E is the energy, m is the mass, and c is the velocity of electromagnetic radiation (for example, light). On the basis of this statement, the first law of thermodynamics is formulated: Mass and *different forms of energy are interconvertible*, or mass *energy may neither* be created *nor destroyed.*

The conversions between mass and energy occur in nuclear fusion and fission reactions. The helium atom has a mass of 4.0026 and the hydrogen atom has a mass of 1.0080; the relationships are shown in the following equations:

4 hydrogen atoms→ 1 helium atom

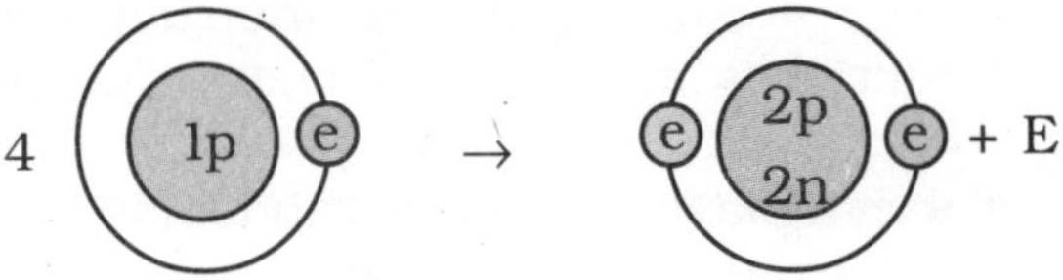

4 (1p) (e) → (e) (2p 2n) (e) + E

$$4 \times 1.0080 \rightarrow 4.0026 + 0.0294$$

(4.0320)

This conversion of four hydrogen atoms to a helium atom thus is accompanied by the disappearance of a small amount of mass; this mass is converted to energy, according to Einstein's equation.

This reaction continuously occurs in the sun at a rate of over 100 million tons of mass converted to energy each second.

ENERGY AND REACTIONS

In order for atoms to be joined by specific bonds into molecules, energy is needed to bring the atoms together to form a stable molecule. When the bonds of a molecule are broken, the energy that holds the atoms together may be used to do work.

When an organism makes or breaks bonds during metabolism, it is important to know whether energy is consumed or liberated.

Consider the schematic reaction of the interconversion between compounds A and B. The reaction will be *exergonic* if energy is liberated and it will be *endergonic* if energy must be supplied to promote the reaction.

These concepts are schematized in Figure elsewhere in this chapter. If energy is given off, not all of this energy is available to do work. That energy actually employed to do work is called free energy.

Although there is no completely satisfactory explanation of chemical reactions, the *collision theory* says that all molecules in a solution do not have the same kinetic energy, for some molecules acquire more energy through collisions than do others.

The molecules that are traveling at a fast rate are more likely to react than the ones that are traveling at a slow rate.

Table 2.1: Free Energies of Hydrolysis of Some Biological Compounds.

Reaction	*Chane in Free Energy (Cal/Mol)*
ATP + H_2O → ADP + H_3PO_4 7300	
ADP + H_2O → AMP + H_2PO_4	7300
Phosphoenolpyruvic acid+ H_2O → pyruvic acid + H_3PO_4	14,800
Phosphocreatine + H_2O → creatine + H_2PO_4	10,300
Glucose-6-phosphate + H_2O → glucose + H_2PO_4	3300
AMP + H_2O → adenosine + H_2PO_4	2200

Thus there is an energy barrier to the reaction of molecules, and this barrier is the *energy of activation.* It is the energy of activation that determines the rate of a reaction; the higher the barrier, the slower the rate of the reaction.

The energy of activation of a chemical is shown in Figure elsewhere in this chapter for the reaction A ± B. In this section the rudiments of the concepts of energy and chemical reactions have been presented.

With respect to biological systems the function of biological catalysts, the enzymes, is to lower the activation energy and therefore speed up the attainment of an equilibrium.

A catalyst does not affect the point of equilibrium; the point of equilibrium depends only on the products and the reactants, assuming that all other factors are constant.

ENERGY, MOLECULES AND OXIDATION

In Chapter 3 the chemical composition of living material was discussed. The lipids, carbohydrates, proteins, and nucleic acids were presented as the four major classes of organic compounds of living systems.

The proteins, lipids, and carbohydrates are significant sources of energy for organisms. The energy content of a molecule depends on the atoms in the molecule and how they are arranged, that is, it depends on the structure of the molecule.

The expression "biological oxidation-reduction" refers to the movements of electrons in living organisms.

Oxidation means the loss of electrons by an atom or molecule, whereas re*duction is* the gain of electrons. A compound that donates electrons is a *reducing agent,* and a compound that accepts them is an *oxidizing agent.*

Thus in an oxidation-reduction reaction the reducing agent is oxidized and the oxidizing agent is reduced.

For living systems oxidation often refers to conversion of organic compounds to carbon dioxide and water. In oxidation, hydrogen atoms (protons and electrons) are removed from compounds.

A molecule that contains a relatively high proportion of hydrogen will release a greater amount of energy than one that contains a relatively low proportion of hydrogen.

Thus the *caloric value* of lipids is higher than that of carbohydrates and proteins. The caloric value of a food is the amount of energy given off (expressed in calories) when the food is completely oxidized.

ENERGY-RICH COMPOUNDS

If a cell or an organism does not trap the energy of the activated complex of an exergonic reaction, then the energy is liberated as heat.

Adenosine triphosphate (ATP) is a compound that is often used to link exergonic reactions with endergonic reactions, that is, the activated intermediate of a reaction drives the synthesis of ATP, and then ATP drives the synthesis of other compounds.

Energy-rich compounds exhibit a large decrease in free energy when they are hydrolyzed, and they are generally destroyed by acid, alkali, and heat.

ATP shows a decrease in free energy of 7300 calories per mole,[2] (cal/mole) when it is hydrolyzed to adenosine diphosphate (ADP); furthermore, ADP also shows a decrease in free energy of 7300 cal/mole when it is hydrolyzed to adenosine monophosphate (AMP).

Since these are relatively large changes in free energy, it is often said that ATP contains two high-energy phosphate bonds. Adenosine phosphates are not the only energy-rich compounds found in cells.

Table anywhere else in this chapter shows the free energies of hydrolysis of some other biological compounds in addition to energy-rich phosphates.

CELLULAR RESPIRATION, ENERGY RELEASE, AND CELL WORK

Consider all the activities that your body has performed today. No matter how long the list grows, it probably will not be complete for many of the body's activities proceed without our consciousness. All the concerted, controlled activities are dependent upon a source of energy.

This energy is produced by cellular processes, collectively termed *cellular respiration.* In cellular respiration, carbohydrates, proteins, and lipids are broken down to simpler compounds with the production of usable energy in the form of energy-rich compounds.

As just mentioned, ATP is a compound that is often used to drive cellular work performed at various levels of the hierarchy of organization: tissues, organs, organ systems, the organism as a whole, and the various levels of organismic interaction.

Since mitochondria produce the vast majority of ATP, they have been referred to as the "powerhouses of the cell." Muscular contraction has been studied extensively with respect to energywork relationships, and the tremendous body of data shows that ATP is rapidly synthesized from ADP by transfer of a phosphate group from phosphocreatine, an energy-rich storage molecule.

Then ATP participates intimately in the process of muscular contraction. ATP drives nervous transmission as well as active transport, where materials cross membranes at a great rate or against a concentration gradient.

The electrical discharge in the electric eel is another type of work produced by living forms. Secretion is another energy-dependent process carried out by specialized cells.

Cellular division also requires the expenditure of energy and is dependent on a supply of ATP.

Table 2.2: ATPs Produced under Aerobic and Anaerobic Conditions.

Conditions	*End Product(s)*	*Number of ATPs*
Anaerobic	Lactic acid or ethanol	2
Aerobic	CO_2 and H_2O	36

All biochemical syntheses of cells require ATP. In fact, ATP is utilized in the first step in the synthesis of proteins, carbohydrates, fats, and nucleic acids. Even the formation of sucrose, the disaccharide of glucose and fructose, requires ATP. The ubiquitous role of ATP in cellular function should be clear now.

Organisms vary greatly in the details of their morphologies; however, most organisms use the same fuels for the production of energy, which is utilized for the various kinds of biological work. Most discussions of cellular respiration center on glucose as one of the most important fuels.

The chemical fate of glucose will provide the axial thread for this discussion of respiration. With glucose as the fuel the overall equation for cellular respiration may be written as follows:

$$C_6H_{12}O_6 + 6O_2 \rightarrow 6CO_2 + {}_6H_2O + \text{energy}$$

Of course this equation is an oversimplification. The breakdown of glucose may be discussed conveniently in four phases:

1. Glycolysis
2. Formation of acetyl coenzyme A from pyruvic acid
3. The Krebs citric acid cycle
4. The hydrogen transport system

Figure elsewhere in this chapter relates the production of ATP in cellular respiration to several types of cell work. What others can you add?

Glycolysis (phase 1) starts with glucose (or carbohydrates that can be converted to glucose). Glucose, a six-carbon compound, is converted in glycolysis to two molecules of pyruvic acid, a three-carbon compound.

In a sense, pyruvic acid is the end product of glycolysis and is the result of breaking glucose apart in its middle between carbon atoms 3 and 4.

First of all, the acetyl (2C) is combined with oxaloacetic acid (4C) to produce citric acid (6C). As the successive reactions occur, a molecule of carbon dioxide is released at two places.

Eventually, oxaloacetic acid is reformed and can then combine with another acetyl group of acetyl CoA. Five pairs of hydrogens are removed as each acetyl group is metabolized. One pair is taken out as pyruvic acid and is converted to acetyl CoA (phase 2) and the other four pairs are removed within the cycle itself (phase 3).

The five pairs of hydrogens are picked up by cofactors of the enzymes that catalyze the dehydrogeneration reactions. From there they are passed down the hydrogen transport system, phase 4 of cellular respiration under aerobic conditions.

The hydrogen transport system is a complex group of protein molecules (cytochromes and flavoproteins) and they pass the hydrogen atoms (protons plus their electrons) along in a series of oxidation-reduction reactions (see earlier in this chapter).

At three places along the transport system ATP is synthesized from ADP and inorganic phosphate (PO_4^{3-}). The energy that drives the synthesis of ATP is derived from the "fall" of electrons from one protein carrier to another. The various protein carriers may be likened to a series of waterfalls.

If the transport of hydrogens and electrons occurred in one step, the delicate biological system would be burned up because too much heat would be produced. Oxygen is the terminal acceptor of the hydrogen transport system. Addition of the hydrogens to oxygen produces water. Returning to the original equation for cellular respiration:

$$C_6H_{12}O_6 + 6O_2 \rightarrow 6CO_2 + 6H_2O + \text{energy (ATP)}$$

it is clear where each component fits into the reaction.

ATP is produced as a result of all four phases of cellular respiration-glycolysis, formation of acetyl CoA, the Krebs cycle, and the hydrogen transport system. Two ATPs are produced in glycolysis. Under anaerobic conditions that is all the ATP formed; under aerobic conditions a total of 36 are produced.

THE METABOLIC MILL

The discussion of respiration has centered around glucose. Indeed, glucose is a focal point of the respiratory scheme, but the participation of other molecules must be considered also. Any intermediate of the glycolytic-Krebs cycle scheme may be metabolized by the scheme even though produced by some other reaction.

For example, pyruvic acid can be produced from the amino acid alanine by a deamination reaction. This molecule of pyruvic acid may be metabolized by the scheme, just as a molecule of pyruvic acid coming from the breakdown of glucose.

This emphasizes the fact that like molecules from several different reactions may contribute to the total amount or concentration of that particular molecule in the cell.

The points stressed in the preceding few paragraphs are that (1) the mitochondria serve as energy converters in the cell and (2) the fuel for the mitochondria is prepared by a large number of reactions.

Admittedly, these reactions are numerous and complex, but this is necessary for the transformation of the many kinds of food molecules into the relatively few kinds of molecules that are intermediates in glycolysis and the Krebs citric acid cycle.

The schematic diagram in Figure elsewhere in this book is intended to summarize these reactions. It is appropriately labeled "the metabolic mill" and is an example of the molecular logic of living systems. The formation of pyruvic acid leads to the consideration of the role of oxygen and the terminal anaerobic reactions in fermentation and glycolysis.

If oxygen is not present in a cell, usually the pyruvic acid is converted to either ethyl alcohol or lactic acid. NAD^+ is a cofactor for dehydrogenation reactions and is converted in glycolysis to NADH + H^+. If the oxidized form of the cofactor (NAD+) is not regenerated, the entire store of the cofactor will be converted to the reduced form.

The lack of oxidized cofactor will bring vital dehydrogenation reactions to a halt, and such a condition results in the death of the cell. Yeast cells regenerate NAD^+ by forming ethyl alcohol; muscle cells form lactic acid.

These relationships are shown in Figure elsewhere in this chapter. Fermentation involves a decarboxylation reaction (removal of a carboxyl group in the form of carbon dioxide) that changes pyruvic acid to acetaldehyde; acetaldehyde is reduced to ethanol, and NAD+ is regenerated.

Regeneration of NAD+ in muscle glycolysis involves the reduction of pyruvic acid to lactic acid.

Phases of Cellular Respiration

The preceding discussion outlined the mechanism of cellular respiration. The four phases now are considered in more detail.

Glycolysis (Phase 1)

Glycolysis is catalyzed by the sequential action of several enzymes that have been isolated, crystallized, and thoroughly studied. The details of glycolysis can be seen in Figure elsewhere in this chapter.

Notice that ATP is used at points A and B and is produced at points D and E. NAD^+ is the acceptor of hydrogens removed at point C. The following information should be gained from the study of Figures elsewhere in this chapter.

1. A six-carbon compound (glucose) is changed into two three-carbon compounds (two molecules of pyruvic acid).
2. A net synthesis of two molecules of ATP occurs for each glucose molecule that is metabolized.
3. Two NADH molccules are produced for each glucose metabolized (C).
4. Under anaerobic conditions, pyruvic acid is converted to lactic acid or ethanol.

Formation of Acetyl Coenzyme A (Phase 2)

In the presence of oxygen (aerobic conditions), pyruvic acid is metabolized in a more complex way. It is converted to acetyl CoA and carbon dioxide; the acetyl group is funneled into the Krebs citric acid cycle. One pair of hydrogens is removed as pyruvic acid is converted to acetyl CoA.

The Krebs Citric Acid Cycle (Phase 3)

A study of Figure elsewhere in this chapter reveals that for each acetyl fragment entering the cycle four pairs of hydrogen atoms are removed from the compounds being metabolized; these points are identified as B, C, E, and F. NAD^+ is the cofactor in three of these reactions, and a flavin compound accepts the hydrogens in the other case (E).

ATP is produced at one place; this is designated as D. Since two molecules of acetyl CoA per original molecule of glucose enter the cycle, two molecules of ATP are produced at this point for each initial molecule of glucose. The following points about this phase of glucose metabolism should be emphasized:

1. Five pairs of hydrogens are removed for each acetyl fragment that is metabolized. One pair is removed in phase 2, and four pairs are removed

in phase 3. Thusfor each original molecule of glucose, ten pairs are removed.

2. ATP is produced directly within the cycle; two molecules are produced for each original molecule of glucose that is metabolized.
3. Two carbon atoms are put into the cycle in the acetyl fragment; two carbon atoms are removed as carbon dioxide.

The Hydrogen Transport System (Phase 4)

In the presence of oxygen the hydrogens are passed through a series of reactions that produce ATP. This is oxidative phosphorylation, since this type of ATP production requires oxygen in the last step of the series.

This series of reactions is shown in Figure elsewhere in this chapter and is frequently called the *main line* of oxidation and reduction in the cell, the *hydrogen transport system*, the *cytochrome system*, or the *electron transport system*.

Each hydrogen atom, consisting of a proton and an electron, is passed to FAD, the prosthetic group (or cofactor) of flavoprotein and then to coenzyme Q. Coenzyme Q liberates the protons (H^+) into the fluid of the mitochondrion while the electrons (e^-) are transferred down the line to successive cytochromes.

The cytochromes are proteins that possess the iron-containing heme group. The last cytochrome is cytochrome a: (cytochrome oxidase), which transfers the electrons to the oxygen that combines with the protons from the mitochondrial fluid to form water.

Thus oxygen is the terminal electron acceptor in the aerobic pathway. Lack of oxygen quickly affects the metabolism of the cell by stopping this energy-release mechanism. Figure elsewhere in this chapter shows that ATP is synthesized at three places in the main line.

Thus each pair of hydrogens that is passed on by the dehydrogenases (NAD+ cofactor) results in the synthesis of three ATP molecules. Each pair that is transferred from the substrate directly to the flavoprotein results in the synthesis of two ATPs.

Thus for the pairs of hydrogens from phase 2 (formation of acetyl CoA) three ATPs are formed. In the Krebs citric acid cycle three pairs of hydrogens enter at the level of NAD^+ ($3 \times 3 = 9$) and one pair (from succinic acid) enters at the level of flavoprotein ($1 \times 2 = 2$).

Thus for each pyruvic acid molecule that is completely metabolized by phases 2 and 3, 14 ATPs are produced in the hydrogen transport system. For each glucose molecule 28 ATPs are produced by the main line of oxidation and reduction.

It is possible to summarize the number of ATPs produced for each original molecule of glucose metabolized to carbon dioxide and water:

Net from glycolysis	2
Hydrogens (2×2) removed in glycolysis and sent through the main line	4
Hydrogens removed in formation of acetyl CoA and in the citric acid cycle	28
ATPs produced in the Krebs citric acid cycle	2
	36

Thus 36 ATPs are produced for each molecule of glucose metabolized to carbon dioxide and water. In muscle glycolysis, free glucose is not the initial substrate; only glycogen (animal starch) serves as the source of glucose. The first step in the sequence of reactions under these conditions is

$$\underset{\text{glycogen}}{(\text{glucose})_n} + \underset{\substack{\text{inorganic}\\\text{phosphate}}}{P_i} \rightarrow \text{glucose phosphate} + (\text{glucose})_{n-1}$$

This reaction is repeated many times and supplies glucose phosphate to glycolysis. ATP is not required as the source of phosphate; therefore the net ATP production from glycolysis with glycogen as the source of glucose is 3 and the total for complete glucose oxidation is 37. The student should not memorize the rather elaborate pathways presented in Figures elsewhere in this chapter, but remember the three phases of glucose metabolism and know the significance of each phase.

An appreciation of the role of glucose and oxygen in the production of ATP and nicotinamide dinucleotide phosphate (NADPH) should be inherent in the study of these schemes.

This discussion on the utilization of energy in biological systems has emphasized the role of ATP. One must keep in mind that the primary storage of energy is in oxidizable compounds (basic foodstuffs such as glucose) and that there are other storage forms such as reduced NADPH and creatine phosphate (in muscle).

Localization of Respiratory Enzymes in the Cell

The mitochondrion is found in virtually every type of eukaryotic cell (mammalian erythrocytes are exceptions). Blue-green algae and bacteria, the prokaryotes, do not have highly organized structures comparable to the mitochondria of eukaryotes.

In the prokaryotes, electron transport and ATP production is associated with the cell membrane. Since there is no mitochondrial membrane and no glycerol phosphate shuttle the total number of ATPs produced per glucose molecule is 38 in prokaryotes.

In eukaryotic cells the mitochondria are in constant motion and they tend to be clustered strategically near structures that require ATP.

High concentrations of mitochondria are located, for example, at the junction of nerve cells where impulses are transmitted across the membranes, regularly arranged in rows in muscle cells along the ATP-requiring contractile elements, around actively beating sperm tails, and near the edges of intestinal cells where absorption is occurring.

Mitochondria also frequently are located near fuel sources such as lipid droplets. The size, shape, structure, and possible evolutionary origin of mitochondria were discussed in other chapter of this chapter. The carbohydrates, lipids, and proteins that serve as metabolic fuels are broken down by degradative enzymes outside of mitochondria into smaller fragments: pyruvic acid, glycerol, fatty acids, and amino acids.

These small molecules can diffuse across the outer membrane. This passage across the inner membrane requires specific transport systems. The enzymes of the citric acid cycle are located in the matrix of the mitochondrion where the breakdown of the small fuel molecules occurs. ATP production is a function of the inner membrane.

There is good evidence that the enzymes of the electron transport system are arranged in an orderly pattern on the cristae of the inner membrane. As previously discussed, the movement of electrons along the transport system is coupled to ATP production.

Isolated mitochondria are capable of carrying out these reactions, and furthermore, mitochon-drial fragments will carry out oxidative phosphorylation also. These fragmented mitochondria will oxidize NADH under the proper conditions; if ADP is absent, the process is halted and oxygen is not consumed.

Thus the flow of electrons is tightly coupled to oxidative phosphory-lation. This is a conservation mechanism since the fuel will not be burned unless the energy is trapped in ATP.

The inner membrane provides part of this conservational control since the inner membrane allows an ADP molecule to pass into the matrix only if an ATP is transported out. This molecule-for-molecule exchange assures a control of the level of ATP in the cytoplasm.

If ATP is being used at a high rate, then the ADP is generated at a high rate also, and this cytoplasmic ADP is exchanged rapidly for ATP across the inner membrane.

PHOTOSYNTHESIS

The overall equation for photosynthesis in green plants is (left to right)

$$CO_2 + H_2O \underset{\text{respiration}}{\overset{\text{Photosynthesis}}{\rightleftharpoons}} \underset{\text{glucose}}{C_6H_{12}O_6} + 6O_2$$

Inspection of this equation shows that photosynthesis and cellular respiration are reverse reactions of each other. Photosynthetic plants capture the sun's energy to drive the synthesis of glucose (and many other compounds).

The animal ultimately depends on the energy trapped by photosynthesis; it consumes plants (or other animals) and derives energy and substance by respiration.

The interlocking of photosynthesis and respiration is fundamental to the understanding of animal nutrition and ecology.

ORGANISMAL RESPIRATION AND CELLULAR RESPIRATION

The introduction to this chapter mentions the general framework and strategy of metabolism in the biological hierarchy: the organismal and cellular levels. The body of the chapter is concerned with the scheme of cellular respiration, however. Although organismal respiration is not emphasized here, the general relationships of cellular and organismal metabolism are clear.

BIOINFORMATION

What is bioinformation? How does it differ from other kinds of information? Strictly defined, bioinformation is any kind of information possessed and processed by living systems.

This would include the information needed and used to control cellular activities, the information concerned with the influences of one tissue or organ on another (hormones and development), the processes involved in the nervous system (learning, memory, and behavior), and so forth. Chapter 3 discusses the proteins and nucleic acids as informational macromolecules, that is, they are specific, linear polymers.

The pattern in which building blocks (amino acids and nucleotides) are put together constitutes a meaningful code-information. The remainder of this chapter considers bioinformation at the subcellular level, with an emphasis on integrating the storage and "reading" mechanisms of the proteins and nucleic acids.

Bioinformation of Macromolecules

Languages, such as English or German, use an alphabet of a few letters which make up sentences, and the sentences, units of coordinated thought, form paragraphs, books, and documents. Bioinformation involves, really, two languages: nucleic acid and protein.

The nucleic acid language is written in nucleotide symbols and it has two "dialects," DNA and RNA.

In DNA there are four nucleotides, A, T, C, and G. In RNA dialect there are also four letters, A, U, C, and G. (Actually, there are more than four kinds of nucleotides in RNA and DNA, but these other nucleotides are exceptions to the general rule.)

The fundamental aspects of the DNA and RNA dialects are similar, but the different functions of the two classes of nucleic acids are related to their different structures- double-strandedness versus single-strandedness, deoxyribose versus ribose, and the nucleotide composition.

After one type of RNA, messenger RNA, has been *transcribed* from DNA, the messengers are *translated* into proteins. Protein language is written with 20 letters (amino acids).

Immediately one sees a definite difference between the information stored in the nucleic acids and proteins (4 letters versus 20). Translation, indeed, involves a change from a 4-letter alphabet to a 20-letter alphabet.

THE GENETIC MATERIAL

A convincing body of data indicates that DNA is the genetic material. These data may be divided into two types, direct and indirect. First, certain observations suggest this, but since they are not strong suggestions, in the absence of any other information, they are termed *indirect* or circumstantial evidences.

One suggestion arises from the fact that the somatic cells of a species contain about the same amount of DNA, whereas the amounts of RNA and protein may vary greatly, depending on the function and the environment of the cells.

Gametes contain about one half as much DNA as do the nuclei of somatic cells; this is to be expected because the gametes have one set of chromosomes while

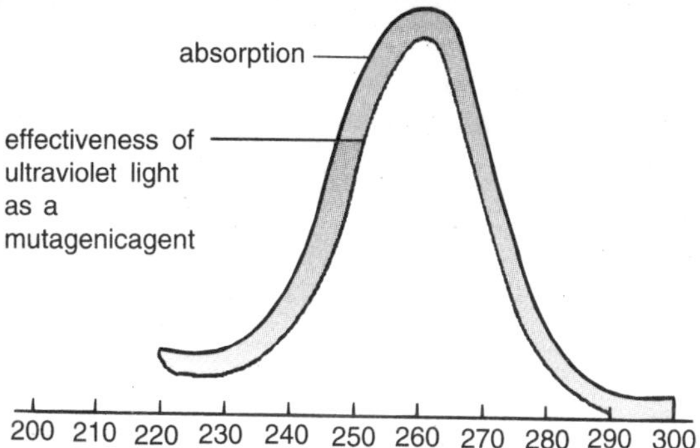

Figure 3.1: Correlation of ultraviolet light absorption by nucleic acids and the action spectrum of induced mutagenesis suggests that the genetic material is nucleic acid.

somatic cells have two sets. In cells of polyploid organisms (those with more than two sets of chromosomes) and in cells with polytene chromosomes (duplicated repeatedly but not separated), there is an increase in DNA content that is related directly to the degree of chromosomal duplication.

Ultraviolet light is one of a number of mutagenic agents. If bacteria or other appropriate organisms (those that have no protective covering to prevent penetration of the cell nucleus by ultraviolet light) are irradiated with various wavelengths of ultraviolet light, then the effectiv-eness of each wavelength in producing mutations can be determined.

The resulting action spectrum shows that the most effective wavelengths are in the 260 nm (10^{-9} m) region. The action spectrum of ultraviolet-induced mutagenesis is similar to the absorption spectrum of the nucleic acids; this is shown in Figure elsewhere in this chapter.

The correlation of these curves suggests that the genetic material is nucleic acid. These ideas support the thought that DNA is the genetic material, a stable but metabolically active control center of the cell. Other bits of evidence indicate strongly that DNA is the hereditary material; these are *direct* or experimental

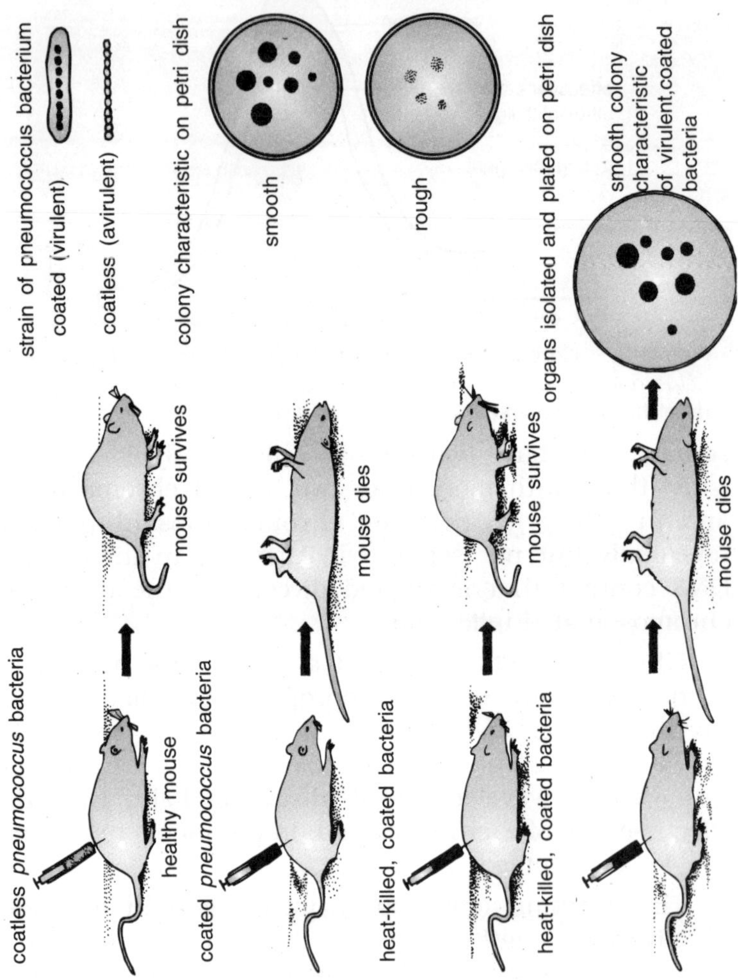

Figure 3.2: Transformation: evidence that DNA is the genetic material.

evidences. The first bit of evidence is the phenomenon of *transformation.*

The pneumococcus bacterium *(Diplococcus pneumoniae)* causes pneumonia in humans and mice and exists as several types, each of which can be distinguished immunologically. Injection of the bacteria or bacterial cell walls into an animal such as a rabbit or guinea pig induces the formation of specific antibodies against the type used for the inoculation.

Some pneumococcal types possess no. tough cell walls or coats, and they produce a "rough" colony on a culture plate; the coated types produce "smooth" colonies. The rough strains are avirulent (the coatless bacteria are easily engulfed by phagocytes in the bloodstream), whereas the smooth strains are virulent, or disease causing.

The first studies on transformation were reported in 1928 by Frederick Griffith, who found that the injection of avirulent bacteria along with heat-killed virulent bacteria caused pneumonia and death in the mouse. Thus some event had changed the avirulent type into the virulent type.

Later workers showed that transformation of type specificity could occur in a testtube culture and that the mouse was not required. After this discovery other workers found that a substance isolated from the virulent type could, when added to a culture of avirulent bacteria, cause the transformation of the avirulent into the virulent type.

All physical and chemical tests have indicated that this transforming factor is DNA. Another bit of direct evidence comes from studies on bacteriophages (bacterial viruses). Viruses possess a protein coat around a core of nucleic acid.

Using T_2 bacteriophage (bacterial virus), A. D. Hershey' and Martha Chase grew cultures of *Escherichia coli* bacteria on ^{32}P or ^{35}S (radioactive isotopes of phosphorus and sulfur), and after adding T_2 to the cultures, harvested T_2 phages that were labeled with ^{32}P or ^{35}S. (In order to label the bacteriophages with radioactive isotopes, radioactive bacteria must be used because bacteriophages do not metabolize independently.)

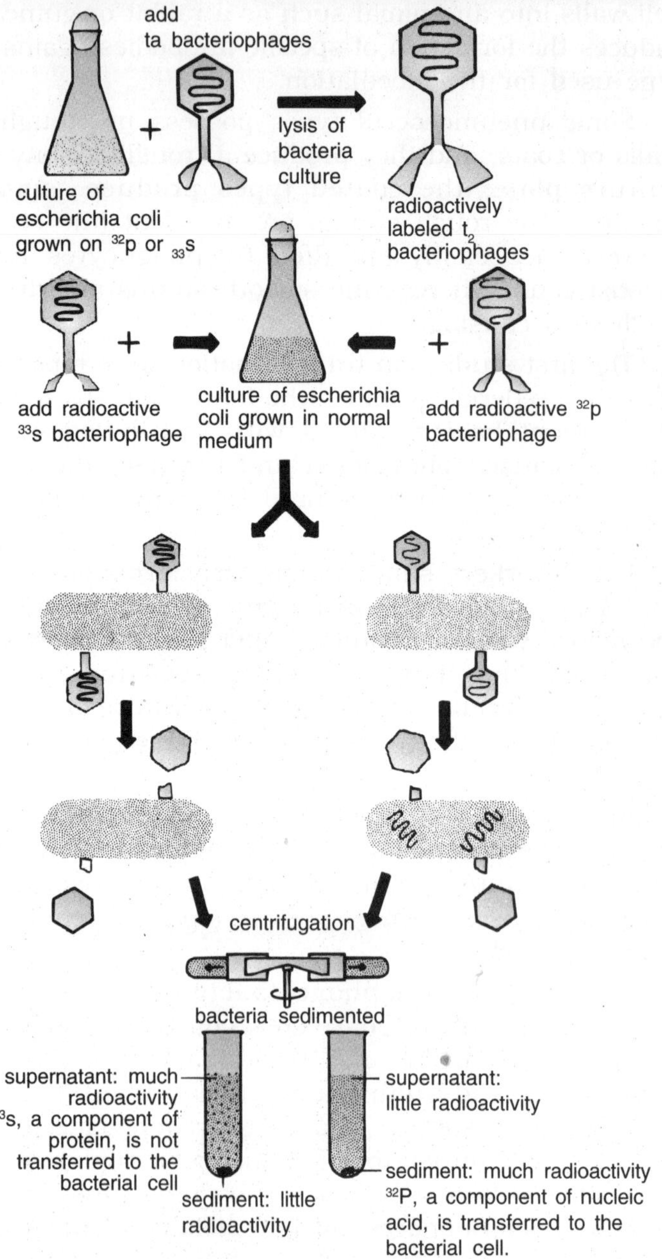

Figure 3.3: Hershey—Chase experiment.

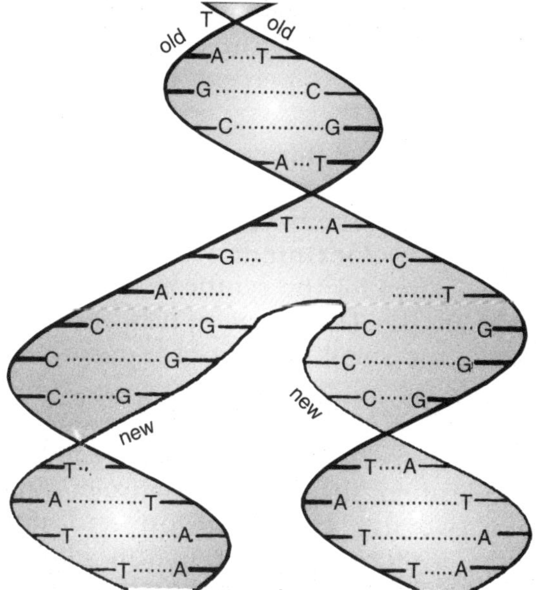

Figure 3.4: Replication of DNA according to Watson and Crick. The two polynucleotide chains of each DNA molecule separate, and each serves as a template for the formation of the complementary chain. The base pairing specificities (A = T, C =- G) tend to insure exact duplication.

Then a sample of radioactive phages was added to unlabeled bacteria. After the phages attached to the bacteria, the phage-bacterium complexes were sheared apart in a Waring blendor.

By differential centrifugation (sedimentation of the bacteria but not of the bacteriophages) the infected bacteria and the empty phage ghosts were separated.

The results of the experiment showed that when ^{35}S was used as the label (sulfur is a constituent of proteins and not of nucleic acids), 80 percent of the radioactivity was found in the ghosts and 20 percent had been transferred to the bacteria.

Furthermore, when ^{32}P was the label (phosphorus is a constituent of nucleic acids but is seldom found in proteins), 85 percent of the radioactivity was transferred to the bacteria. The experiment was later refined to show that almost all DNA of the virus entered the bacterium on infection but only 3 percent of the protein was transferred.

The interpretation of this experiment is that the bulk of the phage DNA is transferred to bacteria in the infection process and the bulk of the protein is not. The Hershey-Chase experiment demonstrated that information required for the synthesis of a virus particle is contained in the DNA that enters the bacterium, rather than in the small amount of transferred protein.

THE REPRICATION OF DNA

One of the three properties of the genetic material is that of replication, the capability of exact duplication. (The other two are transcription and mutation; transcription is discussed later in this chapter while mutation is discussed in other chapter of this book.)

All cells of a multicellular organism are derived from the zygote, and presumably all the cells contain the same genetic material; thus the necessity for the exact transmission of the genetic material from parent to progeny cell imposes a replication requirement upon that material.

James D. Watson and Francis H. C. Crick were aware of the replication requirement and proposed a mechanism for replication at the same time that they proposed a model for DNA structure.

Their proposal for DNA replication was that the two polynucleotide chains of each DNA molecule separate from each other and that each chain serves as a specific surface (a template) for the formation of a complementary chain. The result of this process is two complete DNA double helices.

The schematization of DNA replication is shown in Figure anywhere else in this chapter. Notice the role of base pairing in this template-specific process. The

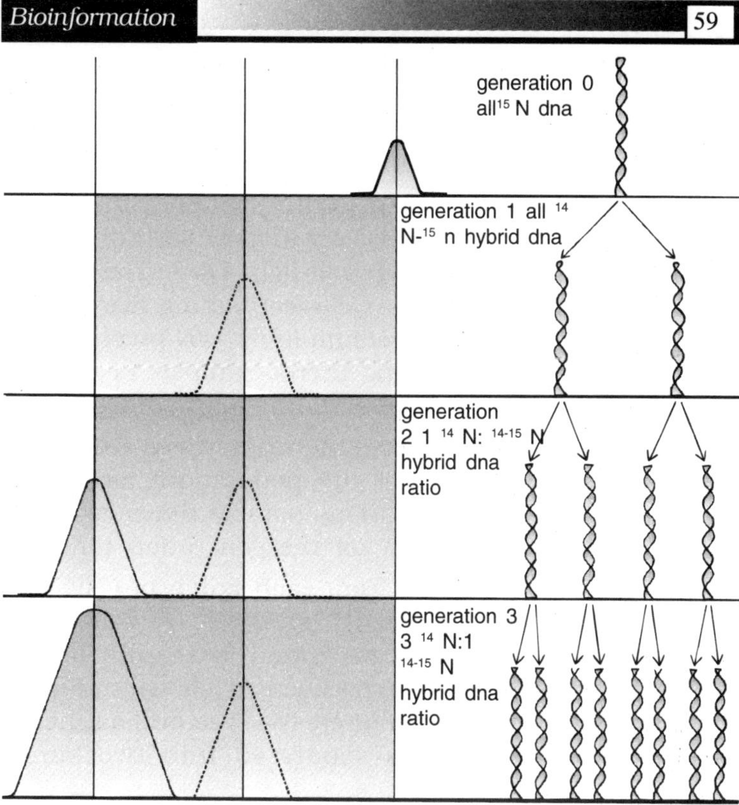

Figure 3.5: Schematic comparison of the Watson-Crick proposal for DNA replication and the Meselson-Stahl-Vinograd experiment

proposal of Watson and Crick for the replication of DNA was tested experimentally in 1958 by Matthew Meselson, Franklin Stahl, and Jerome Vinograd. Bacteria (*Escherichia coli*) were grown for several generations on a medium that contained 15N, the heavy nitrogen isotope, rather than ^{14}N.

DNA extracted from such bacteria and containing the heavy nitrogen is more dense than normal DNA and moves faster in a gravitational field produced by an ultracentrifuge. In this type of centrifugation a tube is prepared with a salt solution that increases in concentration from top to bottom-a density gradient.

When DNA is applied to the top of and is centrifuged in such a density gradient, it moves to the region of its buoyant density. (Where the density of the fluid equals the density of the DNA, the DNA will stop.

Compare density gradient centrifugation with a swim in a salt lake.) Thus heavy DNA will move farther toward the bottom of the tube than will light DNA. The critical experiment was as follows. Cells containing heavy DNA were transferred to light medium (only 14N present) and allowed to continue growing there. Samples of cells in the light medium then were withdrawn at various times.

Since the doubling of generation time (the time neces-sary for doubling of the population) for *E. coli* was known, each of the various sample times could be expressed as some fraction of the generation time.

The DNA was isolated from each batch of cells and ultracentrifuged in a density gradient. A schematic comparison of the proposal and the results of the Meselson-Stahl-Vinograd experiment is shown in Figure 6.5. The figure indicates that each of the original heavy DNA double helices was separated into two single chains.

Upon each original heavy single chain, a new light chain is produced, and the resulting double helix of DNA is hybrid and intermediate in density. A second round of replication produces two hybrid and two light double helices. The replication of DNA logically leads to the question: What are the chemical events in this process?

Arthur Kornberg and associates have devised experiments that permit the cell-free synthesis of DNA. The enzyme *DNA polymerase* (now called DNA polymerase I) catalyzes the synthesis of macromolecular DNA from nucleotide building blocks. The DNA polymerase reaction requires four nucleotides in the form of triphosphates. (As discussed in Chapter 3, three phosphates are attached to the sugar.

This is an energy-rich form.) In addition, DNA polymerase requires some macromolecular (large) DNA as a primer; if the primer is omitted, there is usually no synthesis.

Thus it turns out, as might be expected logically of the genetic material, that *the synthesis of DNA is a highly specific* process.

DNA polymerases have been found in extracts of all cells-bacterial, plant, and animal-where DNA replication has been measured.

The DNA that is synthesized in the cell-free system is similar to the DNA that is used as a primer; the physical properties, such as the sedimentation rate in an ultracentrifuge and the molecular weight, are similar, while the base composition (the percentage of each kind of base) of the product reflects that of the primer.

This ratio is obtained without regard to the extent of synthesis (1-20 times the amount of primer). The interpretation of this observation is that the primer molecules are copied completely and repeatedly. The DNA synthesized in the cell-free system, as described above, has no biological activity.

But in 1967 the cell-free synthesis of a biologically active DNA was accomplished in Kornberg's laboratory. This was done by using the circular single-stranded DNA of a small bacteriophage ((DX-174) as a template. (A single-stranded DNA molecule is found in a few bacteriophages.)

The DNA strand, which is in the bacteriophage, is called the plus strand. It was used to synthesize a double-stranded circle (plus and minus). The minus strand was isolated and was used as a template for the synthesis of plus strands.

The plus strands were then assayed by adding them to bacterial protoplasts. The plus strands did enter the protoplasts and produce complete bacteriophages. An outline of this experiment is shown in Figure elsewhere

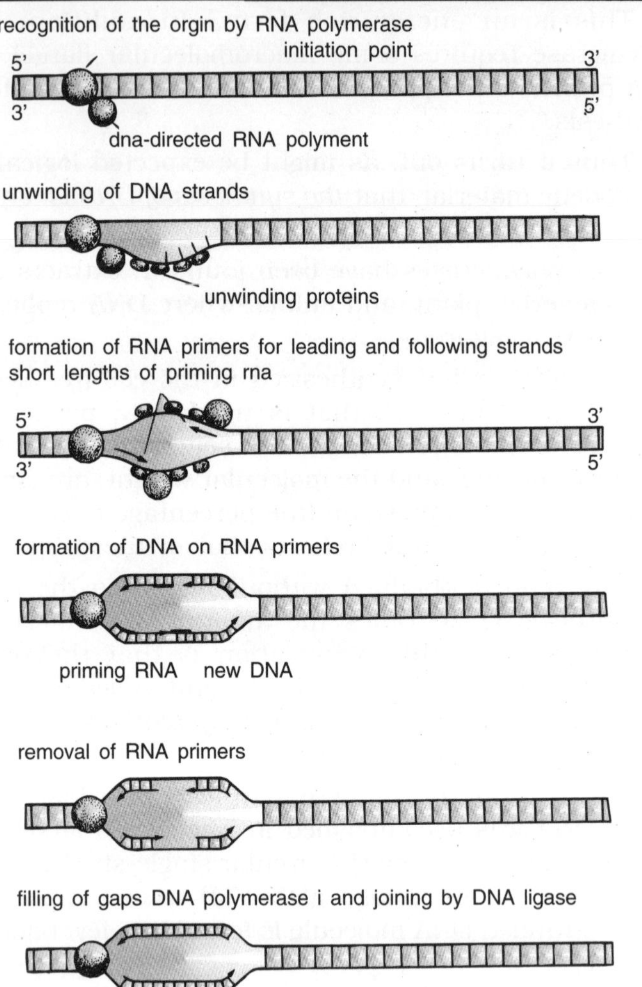

Figure 3.6: General steps of DNA replication.

in this chapter. At this point in the study of DNA replication it was logical to conclude that the basic aspects of the process were well understood.

However, a few months later it was shown that mutations could be induced in the gene which specifies DNA polymerase I. These mutations seriously decreased the enzyme's activity.

The bacteria were not harmed and DNA replication seemed to occur normally in these cells. What could explain these curious observations? Probably DNA polymerase I is not the major enzyme involved in DNA replication, but it is a repair enzyme for broken or imperfect DNA.

Under *in vitro* conditions with high concentrations of nucleoside triphosphates the DNA polymerase is able to do more than repair DNA. It is “forced” to synthesize complete DNA molecules. Which enzyme is the *real* DNA polymerase? Two new enzymes called DNA polymerase II and III, in order of their discovery, have been identified and partially purified.

Many details are yet to come, but DNA polymerase II seems to be the fundamental enzyme involved in DNA replication. DNA polymerases in eukaryotic cells have been studied and they exhibit no unusual properties.

In addition to the nuclei, these polymerases are found in mitochondria and chloroplasts, are associated with ribosomes and are found in isolated, smooth endoplasmic reticulum fractions. Since mitochondria and chloroplasts contain unique DNAs and are semiautonomous cellular organelles, the presence of DNA polymerases is logical.

The significance of DNA polymerases associated with ribosomes and smooth endoplasmic reticula, which do not contain DNA, is not clear. In general, DNA polymerases require a template of primer DNA, all four nucleobases in the form of deoxyribonucleoside triphosphates (base-deoxyribose-P-P-P), and Mn^{++} or Mg^{++}.

The primer DNA directs the specificity of synthesis through the base-pairing relationships, A = T, C = G. Experiments using ^{32}P-radioactive deoxyribonucleoside triphosphates have shown that synthesis always occurs in the 5'→ 3' direction. Since the double stranded DNA molecule has the two strands arranged in an antiparallel fashion, parallel synthesis on each strand would be impossible.

A mechanism of DNA synthesis which accounts for the synthesis in the 5' → 3' direction on both strands is shown in Figure elsewhere in this chapter along with the general reaction and the details of DNA strand extension.

METABOLIC SYSTEMS

Metabolism occurs in orderly pathways. Each step of these metabolic pathways is catalyzed by an enzyme; a good example is glycolysis. If one reaction in a pathway is blocked, then the other reactions may be affected significantly.

If a blocked pathway is an anabolic one, the compound after the block must be supplied in the diet for normal functioning of the organisms. If the blocked pathway is a catabolic one, then the compound before the block accumulates and is excreted (or accumulated).

Some well-known metabolic diseases are directly related to mutant, or altered, enzymes. Such direct influence is called *a primary* block. In the human disease *alcaptonuria* the enzyme that breaks down homogentisic acid into further oxidation products is absent.

The homogentisic acid in the urine of alcaptonurics oxidizes spontaneously to a black pigment. Consequently alcaptonuria was one of the first inborn errors of metabolism to be recognized; it is easily detected in infants by the dark stains in their diapers.

Alcaptonurics slowly deposit the pigmented material in their connective tissues and often have an unsightly staining of the cartilage in the ears and nose; this also causes a relatively benign arthritic condition. *Phenylketonuria,* a very severe mental disease, is due to a primary block that inactivates the enzyme that converts phenylalanine to tyrosine.

In individuals with this disease the phenylalanine

concentration builds up in the body fluids and is excreted in the urine. Another block, responsible for al*binism*, is also shown in Figure elsewhere in this chapter.

This block prevents the formation of the normal pigments of the skin, hair, and eyes. *Galactosemia* is another disease due to a primary block. Infants which have this disease are unable to metabolize galactose, a monosaccharide contained in lactose (a disaccharide), the principal sugar of milk.

As a consequence, the galactose level in the blood is high and galactose is excreted. The deleterious effects of many metabolic disorders cannot be traced directly to primary blocks; rather, the effects seem to come from other reactions that are influenced by metabolites accumulated at the primary blocks.

The accumulation of metabolites above normal levels may result in an inhibition of other reactions; such reactions are secondarily blocked. Examples of secondary blocks can be seen in the diseasesjust mentioned. In galactosemia, galactose probably acts as an inhibitor of reactions involving glucose.

Removal of galactose from the diet of the affected infant permits these reactions to function normally. Adults produce an entirely different enzyme; thus, infant galactosemics outgrow their metabolic disease. In phenylketonuria, phenylalanine is metabolized by other enzymes, and the resulting products serve as inhibitors of the usual phenylalanine pathway.

Thus, a biochemical reaction is not an isolated entity but affects and is affected by many other reactions occurring in the organism.

TRANSCRIPTION: BIOSYNTHESIS OF RNA

The bioinformation stored in the chromosomes of cells must be "read" before this information can influence the operation of the cell. The reading of bioinformation occurs in two distinct steps: transcription and translation. As mentioned earlier, *transcription* is the synthesis of RNA under the direction of DNA. *Translation* is a complex process of protein synthesis involving messenger RNA (mRNA), transfer RNA (tRNA), ribosomes, several enzymes, and other factors.

The three major kinds of RNA (messenger, ribosomal (rRNA), and transfer) are transcribed from specific regions of the DNA.

In eukaryote cells this occurs mainly in the nucleus. Transcription is catalyzed by an enzyme called RNA polymerase, and the reaction requires all four nucleoside triphosphates (ATP, GTP, CTP, and UTP), a divalent ion (Mg^{++} or Mn^{++}), and DNA, which is a primer or template for the reaction:

$$\text{nATP} + \text{nGTP} + \text{nUTP} + \text{nCTP} + \text{DNA template} \xrightarrow[\text{Mg}^{++} \text{ or Mn}^{++}]{\text{RNA polymerase}} (\text{AMP} - \text{GMP} - \text{UMP} - (\text{MP})\text{n} + \text{DNA} + 4\text{n PP}$$

The first demonstration of a mRNA was reported in 1956. When bacteriophages containing DNA as the genetic material infect bacteria, the infected cells synthesize a new kind of RNA molecule.

This newly synthesized RNA has base ratios (A + T)/(C + G) that are different from the DNA of the host bacterial cell.

The experiment was performed in the following manner. *Escherichia coli* were grown and then infected with bacteriophage T_2.

At the time of infection ^{32}P was added to the medium. A large fraction of RNA in the infected cells was found to contain a large amount of radioactive phosphorus.

Hydrolysis of this RNA fraction and subsequent determination of the amount of each kind of nucleobase showed that the base ratio was different from the RNA and the DNA of *E. coli* cells but similar to the DNA of the infecting phage.

This was taken to mean that the infecting DNA had been read several times and that the base sequence of T_2 phage DNA is significantly different from the bacterial chromosome. The term "messenger" was coined to indicate that the RNA molecule could convey a message.

Not all of the DNA of a cell is used as a template for the synthesis of mRNA. Some DNA genes specify rRNA and tRNA. Quantitative analysis indicates that, in a certain strain of bacteria, 0.42 percent of the total DNA is complementary to ribosomal RNA and about 0.03 percent is complementary to tRNA.

Thus the majority of the remaining DNA is presumably complementary to mRNA. The bulk of the RNA in a cell is ribosomal RNA. This means that a small portion of the DNA is transcribed over and overto produce the rRNA.

In higher organisms the regions of DNA that produce rRNA are amplified, and rRNA is abundantly produced. This fact has been used in visualization of the transcription process.

VISUALIZATION OF TRANSCRIPTION

During the early growth of the amphibian egg, the region of the chromosome that contains genes for rRNA synthesis (called the nucleolus organizer region) is multiplied about a thousand times, and these extra copies are released into the nuclear sap.

There is evidence that these ex*trachromosomal nucleoli* function similarly to familiar nucleoli of mature cells in synthesizing ribosomal RNA molecules. Each extrachromosomal nucleolus consists of a compact fibrous core and a granular cortex.

If the cells and their nuclei are disrupted in a hypotonic solution, the extrachromosomal nucleolar cores can be isolated and unwound. The core contains a circular molecule of double'stranded DNA which is about 10-30 nm in diameter. It is periodically coated along its length with fibrillar matrix material.

The structural arrangement of the fibrils and experiments on RNA synthesis indicate that each matrix-covered DNA region is a gene coding for rRNA molecules. Each fibril in the matrix is an RNA molecule, therefore many RNA molecules are simultaneously being synthesized on each gene for rRNA.

PROTEIN SYNTHESIS: TRANSLATION

It is possible to disrupt cells, isolate some cell components, and bring about protein synthesis in cell-free *(in vitro)* preparations.

The components required for protein synthesis are many: amino acids, tRNAs, mRNAs, ribosomes, several specific enzymes, and ATP.

The first step in protein synthesis is the enzyme-catalyzed activation of the amino acids. This reaction requires ATP and forms an activated complex, AMP-amino acid, which is bound to the amino-acid-activating enzymes. There is at least one kind of aminoacid-activating enzyme for each kind of amino acid.

The next step is the transfer of the amino acids to specific tRNA molecules. The amino acid-tRNA complex then interacts with ribosomes and mRNA. The ribosomes are the sites of protein synthesis within the cell, but they are not active in protein synthesis unless mRNA is attached to them.

In fact the ribosome is made of a large subunit and a small subunit. The two subunits do not seem to join unless mRNA and the tRNA bearing the first amino acid are first attached to the small subunit. Several ribosomes may be attached to one messenger forming a polyribosome.

The actual assembly of the protein molecule involves the polyribosome and the tRNAs charged with amino acids. A specific base-pairing mechanism between the tRNA and the mRNA is involved in protein synthesis. This pairing is between sequences of three nucleotides. The three nucleotides in the mRNA constitute *a codon*, and three on the tRNA constitute an *anticodon*.

As an incoming amino acid is transferred to the growing peptide chain, the messenger moves along the ribosome to bring the next codon for rRNA attachment onto the ribosomes. Thus this picture of the formation of peptide bonds involves the relative movement of the ribosome and the messenger, with the addition of an amino acid at each small movement of the ribosome.

The scheme above suggests that the fate of an amino acid is determined once it is attached to its ribosomal RNA. Indeed, this was shown by an elegant experiment: the tRNA specific for the amino acid cysteine was joined to cysteine, the cysteine was changed to alanine while still on the tRNA, and the behavior of this alanine was studied.

The results show that the alanine behaved as cysteine: the alanine was incorporated into protein in the place of cysteine. This is good evidence that the specificity lies in the tRNA and not in the amino acid.

The overall scheme for the synthesis of protein specified by the genetic material is diagrammed in Figure elsewhere in this chapter. In addition to the components of protein synthesis already mentioned there are several other factors involved in the process.

These factors, probably proteins, are involved in the initiation of translation (probably three), in elongation of the chain (probably two), and in the release (probably one). These factors and their functions are currently being investigated.

Messenger RNA formation and the attachment of ribosomes to it has been visualized by lysing bacteria and viewing with the electron microscope. The conclusions from these studies are that most of the bacterial chromosome is not genetically active at any one instant, translation is coupled with transcription in prokaryotes, and the genes for the small and large ribosome subunits occur in tandem on the bacterial chromosome.

Some Details of Protein Synthesis

For several years biochemists thought that the mRNA codon for the first or NH_2-terminal amino acid was distinctive and that the ribosome was able to recognize it as the starting point for the synthesis of a polypeptide chain.

Analysis of the proteins of *E. coli* and several other bacteria revealed that most, if not all, of them begin with methionine, a sulfur-containing amino acid.

Careful studies revealed that the initiating methionine enters as N-formyl-methionine attached to a tRNA molecule. N-formyl-methionine is the result of the addition of a formyl group H-Cto the amino group of methionine.

There are two types of tRNA that can accept' methionine, but the methionine attached to only onetype of tRNA can be formylated. This tRNA is the initiator tRNA.

The blocking of the amino group of methionine by the formyl group prevents the amino group from entering into peptide bond formation and also seems to promote binding of the Nformyl-methionine attached to the tRNA to the ribosome.

The formyl group does not appear in the finished protein but is removed by enzymatic cleavage. The binding of the mRNA and the initiator tRNA with its N-formyl-methionine is the central event in initiation of the polypeptide chain.

Some insight to this binding process resulted from some experiments involving *E. coli* grown on a medium enriched with heavy isotopes of carbon, hydrogen, and nitrogen.

The ribosomes of cells grown for several generations

on such a medium are "heavy"; they have a greater density than ribosomes isolated from cells grown on normal medium.

If *E. coli* cells grown on the heavy medium are transferred to normal medium and allowed to grow further, the ribosomes show two kinds of hybrids; one with a heavy large subunit and a light small subunit, and one with a light large subunit and a heavy small subunit.

It was concluded that the ribosome constantly dissociates into subunits and that the subunits reassociate at random. Other workers were able to demonstrate that the small subunit binds to the mRNA and the initiator tRNA to form an *initiation complex*, which then combines with the large subunit.

Three specific protein factors are involved with initiation. These initiation factors (F_1, F_2, and F_3) can be extracted from the small subunit of the ribosome so they seem to be a normal ribosomal component. But, interestingly enough, as the initiation complex is formed, the initiation factors apparently are released from the small subunit.

This elaborate initiation process is insurance that the ribosomes do not start synthesis in the middle of a messenger. After initiation, the polypeptide chain is elongated in a cycle of three steps for each amino acid that is added. In the first step the next amino acid attached to its tRNA binds to a site on the ribosome.

This site is adjacent to the site at which the initiator tRNA is bound. The binding to the second site requires a protein factor (T, which contains two subunits) and the energyrich triphosphate, GTP. In the second step the peptide bond is formed between the carboxyl group of the first amino acid, N-formyl-methionine, and the amino group of the second amino acid.

This reaction breaks the bond between the N-formyl-methionine and the initiator tRNA. The reaction is catalyzed by a specific enzyme, which is a part of the large subunit of the ribosome. As a result the growing peptide chain is attached to the tRNA bound to the second site. The initiator tRNA remains bound to the first site.

The third step involves a shift of the ribosome and the messenger with respect to each other. As a result, the empty tRNA in the first site is ejected and the tRNA bearing the growing amino acid chain is shifted from the second site to the first.

This complex process is thought to be involved with a conformational change in the ribosome driven by energy from GTP hydrolysis. A specific protein factor, called G, is required. The messenger appears to file through the groove between the two ribosomal subunits.

The threestep elongation cycle is repeated over and over for each amino acid added to the growing chain. A new G factor-GTP complex is used in the third step of each cycle. After the last amino acid is added, the completed polypeptide chain is still attached to the last tRNA.

There is a specific protein release factor (that is, part of the ribosome) that hydrolyses the completed chain from the last tRNA. Little is known about the state in which the completed chain leaves the ribosome in the termination or release step.

Probably the chain has folded to a large degree toward its final three-dimensional shape. After the codon for the last amino acid is reached, the next codon is nonsense, that is, it codes for no amino acid and is a terminator codon.

SOME DETAILS OF THE GENETIC CODE

The genetic code is the dictionary used by cells to translate information written in the 4-letter DNA language into the 20-letter protein language. As mentioned above, the group of nucleotides that codes for one amino acid is a code *word*, or *codon*. The simplest possible code would be *a singlet* code in which one nucleotide codes for one amino acid.

A singlet code would be inadequate for cells because only four amino acids could be specified. *A doublet* code could specify 16 (4 × 4) amino acids, whereas a *triplet* code could specify 64 (4 × 4 × 4) amino acids.

Clearly the triplet code is the simplest code that can account for the 20 common amino acids. Some importa-nt discoveries about the nature of the genetic code were made using synthetic polynucleotides as messengers in cell-free protein-synthesizing systems.

Polyuridylic acid (poly U) which contains only the uridylic acid nucleotide directs the synthesis of a molecule that contains only pjienylalanine. This dramatic discovery started a series of productive experiments that have greatly illuminated molecular genetics, most particularly the genetic code.

In the triplet code, the RNA code word for phenylala-nine would be UUU. There is much evidence that the genetic code is a triplet one. Crick and coworkers have shown by genetic tests that loss or addition of three nucleotides from the end of a gene did not affect its biological activity.

On the other hand, loss or gain of one or two nucleo-tides (or small multiples thereof) near the beginning or in the middle of a gene seriously affected gene function. This suggested that a three-nucleotide change put the reading of the gene back into correct sequence before a critical region of the molecule was reached. Several techniques were used in the deduction of the dictionary of messenger RNA codons.

A particularly important one is based on hydrogen bonding of transfer RNA molecules to the ribosome-messenger complex. Three-letter code words were synthesized and incubated with ribosomes and tRNA that was attached to a radioactive amino acid.

If such a single synthetic codon recognized the tRNA molecule, then the radioactive amino acid was bound to the ribosome. The incubation mixture was then poured onto a nitrocellulose filter that retained the ribosomes but not the smaller components.

Then if the amino acid was bound to the ribosome by the tRNA, the labeled amino acid stayed on the filter. If the codon did not recognize the tRNA molecule, the labeled amino acid (and the attached tRNA molecule) went through the filter.

Thus the presence or absence of the radioactivity on the filter gave a relatively clearcut answer to the question: Is this particular amino acid encoded by this particular codon?

Probably the most direct way to confirm the genetic code is to synthesize a mRNA molecule with a defined base sequence and then determine the amino acid sequence of the polypeptide product of that messenger. Some work along these lines has been done, and it supports the other work on the genetic code.

H. Gobind Khorana has been a pioneer in the synthesis of nucleic acids. After several years of study on how short chains of nucleotides could by synthesized, Khorana successfully synthesized long chains of repeating dinucleotide, UGUGUGUGUG. . . . . ., which contains two triplets, UGU and GUG. The repeating trinucleotide, AGCAGCAGC . . . ., contains three triplets, AGC, GCA, and CAG. Using these long synthetic chains as messengers, polypeptides were synthesized.

In the case of the repeating dinucleotide, two amino acids were found in the polypeptide; these were cysteine (UGU) and valine (GUG). For the repeating trinucleotide three polypeptides were found to be formed: polyserinefrom (AGC)n, polyalanine from (GCA)n and polyglutamine from (CAG)n.

With this technique of using synthetic messengers of repeating sequence, the base sequences of all the codons for amino acids were determined. Another method for checking the code is to discover the anticodon in tRNA.

The complete determination of the structure of a specific tRNA was finished in 1965 after about seven years of work. The tRNA, obtained from yeast, contains 77 nucleotides and is specific for alanine.

The proper sequence of three nucleotides that is complementary to the alanine codon, the anticodon, is located near the middle of the molecule. The two-dimensional structure of alanine tRNA is roughly cloverleaf shaped and is shown in Figure elsewhere in this chapter.

The nucleotide sequences of over 60 tRNAs have now been determ-ined. All results show that the anticodon of a given tRNA is comple-mentary to one of the codons that has been assigned to the particular amino acid.

The threedimensional structure of yeast phenylalanine tRNA has been determined by X-ray crystallography.

The hydrogen bonding relationships predicted from the nucleotide sequence arranged in a cloverleaf are maintained in this three-dimensional structure. The elucidation of the nature of the genetic code has been a fascinating story.

Its basic nature has been established and it shows how the information of nucleic acids is used to control the structure of proteins. The genetic code confirms the theme of molecular genetics.

Genetic information can be stored as a one-dimensional message in nucleic acids and is expressed in the linear structure of proteins.

A linear segment of nucleotides in DNA from an initiator codon to a termination codon that specifies a mRNA molecule is called a *cistron.* Since the genetic code is most probably a triplet one, the cistron that directs the synthesis of a protein containing 100 amino acids would contain at least 300 nucleotides.

THE FLOW OF GENETIC INFORMATION

This chapter has developed the theme that the flow of genetic information in cells is DNA- RNA- protein. Indeed, this logical and reasonable picture is attractive and has been dubbed "the dogma of molecular biology." With RNAcontaining viruses the nature of replication of the RNA to produce more viral RNA has been thought not to involve DNA, that is, RNA serves as a template for RNA synthesis.

For some years several workers have thought that tumor-causing RNA viruses replicate inside of cells by synthesizing a DNA intermediate, which then serves as a template for the production of new RNA molecules that are assembled into new viruses.

In 1970 Howard Temin, a virologist at the University of Wisconsin, and David Baltimore at the Massachusetts Institute of Technology reported the existence of such DNA in cells infected with RNA viruses.

Temin had held this view for several years since he had shown that inhibitors of DNA synthesis would inhibit the replication of RNA tumor viruses in infected cells.

Immediately after Temin's report in 1970, other laboratories found similar evidence to support this idea of RNA-directed DNA synthesis. This is an important exception to the idea that bioinformation flows from DNA to RNA to protein.

What is the significance of these findings? First, the fact that a well established concept has not held up in all cases is a good example of how ideas must change in biology and science as new information is gained. Second, some possible applications of this information may be important in medicine.

Several tumor-causing viruses contain RNA. If the enzyme that catalyzes the synthesis of DNA from RNA (this enzyme is called *reverse transcriptase)* can be selectively inhibited, it may be possible to inhibit viral production, and therefore, the tumors caused by these viruses, without harming the normal cellular functions.

This would be a cure for the cancers caused by these viruses. The situation is quite complex, with many questions to be answered. For example, is the reverse transcriptase an enzyme peculiar to RNA viruses which cause tumors?

Docs the reverse transcriptase occur in normal cells and has it just not been detected heretofore? There is some evidence that the reverse transcriptase may function in the multiplication of RNA-containing viruses that do not cause tumors.

Also, some recent studies indicate that normal cells do contain small amounts of the enzyme. As this story unfolds in the next few years, it will be reported, undoubtedly, in newspapers and news magazines. Thus many people will be able to follow this example of application of basic research to the benefit of human welfare.

REGULATION OF INFORMATION FLOW

If a culture of bacteria is growing in minimal medium (a simple medium containing a few compounds that satisfy the barest nutritional requirements) with glucose as a carbon source, the presence of the enzyme β-galactosidase can be detected only in minute amounts. (β-galactosidase catalyzes the hydrolysis of lactose into galactose and glucose and is also called lactase.)

If lactose is then added to the culture medium, β-galactosidase molecules appear very shortly thereafter and can be detected easily. Such an enzyme is called an *inducible* enzyme because its synthesis is induced by a specific small molecule.

On the other hand, a culture of bacteria growing on

minimal medium synthesizes the amino acid histidine from carbohydrates by a relatively complicated pathway. All enzymes of this pathway can be shown to be synthesized by the cells under these conditions.

If histidine is added to the medium, the synthesis of the histidine enzymes is turned off. Such enzymes are called *repressible* enzymes because their synthesis is repressed by a specific small molecule.

These are two cases of differential gene activity in which the synthesis of gene products is sensitive to environmental conditions. Such cellular control mechanisms have been studied, and a model for these phenomena has been proposed.

This proposal, called the operon model, involves the following com-ponents: regulator genes, operator genes, repressor substances, corepre-ssors, inducers, and structural genes.

The regulator gene (RG) produces the repressor substance (R), a protein. The operator gene (OG) turns the transcription of structural genes (SG) on and off in response to the repressor substance. The structural genes (cistrons) function in specifying a protein via mRNA.

The inducer or corepressor (for example, lactose or histidine, respectively) combines with the repressor substance to change its ability to co(nbine with the operator gene.

Transcription of structural genes occurs when the operator gene is not associated with the repressor substance. The inducible and repressible systems differ in the form of the repressor substance that will associate with the operator gene.

In an inducible system the repressor substance normally associates with the operator gene (no transcription); the addition of inducer prevents the association and turns on transcription.

In a repressible system the repressor substance normally does not associate with the operator gene (transcription); the addition of the corepressor allows the association of the repressor with the operator gene and turns off transcription.

Thus the inducer and corepressor function differently in the two systems. They are small molecules and may be obtained from the outside or from metabolism within the cell.

No matter what the source, the concentration of those substances controls transcription within the cell. If a cellular metabolism raises the concentration of a corepressor, this elevation will turn off the production of more corepressors.

This mechanism is a sensitive control system, and it helps regulate the concentration of small molecules in the cell. The mRNA produced by the structural genes that are controlled by one operator gene probably is one long "giant messenger" transcribed from contiguous cistons.

The regulator gene is not necessarily adjacent to the operator gene that is regulated. The operator genes and the structural genes under their control constitute an *operon,* which is the unit of transcription. The operon model for the regulation of gene activity is based on studies done primarily with microorganisms.

This model has served as an important stimulus in thinking about ways in which eukaryotic cells might become different from each other as a result of changes in their environment.

Recent work indicates that the operon model, although of fundamental importance in understanding regulation of the flow of bioinformation, does not spell out the whole story. Refinements, extensions, and alternatives of this model are even more complex and beyond our scope in this introductory text.

Chapter 4 CHROMOSOMES, MITOSIS, AND MEISOSIS

In the discussion of the cell nucleus in other chapter of this book the chromatin material was described as condensing into stainable chromosomes at the time of cell division. The term "chromosome" means colored body (Gk. *chrome*, color; soma, body); the name is related to the fact that cells with definite nuclei have chromosomes that stain easily with a variety of biological stains.

CHROMOSOMES

Viral Chromosomes

The viruses do not qualify as cells for several reasons. They do not have cytoplasm and therefore do not undergo cell division. Their reproduction occurs only within living cells, where they use materials and energy from the host cell.

A virus possesses all the genetic information necessary for the production of new viruses but none or only a little of the machinery necessary for such production. The chromosomes of a few viruses have been well studied. Generally they are naked nucleic acids-DNA or RNA.

The nucleic acid of bacterial viruses (bacteriophages) is packed tightly into the capsule of the virus. As present in the mature virus particle, the linear double-stranded

DNA helix is about 17μm long in phage lambda and 52 μm long (52,000 nm) in T_2 and T_4 bacteriophages. In T_2 and T_4 the DNA is packed into a head that is 95 nm long.

This is a packing ratio of over 500:1. The packing ratio is the degree of shortening because of coiling, supercoiling, and folding of the DNA. Replication of doublestranded DNA viral chromosomes is by a mechanism of separation of the two strands from each other, with synthesis of a new strand on each old separated strand.

Some viral chromosomes are single-stranded circular DNA molecules, and replication is somewhat different. The viral chromosomes in solution, outside of the virus, are influenced by the temperature and the kinds of ions that are used to neutralize the negative charges on the phosphate groups of DNA.

The viral chromosomes will coil and supercoil in response to changes in the salt concentration in the solution. The chromosome of the tobacco mosaic virus (TMV) is a single strand of RNA coiled inside a coat of protein subunits. All plant viruses and some bacterial and animal viruses possess RNA rather than DNA.

At one time it was thought that viruses could possess only one kind of nucleic acid; recently some RNA tumor viruses have been shown to contain small amounts of DNA in addition to RNA, and one report gives evidence that a bacteriophage contains both DNA and RNA.

The Chromosomes of Prokaryotes

The nucleoid area, or the chromatin of the prokaryotes, may be detected by staining and viewing with the light microscope or by using the electron microscope.

There appears to be one bacterial chromosome per nucleoid area (some bacteria have more than one nucleoid area). The chromosome of the bacterium *Hemophilus influenzae* is about 860 μm long and

Table 4.1: DNA Content of Some Viruses, Prokaryotic Cells, and Eukaryotic Nuclei.

	Daltons	Nucleotides
Viruses		
Φ X-174	1.6×10^6	5500
T_2	130×10^6	400×10^3
T_2	85×10^6	260×10^3
Prokaryotic cells		
Hemophilus influenzae	0.7×10^9	2×10^6
Escherichia coli	2.6×10^9	7.4×10^6
Eukaryotic nuclei		
Drosophila melanogaster (fruit fly)	0.12×10^{12}	0.4×10^9
Frog	28×10^{12}	90×10^9
Carp	2.0×10^{12}	6.6×10^9
Mouse	3.0×10^{12}	8.6×10^9
Human	3.6×10^{12}	11.2×10^9

appears to be linear, naked DNA. The chromosome of the colon bacterium, *Escherichia coli*, is about 1000 μm long and is a closed circle.

The DNA of *E. coli* is packed into a nucleoid less than 1 μm long at a packing ratio of about 1000:1. Since viral and prokaryotic chromosomes are simple in comparison to eukaryotic chromosomes, some workers have suggested that they be termed prochromosomes.

The Chromosomes of Eukaryotes

The structure of the chromosomes of the eukaryotes is extremely complex. Table elsewhere in this chpater shows the DNA content of some viruses and prokaryotes in comparison to some eukaryotes. From these data it is clear that a eukaryotic nucleus will contain about 1000 times more DNA than a virus or prokaryotic cell.

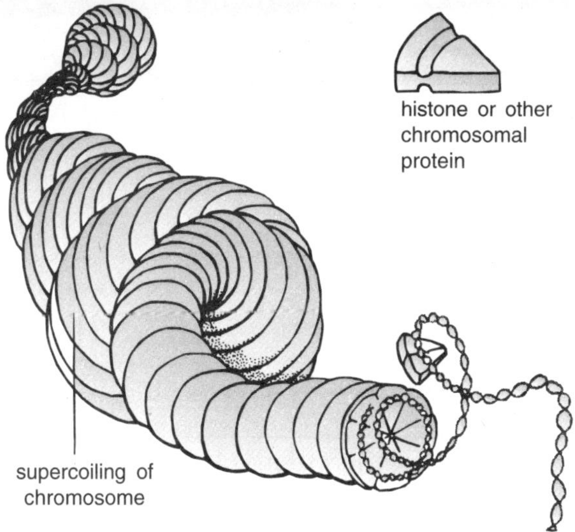

Figure 4.1: Chromosome model. Inside each chromosomal fiber, a single DNA double helix is tightly packed by supercoiling. The DNA molecule is held in place by histones and other proteins which are shown as wedge-shaped molecules.

In addition to a complex chromosome structure, the eukaryotes possess a mitotic apparatus, a nucleus enclosed by a membrane, and a drastic increase in chromosome size over the prochromosomes of viruses and prokaryotes. Furthermore, parts of the eukaryotic chromosome sometimes are metabolically inactive, while at other times they are active-some chemical components are rather constant for long periods and others fluctuate greatly.

Chemically, the chromosome contains DNA, RNA, and proteins. There have been several suggestions as to how the DNA is ordered in the eukaryotic chromosome. The suggestion in current favor is that it is a continuous strand from one end to the other with proteins and other materials attached along its length.

Figure elsewhere in this chapter shows a model of the structure of a chromosome that illustrates the coiling and supercoiling to give a packing ratio of 56:1. Whate-

Table 4.2: Chromosome Numbers of Selected Organisms.

Organism	*Diploid (2n) Number*
Dog	52
Chicken	18
Fruit fly	8
Planaria	14
Hydra	12
Crayfish	200
Frog	26

ver the structure of the eukaryotic chromosome should turn out to be, it must provide for some elaborate and precise movements.

These movements are associated with two processes, mitosis and meiosis. As noted in other chatper of this book, these complex chromosomal events are means for passing on the same sets of chromosomes to somatic or body cells (mitosis) or reducing by one half the number of chromosomes in a gamete (meiosis).

At certain regions there are constrictions of the chromosome; the primary constriction is the region of the *centromere* (sometimes called the kinetochore), and the other regions are called *secondary constrictions.* The centromere is easily distinguished in stained preparations of cells, since it does not stain or stains only lightly.

The centromere has been studied by electron microscopy, and it is thought to be a structureless segment of the chromosome in some species and a set of complex granules or tubules in others. The centromere functions in attaching to the spindle fibers that form in mitosis and meiosis.

Karyotypes

All body or somatic cells (not sperm or eggs) in an

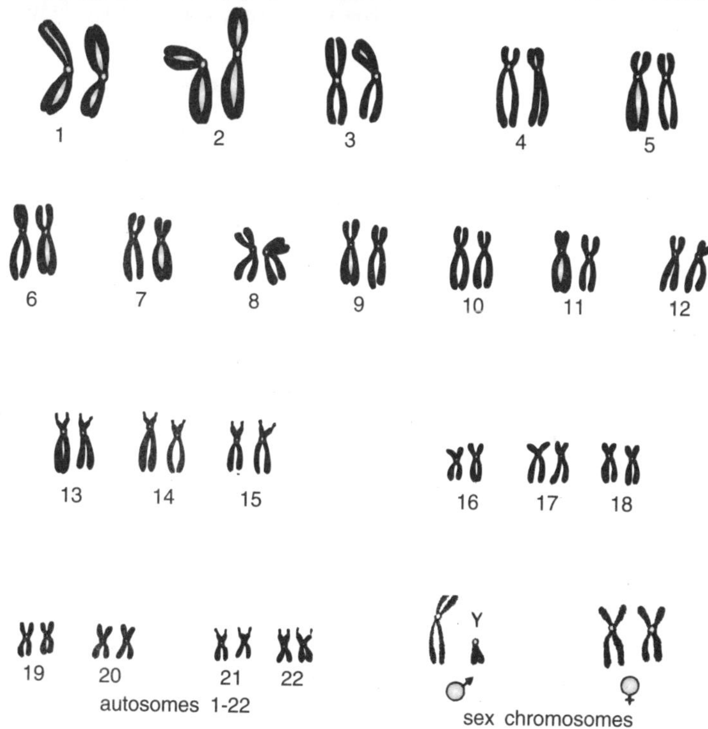

Figure 4.2: Mitotic metaphase chromosomes of the human arranged according to the "Denver classification." Chromosomes are grouped according to the position of the centromere, size, and ratio of arm lengths. Such an arrangement of photographs of chromosomes is the karyotype. The twenty-third pair of human chromosomes is the pair of sex chromosomes, XX in the female and XY in the male.

organism normally have the same number of chromosomes. This number ranges from two to several hundred in different species.

The human chromosome number is 46. Some other chromosome numbers are given in Table anywhere else in this chapter. The chromosomes of body cells occur in pairs. In the formation of the fertilized egg one member of each pair of chromosomes is contributed by the egg, and likewise, one member of each pair is contributed by the sperm.

Except for a pair of chromosomes associated with sex in most animals, the members of each pair of chromosomes are normally alike in size and shape. The members of such a pair are called *homologous chromosomes.*

In most species the chromosomes of different pairs tend to differ in size and shape. Thus the chromosomes exhibit individuality, and it is possible to study individual chromosomes during the division process. The *karyotype* is the term applied to the description of the chromosome composition of a species as illustrated in Figure elsehwere in this chapter.

Usually karyotypes are established by cutting the individual chromosomes from a photograph and arranging them by homologous pairs. Each kind of gamete, sperm or egg, contains one set of chromosomes, that is, one of each chromosome in a homologous pair.

This chromosome set is a *haploid* set and is abbreviated by the symbol n. Somatic cells, on the other hand, are 2n or *diploid* since two chromosome sets are present in the nuclei. Recently methods for studying chromosomes in somatic cells of humans have been improved.

This has permitted an accurate and detailed description of the normal karyotype and the discovery of abnormalities responsible for certain congenital malformations. Several techniques have helped greatly in this regard:

1. Treatment of cultures of cells with the alkaloid drug, *colchicine,* which prevents the formation of the spindle, with the result that many cells arrest at metaphase with definable chromosomes.
2. Treatment of cells with a hypotonic solution that causes nuclei to swell and makes the spreading of the chromosomes much easier.
3. Cells used in karyotype preparation are often obtained from bone marrow, skin, or connective tissue by biopsy. White blood cells are widely

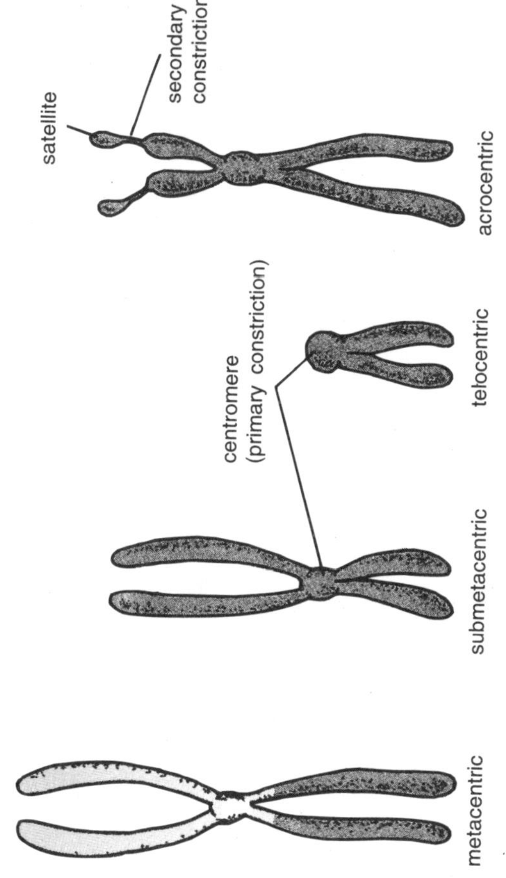

Figure 4.3: Types of metaphase chromosomes.

used also. The addition of phytohema-glutinin (a substance derived from the broad bean) agglutinates the red blood cells, and also stimulates division of white cells.

4. Tissue culture methods have been important in chromosome analysis.

These procedures have led to a rather rapid advance in human chromosome methodology and in the understanding of the relationship of abnormal chromosome structure to pathology. The chromosomes are classified

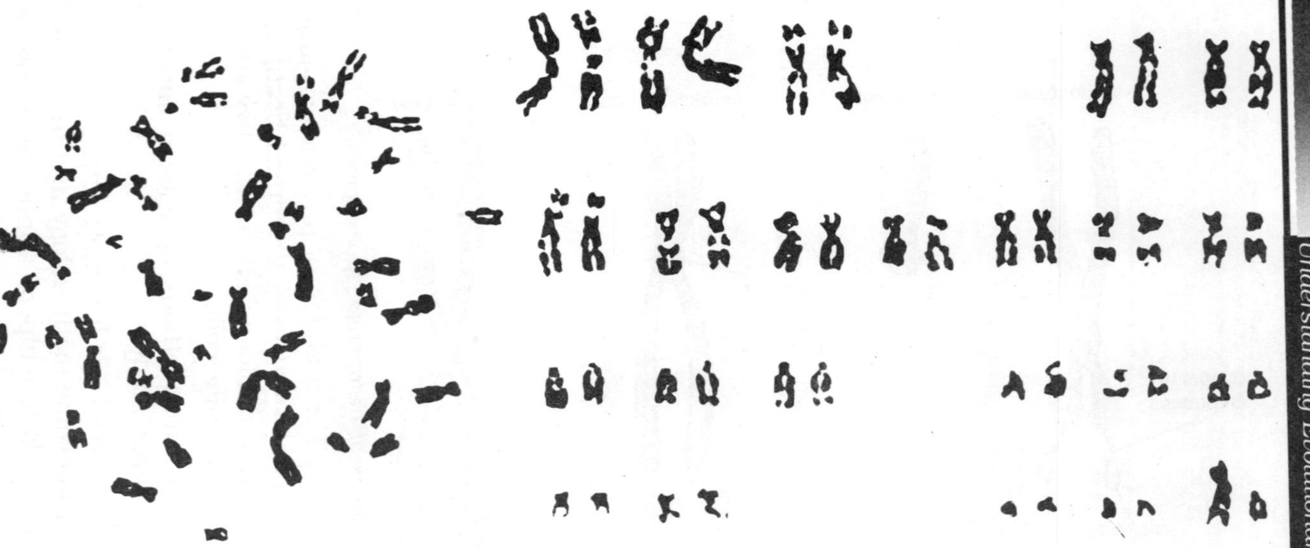

Figure 4.4: Karyotype of a normal human male.
The Giemsa stain banding pattern is characteristic for each chromosome.

according to size: small, medium, and large. Additionally, chromosomes are recognized according to the position of the centromere (the primary constriction) and the resulting relative length of the arms. If the centromere is in the center, then the arms of the chromosomes are the same length.

The centromere may be asymmetrically located in the chromosome, or it may be placed at the end. Some chromosomes have secondary constrictions. This makes the chromosomal arm appear as if it contained a stalk with a bulb of chromatin attached.

The bulb of chromatin is called a satellite and is useful in identification of chromosomes. The karyotype of the human female has 23 homologous pairs including a pair of X chromosomes; the male has 22 homologous pairs and an X and a Y chromosome.

The X and Y chromosomes are called *sex chromosomes* while the others are termed autosomes. Karyotyping of cells by the traditional methods of photographing a stained preparation of mitotic cells and arranging the individual photographs of the chromosomes in order of size and centromere position has allowed cytologists to identify postively only 4 of the 23 pairs of human chromosomes.

In the late 1960s karyotyping was advanced by the development of chromosome analysis under a fluorescence microscope. The Y chromosome fluoresces when treated with a class of compounds called quinacrine dyes (normally used in the treatment of malaria). Sperm and cells taken from certain extraembryonic membranes (the amnion and chorion) can be distinguished as to their sexual type.

This staining technique can be used for the prenatal determination of the sex of a baby. Cells in the amniotic fluid may be withdrawn through a syringe needle (the human female reproductive system is discussed in other chapter of this book). The amniotic fluid cells originally were sloughed from the lower intestinal tract of the baby.

This process of withdrawing amniotic fluid cells is called *amniocentesis*. In addition to staining the chromosomes of the cells for determination of the sex of the baby or detection of chromosome abnormalities, the amniotic cells may be cultured and metabolic deficiences of the baby determined.

Since there is a slight chance of miscarriage associated with amniocentesis, it is seldom used for prenatal sex determination exclusively. In 1970 a truly remarkable discovery in karyotype preparation was made.

Treatment of chromosomes with hydrochloric acid to remove basic proteins, with ribonuclease to remove RNA, and with sodium hydroxide (pH 12) to denature the DNA produces a chromosome that shows a specific banding pattern with Giemsa stain (long used for staining blood cells).

Precise identification of every human chromosome is possible with this technique. This new technique should allow the identification of chromosome abnormalities involved in birth defects, drug and pollution damage, mental retardation and illness, aging, and cancer.

The quinacrine and Giemsa stain techniques set off an explosion of reports of new information on the karyotypes of many kinds of organisms. Additionally, other staining techniques have been shown to give banding profiles when used on chromosomes that have been "relaxed" by the above or similar techniques.

MITOSIS

Ordinary cell division often is called mitosis. Strictly speaking, the term mitosis refers to nuclear changes during cell division, whereas the division of the cytoplasm more properly is called *cytokinesis*. As mentioned in other chapter of this book, mitosis is a mechanism that normally produces two daughter cells, each with the same chromosome complements. This means that the two cells so produced have the same hereditary material, since the chromosomes are the locations of DNA in the nucleus.

Stages of Mitosis

The changes occurring in mitosis are continuous, but for analytic purposes the process is divided into stages. The stage between divisions is known as the *interphase*. The process of division is divided into *prophase*, metaphase, anaphase, and *telophase*.

Although the process may be studied in living cells by using a polarizing microscope or a phase microscope, in ordinary studies the cells are killed and stained; thus each cell is analogous to a single frame of a moving picture film. Below are described the stages of mitosis as they occur in a typical animal cell.

Interphase

Although the interphase stage is not a part of the division process, it is a very important stage in the *cell cycle*. In this stage the individual chromosomes cannot be seen as such. Each chromosome is greatly elongated, and the chromatin material (after staining) appears diffuse in the nucleus.

There is evidence that the replication of the chromosome occurs during interphase. This means, of course, that the synthesis of more DNA and more protein, the main constituents of chromosomes, occurs in this period.

Three steps of interphase are recognized: the G_1 (gap) stage, which is the period preceding DNA synthesis; the S (synthesis) stage, during which DNA synthesis occurs; and the G_2 stage, a period of preparation for actual division.

The cell cycle is diagrammed in Figure elsewhere in this chapter. There also is evidence that the synthesis of the proteins that go into the formation of the spindle (described below) occurs during interphase. With this in mind it can be said that mitosis is a phenomenon that results in the orderly distribution of the already duplicated chromosomes to daughter cells.

In addition to the chromatin, the nucleoli are often conspicuous in the stained interphase nucleus. Figure elsewhere in this chapter gives a schematic view of the mitotic process in a cell containing two chromosomes (one homologous pair).

Prophase

The first visible change at the beginning of *prophase* is the appearance of the chromosomes as long, thin threads. This is due to the shortening and thickening of the interphase chromatin. These changes result from the loss of water by the chromosomes and by the coiling of the constituent elements.

The chromosomes in prophase are double structures except for the centromere (mentioned already as the primary constriction), which holds them together and which will be the point of attachment to a spindle fiber.

The doubling of the chromosomes occurred in interphase (S stage) when they were dispersed as chromatin.

The two members of each double chromosome are known as chromatids, the term used for them until division of the centromere occurs at the end of metaphase. Chromosome movement is associated with the microtubules called *spindle fibers.*

One end of a fiber may be attached to the centromere of a chrom-osome, while the other end may terminate near a small structure at the pole of the spindle; this structure is *a centriole.* Other fibers may run from pole to pole without attaching to chromosomes.

The centrioles originate just outside the nucleus. Each centriole is a cluster of nine groups of triplet microtubules whose structure is identical to basal bodies found at the bases of cilia and flagella.

At the onset of prophase there is a pair of centrioles near the nuclear membrane. Each centriole replicates and each pair of the resulting two pairs moves in opposite direction as the nuclear membrane breaks down. Thus a pair of centrioles is located at each pole.

Their dimensions are close to the lower limit of the resolving power of the light microscope. As a result, the centriole appears as a very small dot under a light microscope, and in some cases it is not visible at all.

As the centrioles move toward the poles, fibrillar structures begin to differentiate from each centriole. Each radiating fibrillar structure is called an aster, and the fibrils themselves are *astral rays.* Between the two asters the spindle fibers appear.

The structure formed by the centrioles, asters, and spindle is called the *mitotic apparatus*, and it is involved intimately in the division process. Figure elsewhere in this chapter shows asters and spindle fibers in cells of a developing whitefish embryo.

Returning to the events that occur in the nucleus, the chromosomes continue to shorten and thicken, the nucleoli disappear, and as mentioned before, the nuclear membrane disintegrates during late prophase. Then the chromosomes move to the center of the disintegrating nucleus and begin to arrange themselves in the central plane of the spindle, known as the equa*torial plate.*

Metaphase

When the nuclear membrane has broken down and the chromosomes have become arranged on the spindle in the equatorial plate, *metaphase* begins. A spindle fiber from each pole appears attached to the centromere of each chromosome. The simultaneous splitting of the centromeres of all chromosomes signals the end of metaphase.

Anaphase

Anaphase begins as soon as the centromeres split;

the chromatids (now called *daughter chromosomes)* move to opposite poles. The movement of the daughter chromosomes is not really understood. They seem to be pulled to opposite poles by the spindle fibers.

Some chromosomes have their centromeres in the middle, some near one end, and occasionally one is found with a terminal centromere. In the movement of the chromosomes they appear as V, J, or as rods. This is taken by many biologists to indicate that the chromosomes are being pulled along by contraction of the spindle fibers.

Recent work suggests that small amounts of actin and myosin, contractile proteins characteristically found in muscle cells, are present in spindle fibers. Although much remains to be learned about this movement of chromosomes, it can be said that both centromere and spindle fibers are essential.

A chromosome without a centromere does not move, and one with a centromere but not attached to a spindle fiber does not reach one of the poles.

Telophase

The chromosomes approach the poles and become less compact as the nuclear membrane is reformed and the nucleoli reappear.

As the daughter chromosomes approach the poles, a furrow appears at the surface of the cell in the equatorial region, and constriction into two cells begins.

No clear understanding of the controlling conditions for the formation of this furrow exists at present, although several hypotheses have been proposed.

Duration of Cell Division

The time required for completion of mitosis varies from cell type to cell type and is related to the length of the G, phase. Temperature, within certain limits, also affects the duration of the process.

In general the metaphase and anaphase stages are

of short duration; most of the time of cell division is spent in prophase and telophase stages.

It must be remembered that the period between cell division, interphase, is usually long. For instance, in some mammalian cell cultures 16 to 20 hours between cell divisions is a common occurrence. Many cells of both plants and animals studied in tissue culture show the following durations in the cell cycle.

G_1	10-20 hours (usually less than 50 percent of the total)
S	6-8 hours
G_2	1-4 or more hours (usually less than 20 percent of the total)
M	1 hour
Total	18-33 hours

Control and Regulation of Cell Division

Just what initiates the division process has not been determined definitely. Usually it is assumed that the surface-volume relationships of a cell play an important role. As a cell grows in size, its surface increases in proportion to the square of its radius, while its volume increases in proportion to the cube of its radius.

Since a living cell must obtain through its surface all materials needed for maintenance and growth, there will come a point at which the surface area is inadequate to supply the large volume. It has been proposed that there is a critical point in the surface-volume relationship at which the division process is initiated.

This proposal seems plausible, but it does not explain the initiation of cell division in all cells, since some cells divide at a size at which others continue to enlarge. Changing the temperature will, within certain limits, speed up or slow down the process.

Also spindle formation can be prevented by placing

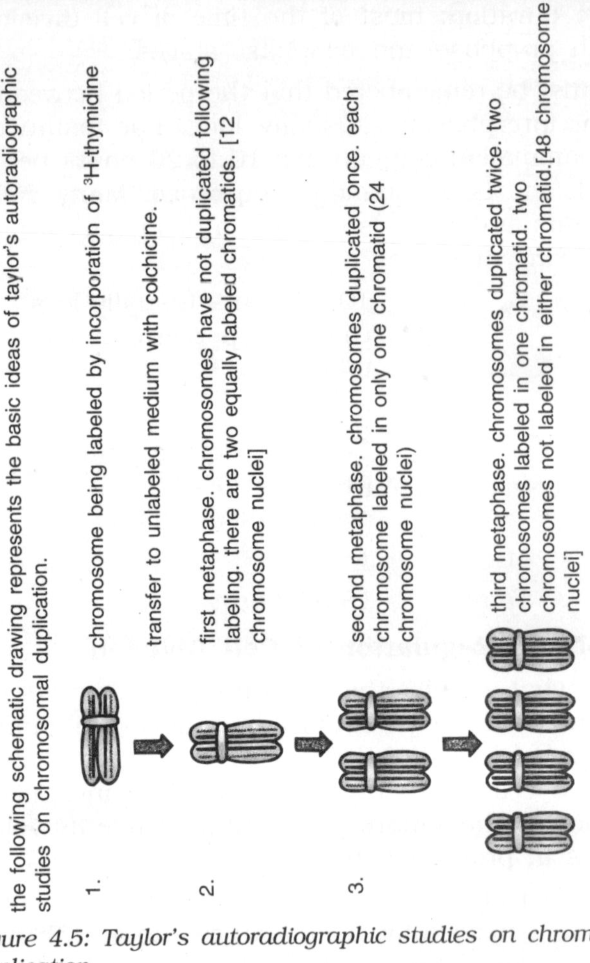

Figure 4.5: Taylor's autoradiographic studies on chromosomal duplication.

cells in a solution of the alkaloid drug colchicine. In this situation the chromatids of the double chromosomes (not to be confused with doublestranded DNA) are unable to separate because of the disruption of the microtubules composing the spindle fibers.

The Significance of Cell Division

Mitosis is the universal process associated with eukaryotic cell reproduction. Two cells are formed, each usually half the size of the original cell and each containing the same complement of chromosomes. Between cell divisions, cell growth occurs through the assimilation of materials from the outside and their synthesis into new cell parts.

Usually, cells must have their normal complement of chromosomes for normal functioning. Addition or loss of chromosomes or parts of chromosomes may lead to malfunction of the cells.

As indicated in other chapter of this book, these changes may also lead to evolution. In cell replacement, wound healing, and regeneration, new cells are produced by cell division.

Although many of the highly specialized cells that result from cell differentiation lose the ability to divide, cell divisions occur throughout life in such regions as the blood-cell-forming tissues, the epithelial tissues of the skin and the intestine, and the gamete-forming tissues of the ovaries and testes.

Once differentiated, many cells such as nerve cells may never undergo mitosis. The process of mitosis is significant in another way.

The basic unit of all organisms is the cell, and that the process of cell division in many kinds of organisms is essentially the same is a potent argument for the basic relationship of all living things.

Autoradiographic Studies on Chromosomal Duplication

Autoradiography is a useful technique for cell studies that involve small amounts of materials. Radioactively labeled compounds are used.

After the experiment has been performed, the radioactive atoms are localized by putting a photographic film against the fixed (chemically killed and immobilized) cells.

The β rays (electrons) emitted by the radioactive

atoms expose the silver grains in the photographic emulsion. Thus by looking at the dark spots on the developed film, one can see the pattern of radioactive compounds in the biological material. J. Herbert Taylor and his associates studied the transfer of atoms of DNA in the chromosomes of the English broad bean (*Vicia faba*) during mitosis.

DNA in the root tips of the broad bean was labeled with tritium (^3H), the radioactive isotope of hydrogen, by exposing the growing tips to a solution containing ^3H-labeled thymidine (the dexoyribonucleoside of thymine).

After about one third of a division cycle the seedlings were transferred to a growth medium without labeled thymidine but containing colchicine. After periods equal to one or two division cycles, the root tips were fixed and pressed against the photographic film.

The electrons emitted by the incorporated tritium are of such low energy that they do not penetrate deeply into the film, and they therefore produce images only at their point of entry into the film emulsion.

The chromosomes and their autoradiograms can be viewed simultaneously with the light microscope. The broad bean contains 12 chromosomes (2n = 12, n = 6). Some nuclei treated in this experiment contained 12 chromosomes, some contained 24, and some contained 48. The chromosomes in cells with 12 metaphase chromosomes have not duplicated following labeling.

The chromosomes in cells with 24 and 48 metaphase chromosomes have duplicated once and twice, respectively. The chromosomes in the nuclei containing 12 chromosomes were equally radioactive in the two chromatids.

Those chromosomes that had experienced a division and were in the second metaphase after labeling (24 chromosome nuclei) were labeled in one chromatid only. In those cells with 48 chromosomes, two sets of chromosomes were completely unlabeled and the other two sets were labeled like those that had undergone only one division.

Figure elsewhere in this chapter outlines the basic ideas of Taylor's autoradiographic studies on chromosomal duplication. Although the actual arrangement of DNA in chromosomes is yet unknown, the transmission of atoms to daughter chromosomes supports the idea that a DNA double helix runs the entire length of the chromosome.

For simplicity of presentation the metaphase chromatids in Figure elsewhere in this chapter have been represented as containing two linear DNA molecules rather than a double helix.

Unsolved Problems

Although the process of cell division has been studied rather intensively for many years, it has been necessary in the preceding discussion to point out in many places that this or that aspect of the process is not fully understood. In sum, this is true for:

(1) the initiation of the process;

(2) the movements of the chromosomes to the equator of the spindle and their subsequent movements to the poles of the spindle;

(3) the formation of the spindle;

(4) the constriction of the cytoplasm in animal cells; and

(5) the apparent need of centrioles in animal and lower plant cells but not in higher plant cells.

At times, masses of cells become abnormal and divide without normal organization. This results in tumors, both benign and cancerous. What causes this abnormal behavior of cells is still not completely understood.

It thus seems that an understanding of the factors that initiate and regulate cell division is essential to the solution of the cancer problem. As a rule the division of the nucleus and the division of the cytoplasm is synchronized.

Yet there are situations when this does not happen. In some of the protozoa, such as the malarial parasite, many nuclear divisions occur before membranes finally are formed around each nucleus. Since normally the division plane for cytokinesis coincides with the equatorial plane of the spindle, how such membranes are formed in the absence of a spindle remains unknown.

MEIOSIS

The discussion of mitosis indicated that the body of cells of each species contain a characteristic number of chromosomes.

It was indicated also that this characteristic number is the diploid, or 2n, number, that is, it is made up of homologous pairs of chromosomes.

In addition, it was pointed out that this diploid condition is the result of sexual reproduction. This means that the germ cells that unite in fertilization must be haploid and that the process of their formation from diploid cells must involve a mechanism for reducing the number to the haploid, or n, number.

As mentioned in other chapter and earlier in this chapter, the mechanism for this reduction is meiosis. Meiosis actually involves two special cell divisions, and the products of these divisions are four cells, each one of which contains one of each pair of chromosomes that characterizes the diploid cells of the species.

Were this not so, the number of chromosomes in sexually reproducing organisms would double with each new generation.

Meiosis and subsequent fertilization, however, normally maintain the constancy of the chromosome number of the species. Meiosis in multicellular animals occurs in the testes in the formation of sperm and in ovaries in the formation of eggs.

Meiotic Divisions

First Meiotic Division

Both meiotic divisions may be viewed as a series of stages similar to those in mitosis: prophase, metaphase, anaphase, and telophase. The prophase of the first meiotic division is quite long in duration and differs in several respects from the prophase of mitosis. When the chromosomes become visible in early prophase, they are exceedingly long and thin.

Although there is no evidence at this time of the replicated state of the chromosomes, our knowledge of DNA synthesis suggests that replication has occurred by the time this stage is reached.

The pairs of homologous chromosomes move together and unite throughout their lengths in a process known as *synapsis.*

Many early studies with the light microscope and recent studies with the electron microscope have revealed that synapsed chromosomes are associated in a very precise way. After pairing, the united chromosomes shorten and thicken, and each fused pair looks like a single entity at this stage.

In later prophase the united chromosomes separate slightly, and it is possible to see that each chromosome is now double, composed of two chromatids that are held together at the centromere.

Since the fused homologous chromosomes are now made up of four parts (two chromosomes consisting of two chromatids each), each such unit is called *a tetrad.*

The number of tetrads is always equal to the haploid number of chromosomes. As in mitosis, while the nuclear changes described above are occurring, spindle fibers appear, and there may be centrioles and typical asters as well.

The end of prophase of the first meiotic division is marked by the disintegration of the nuclear membrane and the movement of the tetrads to the equatorial plate of the spindle.

When the tetrads become aligned on the equatorial plate, the metaphase stage is reached. In anaphase the homologous chromosomes, which fused during early prophase in synapsis and which are made up of two pairs of chromatids, each held together at the centromere, separate and move to opposite poles.

These double structures, each one of which is one half of a tetrad, are called *dyads.* As in mitosis, the telophase is marked by the beginning of cytokinesis, which occurs by constriction.

Following the telophase, each daughter cell may enter an interphase condition similar to that seen in mitosis. However, in many cells the interphase is quite short and in others it is lacking entirely.

Second Meiotic Division

If the second meiotic division occurs immediately after the first division, as will be seen for *Ascaris* eggs later in this chapter, the dyads soon orient on a second spindle.

The division that follows resembles mitosis in that the centromeres divide and the sister chromatids are separated, one of each pairgoing to each pole as a daughter chromosome.

If an interphase occurs between the first and second meiotic divisions, there will be a prophase, as in mitosis, ending in the breakdown of the nuclear membrane and the completion of the spindle.

During anaphase the sister chromatids separate and move to the poles, followed by cytokinesis and the formation of two cells in telophase.

Since the complete meiotic process involves two successive divisions, four haploid cells are produced for each cell that undergoes meiosis.

Comparison of Mitosis and Meiosis

In each mitotic division of diploid cells the number of chromosomes characteristic of the species is maintained; in the two successive divisions of meiosis the diploid number is reduced to the haploid number.

The basic differences in the two processes can be seen in a comparison of mitosis and the first meiotic division. In mitosis the replicated chromosomes line up on the spindle, the centromeres divide, and the sister

Chapter 5 REPRODUCTION

That "Life begets life" is a truism. The process for sustaining life from one generation to another is reproduction. Organisms have various adaptations that function in the reproductive process.

In the absence of true immmortality, here are a few of the ways in which continuity from one generation to the next is maintained. In some organisms, the entire animal undergoes division, much as do single cells in our bodies; this is especially true of protozoa.

Other animals reproduce by developing localized buds that pinch off as new individuals; coelenterates characteristically often do this. Some animals increase their reproductive potential by having several stages in their life cycles, each of which can produce many copies of itself or the next stage; this method of reproduction is common among some of the flatworms, especially the parasitic ones where survival of the species depends on the production of large numbers.

Other animals have the labor of feeding concentrated in one stage of a life cycle, a larval stage, and confine reproduction to another stage, adult, where feeding may be absent; some forms of insects practice this "division of labor." A very important aspect of reproduction in most animals is the presence of two sexes*bisexuality-a* very significant aspect of reproduction.

Why is bisexuality considered to be so important? Certainly the capacity to reproduce asexually appears to be an economical way to produce new members of the species, and it is. But it ignores a condition in the natural world, namely, change.

Asexually reproducing animals usually make almost exact copies of themselves; this offers little opportunity for variation and variation in organisms is essential in order to cope with change. For this reason nearly all living things have developed two sexes and reproduce sexually. Each sex produces gametes that are haploid.

The union of gametes, eggs and sperm, results in the production of a zygote that has a genetic contribution from both parents. Thus the new, sexually produced individual will be different from either parent. There is variation.

With variation there is an increased chance that some members of the new generation will· be better able to cope with changes in the environment. This explanation does not appear to come to grips with the possibility that eggs and sperm'm could be produced in the same animal, a condition called *hermaphroditism.*

There are functional hermaphrodites among the animals, but:' they are relatively rare. Also, even though both sexes may be represented in some animals, there may be different timings at which the male and female organs become sexually mature.

While self-fertilization can occur in some hermaphr-odites, it is uncommon and usually cross-fertilization occurs. The more common condition of separate sexes has the adaptive advantage of creating a division of labor between the sexes. Just one manifestation of this is seen in the production of eggs versus the production of sperm.

Eggs are usually produced in fewer numbers than sperm and tend to conserve their cytoplasm as food-storing reservoirs (yolk) while sperm are much more numerous, restrict their cytoplasm, and usually have large capabilities for movement.

In this chapter vie will place strong emphasis on bisexual reprodu-ction. However, you are reminded that a normal cell cycle is a reflection of one kind of reproduction. Also, meiosis is an essential part of preparing for the production of eggs and sperm. Consistent with the approach developed in Part II, we shall examine reproduction in the human before proceeding to examine development in the next chapter.

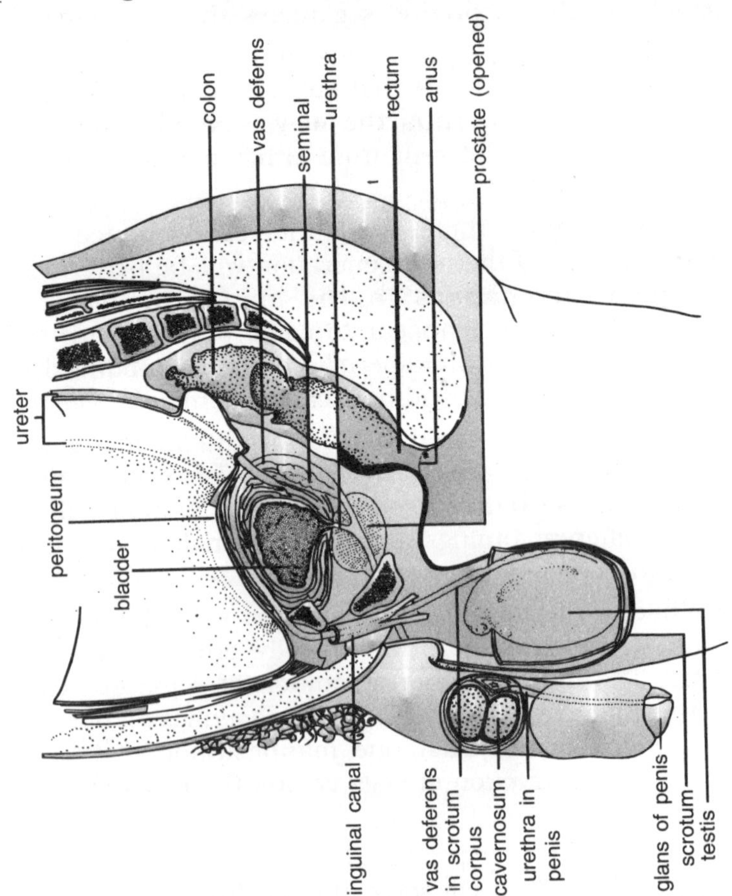

Figure 5.1: Reproductive organs of human male.

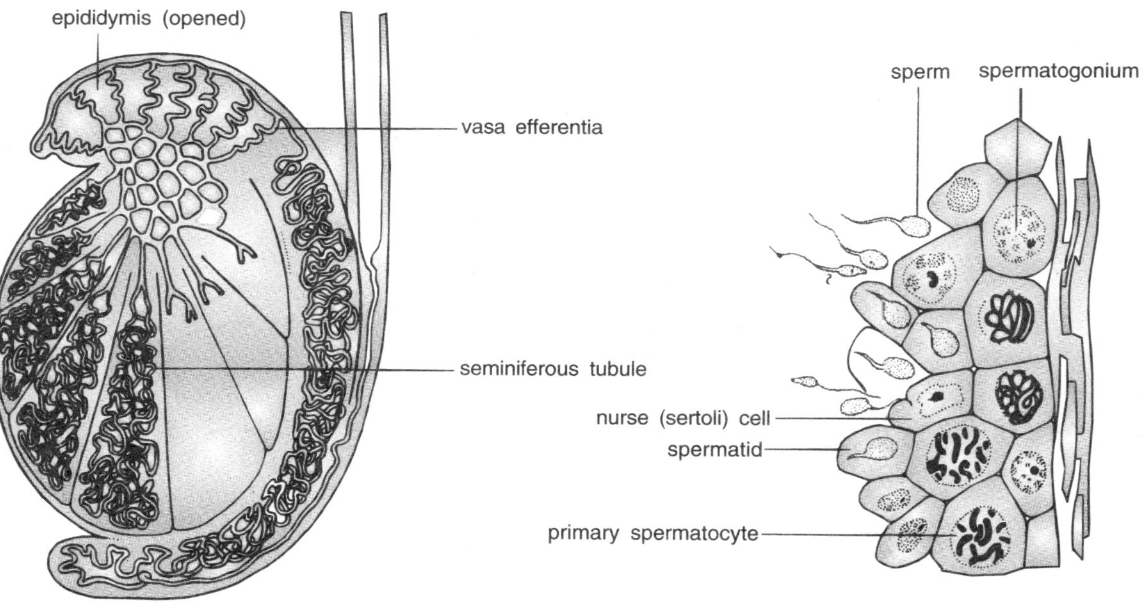

Figure 5.2: Section of human testis and the development of sperm in seminiferous tubules.

REPRODUCTION OF AN ADVANCED ANIMAL: THE HUMAN

Mating in most animals is accompanied by physical and behavioral changes; many of these are under hormonal control and may be quite stereotyped. In

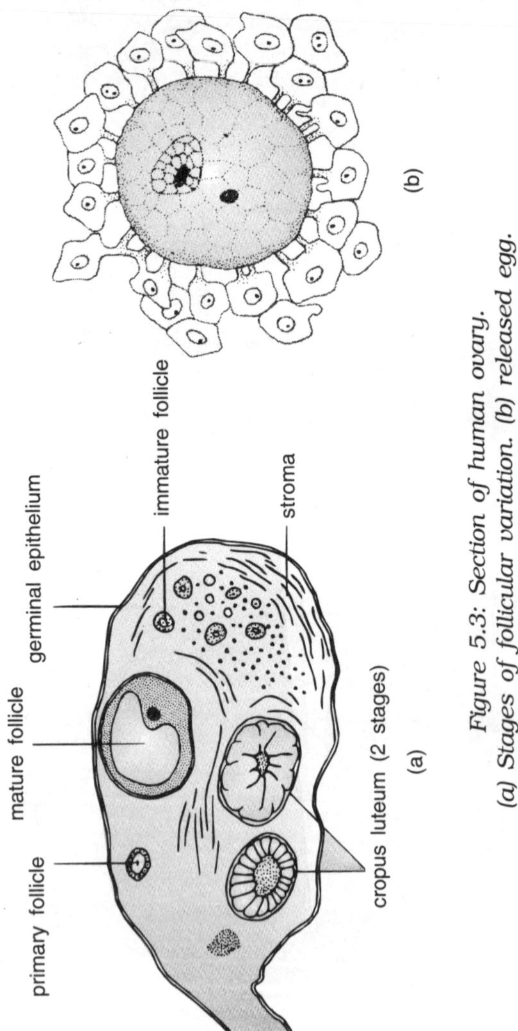

Figure 5.3: Section of human ovary.
(a) Stages of follicular variation. (b) released egg.

humans, however, there is considerable variation in mating play, posture, and frequency of mating. The human female is subject to sexual arousal in no pattern and at relatively frequent intervals.

It has been postulated that this is a naturally selected condition corresponding with the male's relatively continuous sexual drive.

In the copulatory embrace the erect penis is inserted into the vagina and approximately 3 ml of semen containing 300 million sperm are discharged from the male through a series of reflexive spasms of male ducts and glands. The erogenous areas of the penis and the clitoris are stimulated in the sex act to a peak of excitement that then ebbs.

Organs of the Human Male

The *scrotum,* a sac hanging from the lower wall of the abdomen, houses the pair of testes, the sites of sperm production. The testes originate in the body cavity but descend into the scrotum through the inguinal canal.

This route normally becomes blocked off by connective tissue but sometimes is a site of weakness at which an inguinal hernia can develop, in which case a part of the intestine may tend to push into the scrotum.

The testis is composed of coiled *seminiferous tubules* lined with epithelial cells that produce sperm cells; also interstitial cells around the tubules produce the male sex hormone, testosterone, which controls male secondary sex characteristics.

Sperm leave the seminiferous tubules in the testes and pass through a set of ducts, from the *vasa efferentia* to the *epididymis,* derived from embryonic kidney, and into the *vas deferens.*

The vas deferens leaves the scrotum by the inguinal canal and empties into the *urethra,* the duct that leads from the bladder. Fluids of the semen are added to the sperm en route from three sets of glands.

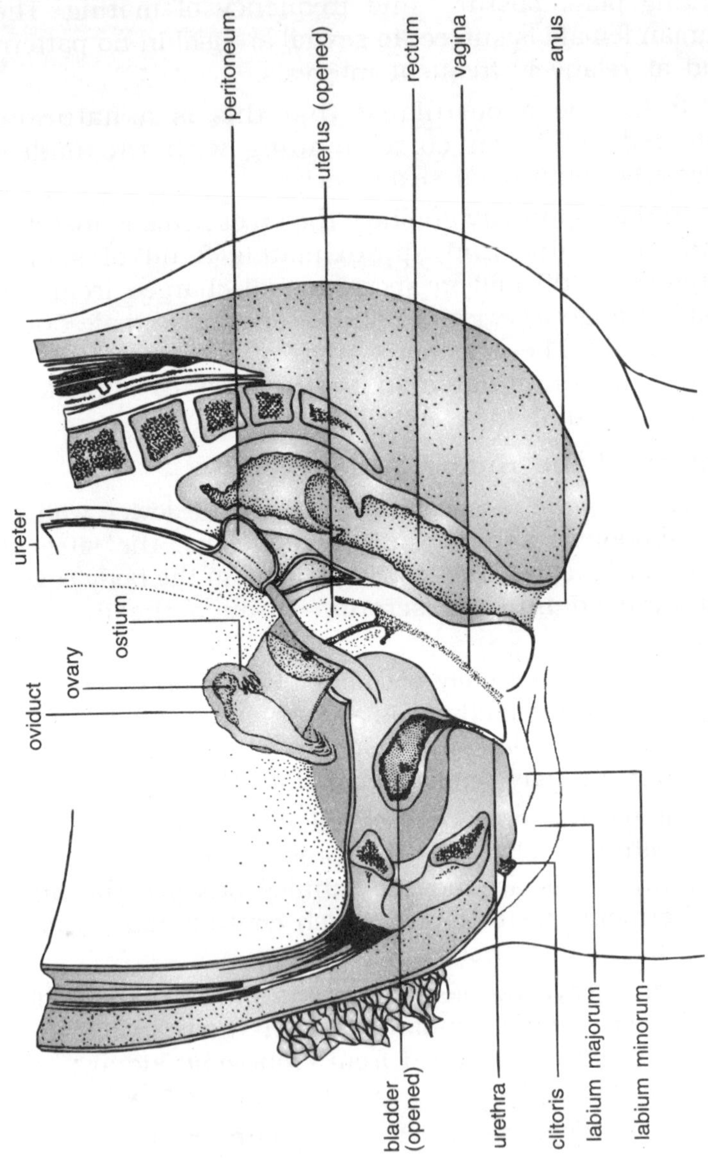

Figure 5.4: Reproductive organs of human female.

A pair of *seminal vesicles* empties into each vas deferens before it connects to the urethra; a single *prostate* gland surrounds the urethra near the junction of the vasa deferentia, and *Cowper's glands* are connected to the urethra near the base of the spongy tissue of the penis.

In the penis the urethra is surrounded by three columns of spongy tissue permeated with blood sinuses that engorge to erect the penis.

Organs of the Human Female

At the midpoint of each menstrual cycle, the human female usually releases one egg from only one of a pair of almond-sized *ovaries* lying in the pelvic part of the body cavity.

Each ovary is surrounded partially by the expanded opening of an *oviduct* (Fallopian tube). The pair of oviducts lead to a central pear-shaped uterus of about 5 by 10 cm (2 by 4 inches).

The uterine wall is thick and is the site where development will take place in the event of fertilization. The uterus is connected to the vagina, whose external opening is flanked by an inner pair of moist folds, the *labia minora*, enclosed with the fleshier hair-covered outer labia majora.

These structures enclose the clitoris, mentioned earlier, and conceal the opening of the urethra that drains the bladder. If semen is deposited in the vagina, the sperm rapidly travel through the uterus and into the oviducts.

If an egg has been released recently from the ovary and has started down the oviduct, fertilization may occur to produce the zygote.

In recent years the biological, psychological, and sociological problems associated with inducing or thwarting such fertilization have received much attention relative to family planning and population control.

SEX ORGAN HOMOLOGIES

While the structures of the male and female reproductive systems seem quite different, each mammal develops similarly up to a point, a period sometimes called the indifferent phase of development. During this period the following structures are in common.

There are paired mesonephric kidneys whose mesonephric ducts (also called Wolffian ducts) drain into the cloaca. Adjacent to the mesonephric kidneys and supported from them by a mesentery, *genital ridges* give rise to the gonads.

Running parallel to each of the mesonephric ducts is a paramesonephric (Mullerian) duct. Externally a small structure, the *genital tubercle,* develops just anterior and ventral to the part of the cloaca that persists in association with the urogenital structures. On each side of this opening are genital folds and genital swellings.

The events between this indifferent phase and the development of the definitive male or female sex are complex, under hormonal control, and develop depending on the genetics of the embryo. Only a brief summary of these events is described and tabulated.

If the embryo develops as a female, the mesonephric kidney and mesonephric ducts regress. The genital ridge areas become ovaries. The paramesonephric (Mullerian) ducts persist as the oviducts, the uterus, and part of the vagina; the urogenital sinus becomes the rest of the vagina.

The genital tubercle undergoes relatively modest growth to form the *glans clitidoris* of the clitoris. The genital folds and swellings become, respectively, the labia minora and labia majora.

If the embryo develops as a male, part of the mesonephric kidney persists and ducts connect it and the developing testis. The part that was mesonephric kidney becomes the epididymis. The mesonephric ducts

Table 5.1: Homologies between female and male reproductive structures.

Female	*Indifferent Stage*	*Male*
Ovary	Genital ridge	Testis
Vestigial	Mesonephric kidney	Epididymis
Vestigial	Mesonephric duct	Vas deferens
Lower vagina	Urogenital sinus	Proximal urethra
Oviduct,	uterus, Paramesonephric upper vagina	Vestigial duct
Labia minora	Genital folds	Dorsal shaft of penis and penile urethra
Labia majora	Genital swellings	Scrotum

persist as the vas deferens that drains into a section of the original urogenital sinus.

The genital tubercle becomes displaced to the tip of the developing penis as the *glans penis.* The shaft of the penis is produced normally by the extended fusing of the paired genital folds.

The genital swellings enlarge in the male, incorporate a part of the body cavity, and are the site into which the testes grow to form the scrotum.

Thus, as shown in Table elsewhere in this chapter, there are true homologies between male and female reproductive structures.

VIVIPARITY

The Uterus

When an egg is fertilized high in the oviduct, it becomes *a zygote* with the diploid number of chromosomes reestablished. During a period of three or four days, as it passes down the oviduct, the zygote divides frequently and enters the lumen of the uterus as *a blastocyst*.

Its fate is partially dependent on the conditions existing along the uterine walls. Some blastocysts that may have developed abnormally never establish a relationship with the lining of the uterus and are discharged without the woman even recognizing that an egg may have become fertilized.

The critical importance of the condition of the uterine lining is that it is the site where the blastocyst becomes embedded and which nourishes the development of the embryo.

Humans are examples of animals that develop their young internally for a period of *gestation*. Thus we are viviparous animals.

Viviparity is not a trait restricted to mammals, however. For instance, some sharks develop internally. In fact, even mammals have varying periods of development that they support in the uterus.

For instance, mice, rats, and rabbits are born hairless, with their eyes closed, and quite helpless.

Calves and colts, on the other hand, can stand and nurse very shortly after birth, and guinea pigs are so well developed that they resemble miniature adults shortly after birth.

Human babies are better developed in a number of ways than rodents, but they are still quite dependent on adult care.

A whole subclass of the mammals, the Metatheria or marsupials, remain in the uterus for only part of their development.

When young marsupials are born, they may not have completed the development of all their appendages, for instance.

However, they can reach the marsupial pouch where

the mammary teats are located and complete development there.

The Structure of the Uterus and Its Hormonal Regulation

The uterus of mammals varies in its general shape. Two shapes are especially worthy of description. Most mammals have *bicornuate* uteri, that is, the two short oviducts lead into long uterine horns where the developing young are implanted.

These horns join before they lead to the vagina. In humans, during the development of the female, only the oviducts remain paired and the uterus is fused into a single pearshaped, *simplex* uterus. The uterus is thick-walled and muscular.

It is lined by an epithelium that, in humans, undergoes a rhythmic increase in thickness followed by a brief period of discharge of the uterine lining. This period of discharge is called *menstruation,* lasts four to five days, and reoccurs generally about every 28 days.

Menstruation is a trait that occurs only in higher apes and humans. Its repeated appearances are called *menstrual cycles.* Nonprimate mammals do not show such cycles. Instead, they have estrous *cycles* that are spaced further apart.

Some animals "come into heat" only once a year, others several times a year, and others may not be sexually receptive over more than the span of a year.

Estrous cycles have in common with menstrual cycles a period when the lining of the uterus is in an appropriate condition for the implantation of the developing embryo.

However, if implantation fails to occur, there is no sudden loss of uterine lining as there is in higher primates. Instead, the uterine lining returns to an inactive and nonreceptive state.

In animals with estrous or menstrual cycles, the

regulation of the uterus is under hormonal control. While it is difficult to analyze critically the endocrine controls in humans, the following description seems to fit the combination of evidence drawn from experimental animals and from testing of humans.

The condition of the uterine lining, the en*dometrium*, is controlled by the interaction with hormones produced by three other areas of the body, the ovaries, the pituitary gland, and a section of the brain, the hypothalamus.

These organs not only control the condition of the uterus, but also influence the development of the gametes in both females and males and condition the responses of sexual partners.

Because of the complexity of the interactions, the description of endocrine controls that ultimately influence the uterus will not begin with the uterus but will start with the pituitary and its controls.

It should be emphasized that while the description emphasizes the female endocrine pattern, the male is controlled by the same glands and hormones.

The pituitary produces many hormones, but the ones we consider here are called *gonadotrophins.* These are the *follicle-stimulating hormone* (FSH) and the *luteinizing hormone (LH).*

(A third hormone, *prolactin,* may be involved in the complex steps but for our purposes it will be described as principally stimulating milk secretion from the mammary gland after birth.)

Let us describe the events in a stepwise fashion. When the hypothalamus releases a hormone to the pituitary through a small portal system, this hormone, *follicle-stimulating* hormone *releasing factor* (or *hormone)* (FSH-RF), triggers the release of FSH into the blood.

On arrival at its target organ, the ovary, development of a follicle is initiated. The follicle bears in it one egg. During the expansion of the follicle, its cells synthesize an *estrogen,* principally *estradiol.* This hormone enters the blood stream; its principal target organ is the uterine epithelium (mucosa).

It stimulates this to proliferate. Thus during the ten days after the last menstruation, the estrogen increases with the expanding follicle and the endometrium thickens and develops narrow tubular glands.

When the estrogen in the blood reaches a certain concentration, it also acts on the pituitary to shut down FSH production and on the hypothalamus to result in the discharge of *luteinizing hormone releasing factor* (LH-RF) to the pituitary.

The pituitary now release LH to the circulation. In combination with the residual FSH, it results in *ovulation,* the rupture of the follicle and the release of the egg, which normally is drawn into the open end of the oviduct.

Here it may or may not be fertilzed by a sperm. The LH also causes the cells lining the follicle to alter, enlarge, and fill the old follicular cavity.

The structure formed is the *corpus luteum.* The corpus luteum produces a hormone, *progesterone,* whose principal target is the thickened endometrium. Its action is to increase the vascularization and glandulari-zation of the endometrium.

Also, the level of progesterone in the blood feeds back information to the hypothalamus in the event no implantation occurs.

Luteinizing hormone release is shut down, progesterone is shut down, and support of the uterine lining fades, leading to menstruation.

However, if implanation occurs, the membranes surrounding the developing embryo embedded in the uterine lining contribute to the formation of the placenta and begin to secrete a progesteronelike hormone that finally replaces that produced by the corpus luteum.

This prevents the uterine lining from sloughing and supports pregnancy. The interrelationship between organs and hormones in the menstrual cycle is illustrated in Figure elsewhere in this chapter.

The hormones estrogen and progesterone, produced by the developing placenta, also stimulate enlargement of the breasts.

These hormones do not lead to actual milk secretion, which is regulated by the anterior pituitary hormone, *prolactin*, and the hormone stored in the posterior pituitary, *oxytocin*. These hormones are released after the inhibitions of the placental hormones are removed at birth.

Male Reproductive Capacity

The same hormones, FSH and LH, that regulate female reproductive capacity influence the development of the testes.

The hormone produced by interstitial cells in the testes is testosterone. These hormones must function properly for males to be reproductively competent.

Puberty

In both males and females the arrival of sexual maturity, the onset of sex organ function, is achieved under the control of the pituitarygonad axis. In females the changes in skeletal structure, fat deposition, breast development, and pubic and axillary hair are principally controlled by estrogens.

In males, testosterone controls the development of the penis, the characteristic hair pattern, and changes in the voice, in muscular, and in skeletal development.

Hair pattern not only involves the axillary area and the pubic hair, where the pattern differs from the female in tending to extend in the midline toward the navel, but it also involves development on the face and chest to varying degrees, depending on the individual genetics of the man, as well as his race.

SEXUAL RESPONSE

With the development of the biological subscience of behavior (ethology) and the growing awareness of the human as another animal worthy of analysis, attention has in recent years been directed to the human sexual response.

This has been examined as a strictly physiological problem and as a societal problem. As becomes obvious in other chapters, much of the societal aspects of animal populations revolve around reproductive drives as adaptations for survival.

Furthermore, the currently acceptable patterns of human behavior permit a franker and more objective examination of human sexuality.

In past decades, sexuality was identified so closely with concepts of sin and with concepts of aggression that open discussion was inhibited.

With the growing dignity given to women as an outgrowth of the women's liberation movement, sexual response has come to receive attention in a more complete and realistic light.

Furthermore, with the development of more reliable contraceptive methods, such as "the pill" and the IUD (see below) in humans, sexual response has become somewhat divorced from concepts of procreation.

Sex, therefore, is now viewed by many as are other human endeavorsa matter of choice on the part of both partners of the sexual act. In recent years the issue of choice has extended even to the choice of the sexes of the partners; this is not a new situation in human societies, but only one that has been openly practiced rather than covertly practiced or examined.

Male Sexual Response

In both males and females, sexual arousal usually follows preplay of varying forms and intensities. When fully aroused, the penis becomes engorged with blood and enlarges from an average of approximately 7.5 cm to 15 cm (3-6 inches) and achieves a diameter of about 3 cm (1¼ a inches). This is the period of excitement.

When in copulation with a female and with movements of the penis in the vagina, the male enters a plateau period when the breathing and heart rates accelerate. Also, the accessory reproductive glands, such as the seminal vesicles, prostate, and urethra, become especially well vascularized.

When continued stimulation of the glans penis occurs, this triggers the spasm of muscles of the genital organs creating the orgasm and resulting in the discharge of semen from the urethra.

Shortly thereafter the penis usually shrinks to near its unstimulated size. Under appropriate conditions after a refractory period, the man may be induced to reestablish an erect penis and repeat the sequence.

Female Sexual Response

While the female usually passes through the stages of excitation, plateau, orgasm, and often refractory period, her patterns are more variable and complex than are those of the male. The phase of excitement not only includes clitoral and genital fold swellings, but the vaginal wall secretes and creates a moist lubricant.

Also, the breasts usually swell and the nipples become erect. On entering the plateau phase, her breathing and heart rates increase.

It is now also recognized that clitoral and vaginal stimulation can both be elicited. The stimulation usually starts at the clitoris but spreads over the vagina and external genitals.

Orgasm in the human female is usually associated with contractions of the vaginal wall. These may be spasmodic. Also, the result of an orgasm in the female is often to create a syringing action on the pool of semen deposited by the male near the cervix of the uterus; this acts to aspirate sperm into the uterus.

In human females there may be two striking differences from the usual performance in males. First, under some circumstances the female may proceed rather rapidly from excitation to orgasm.

Second, the female may have repeated orgasms without the usual refractory period seen in males. These reviews of human sexual behavior can only be considered as brief surveys.

Since the studies of Alfred Kinsey in the 1940s and the more recent studies of Masters and Johnson, much has been learned about the great variety of sexual expressions that exist in human populations and in different human societies.

The noteworthy theme that is in common with most of these events is, as said before, the dissociation of sexual behavior from childbearing.

Two things follow logically from this. One is that sexual partners need to understand each other and the implications of their activities.

Among the larger problems that seem to exist are those revolving around whether orgasm is a minimal requirement for sexual satisfaction.

A concensus of students of human sexuality is that the mental attitude of sexual partners is a very important aspect of a sense of sexual gratification and can produce gratification independently of orgasm.

The second point that follows current attitudes is the implication that pregnancy can be a matter of choice. Controls on pregnancy, therefore, become important.

Contraception

Applied reproductive physiology has been under public scrutiny in recent years in relationship to the control of pregnancy, the right to determine family size, and the social responsibility for population control. Some believe that true population control comes from the will of the people not to have children.

It is agreed that continence rather than artificial means played a significant role in lowering the birth rate during the economic depression of the 1930s.

Today, however, restraint is assumed to be an unrealistic approach. Therefore three major methods that allow intercourse and prevent childbearing are used: physical interference, restraint, or chemical inhibition of conception.

Physical interference can be accomplished by the unreliable act of withdrawing the penis from the vagina before ejaculation, by ensheathing the penis in a condom, or by damming the route of passage of the sperm with a diaphragm. More radical is the tying and severing of sections of the ducts of males or females.

In males this is accomplished by a small incision in the scrotum, and in females by small punctures either through the abdominal wall or through the vagina alongside the cervix of the uterus. In both males and females these procedures can be done quickly and without hospitalization.

Intrauterine devices (IUDs), small inserts of loops or coils (usually of plastic) into the uterine cavity, can be used to prevent implantation of the developing embryo.

Restraint, or commonly "the rhythm" method, assumes that abstinence from intercourse will be practiced during the period of receptivity of the ovulated egg for sperm.

If one assumes a three day variation in ovulation from the normal midpoint at 14 days, abstinence between approximately days 11 through 17 is required.

This is an unreliable procedure because of error in memory, error in calculating the day of the cycle, or irregularity of the menstrual cycle. Chemical interference has become a major means of employing or mimicking the female hormones.

This has largely supplanted older chemical means that used douches, oils, and jellies. The most widespread means of chemical contraception in North American is oral contraception by use of synthetic estrogens and progesterones, commonly called "the pill."

As Figure elsehwere in this chapter shows, the estrogen-progestin "pill" prevents FSH and LH secretion among other things to sustain the postovulatory phase because the dosages of the estrogenlike and progesteronelike substances are controlled.

In one popular form, the woman begins taking one pill a day for 21 days, then waits 7 days before taking them again. During the 21 days she takes the pill, she passes her normal period of ovulation without releasing an egg, yet this allows relatively normal uterine wall development.

During the seven days after the 21st pill, the level of the synthetic hormones in the circulatory system drops and menstruation occurs. The clue to the success of the procedure lies in the balance between the two hormones in the pill and the physiology of the woman; in some cases pills containing only estrogens or only progesterone may be used.

Recently prostaglandins have been employed as postcoital contraceptives by causing contractions of the uterine wall to prevent implantation. At present this method does not have the same widespread public usage as does the progestin-estrogen pill.

Also, research in recent years has been directed to finding a male contraceptive.

Chapter 6 DEVELOPMENT

The topic of development has no physical or temporal time span. In humans, it is true, it has been a convention for biologists and physicians to consider development up to birth. Psychologists, however, extend the study of development at least through the prepubertal years.

Also, biologists sometimes vary in the scope of their study of development. For instance, students of amphibian or insect development may examine early development from the egg to the acquisition of body form and think of it as embryology.

But development in these two examples extends beyond embryology to studies of problems associated with metamorphosis from tadpole to frog or salamander, or from larva to pupa to adult in insects.

Thus development has a large scope and cannot be covered fully in one chapter. We will confine ourselves to a rather restricted survey that not only describes physical changes during development but also exposes some of the questions that remain to be examined in order to better understand this complex subject.

It should be emphasized at the outset that many, many events, usually under specific genetic control, must occur with exquisite precision in order for a normal individual to be produced.

This becomes obvious if one simply thumbs through a treatise on medical genetics and observes the large number of kinds of abnormalities in development that can occur in humans. There is evidence that similar relationships exist in other organisms also.

From other chapters we see that the cells that unite to form a new individual, a zygote, are the eggs and sperm. Two conditions are created when this occurs in any animal: the diploid chromosome constitution is reestablished and the egg is activated to develop into a new individual. In its development, cell divisions, called cleavages, occur.

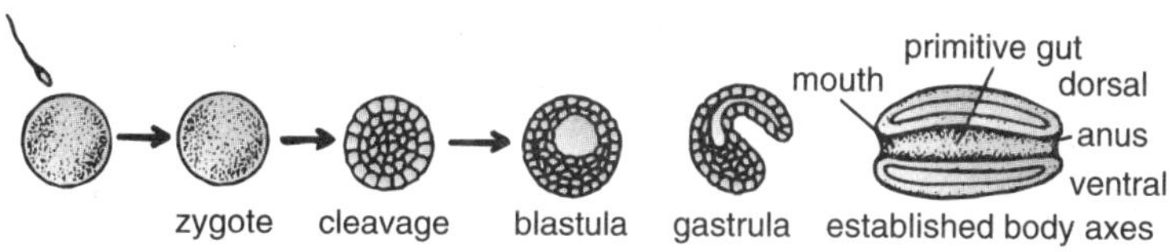

Figure 6.1: Representative stages of development from fertilized egg to establishment of basic body form.

When the large number of cells are produced by cleavages, a stage called the *blastula* is reached. This is a round hollow sphere in many animals. However, some animals produce a blastula with a cellfilled center.

The blastula stage is followed by one in which there is a striking rearrangement of cells through *formative movements* of these cells in relationship to each other.

This process is called *gastrulation* and the product is a *gastrula*. In the gastrula stage, cells or groups of cells establish new relationships with each other.

The subsequent development of the animal is often dependent on the influence of one group of cells on another, a process called *induction*.

Our objective here will be to discuss development briefly from gametoge-nesis through fertilization and zygote formation, cleavage, blastula formation, gastrulation, and the establishment of body form.

How we discuss this for individual species of organi-

Table 6.1: Classification of Egg Types.

Egg Type	*Description*	*Examples*
Isolecithal, alecithal	Having a small amount of yolk distributed in the cytoplasm; or lacking visible yolk	Sea urchins, humans
Telolecithal	Having the yolk more highly concentrated at the vegetal pole than at the animal pole; cytoplasm concentrated toward the animal pole	Moderately telolecithal: frogs, sala manders Strongly telolecithal: birds, rep tiles, some sharks
Centrolecithal	Having the yolk located in the center of the egg and surrounded by cytoplasm	Insects

sms depends on the kind of eggs one starts with and the variations that occur during the stages outlined.

GAMETOGENESIS

The eggs and sperm mature in the ovaries and testes, respectively. Each gonial stage (oogonia orspermatogonia) ceases to proliferate by mitosis, and two meiotic cell divisions produce, respectively, the eggs and the sperm. Our attention is called here to the differences between these two kinds of gametes.

Eggs

Eggs are often large and laden with yolk (for example, the yolk of a hen's egg), although not all eggs are. Table elsewhere in this chapter shows ways in which eggs are classified depending on their yolk concentration.

We will see that the concentration and distribution of yolk influences the cleavage pattern following fertilization. One mature egg develops from each primary oocyte. Depending on the species, eggs may be liberated from the ovary at stages ranging from primary oocytes, where the first meiotic division has not started, to completion of meiosis.

For instance, sea star eggs are released prior to onset of meiotic divisions while vertebrate eggs stop at metaphase of the second meiotic division. The zygote must contain the nutrients to support development until nourishment can be obtained from the environment.

Sea urchins and sea stars have only a small amount of stored nutrients in the zygote but they develop rapidly to freely feeding larvae. Frog larvae are late in developing, but the egg is supplied with a considerable store of yolk to support development until the tadpole can feed.

Human eggs have little yolk, but the early embryo becomes embedded in the wall of the uterus, from which it draws nourishment until the placenta is established and food from the mother's blood passes across the placenta to the embryo's blood. Where yolk is present, it is deposited in the developing egg while it is in the ovary.

The source of the yolk is from surrounding follicle cells that assist in the transfer of yolk into the cytoplasm of the egg. The egg proteins and phospholipids that contribute to the formation of yolk are produced in the livers of vertebrates as can be shown by using radioactive phosphates.

Preparation of the egg for cleavage can be traced back to the prophase of the first meiotic division. During cleavages there are three important events that occur which depend on the appropriate biochemical machinery: increased amounts of mitotic spindle assembly, increased amount of plasma membrane, and increased number of nuclei.

In the frog egg the efficiency for accomplishing these events is achieved by concentrating over 1000 times the normal somatic cell's amount of rRNA in the egg. This is achieved by repeated transcriptions, extra copies, of rRNA being made during oogenesis and concentrated in multiple small nucleoli that deliver the rRNA to the cytoplasm.

This is a unique trait of oogenesis and does not occur in somatic cells. As a result of this, a mature frog's egg comes equipped with a reserve of rRNA that it uses in the translational processes which occur all through cleavage and blastulation.

Thus while the frog's egg is proceeding rapidly to a multicellular stage, no energy is required for rRNA production, and this energy can be employed in other developmental events such as making DNA synthetase enzymes, manufacturing new plasma membrane, and so forth.

Furthermore it now seems that mRNA may be present in an inactive or "informational" form which becomes active during development. In summary, the egg has a "dowry" of energy reserves in the form of yolk and an important part of its genetic equipment, rRNA, provided to it in the ovary prior to ovulation.

Sperm

Sperm differ from eggs in having completed meiosis by the time they are released. Furthermore, four sperm normally develop from each primary spermatocyte.

After passing through the two meiotic divisions the spermatids produced undergo a metamorphosis in which they become highly elongated, have only a very small amount of cytoplasm, and in many animals can be

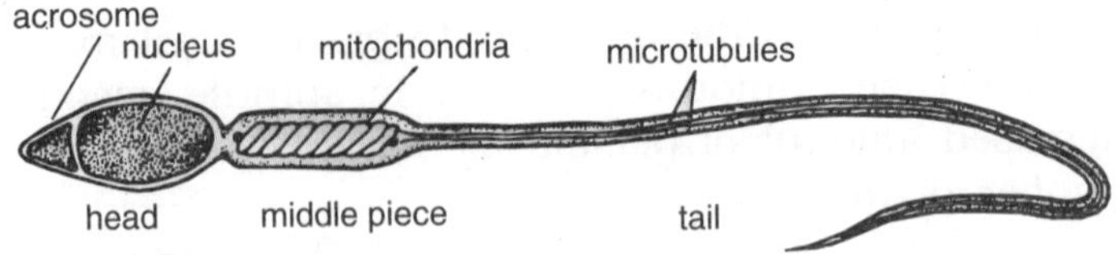

Figure 6.2: Diagram of the structure of a sperm.

subdivided into three regions: a head containing the nucleus and an acrosome; a middle piece containing centrioles, microtubules, and a high concentration of mitochondria; and a tail mostly made up of microtubules, seen in cross section to have a "9 + 2" arrangement.

Not all animals have sperm shaped as described. For instance, the sperm of arthropods have several configurations and are often immotile.

FERTILIZATION AND ZYGOTE FORMATION

The process of fertilization in animals is better appreciated if some adaptations associated with bringing eggs and sperm together are discussed. Many animals release their gametes directly into their aqueous environment.

However, even here there are adaptations and synchronies that increase the chances that a sperm will reach a short-lived egg and activate its continued development. Some animals such as sea urchins and sea stars seem to release their eggs and sperm freely into the sea.

However, usually the releasing animals are quite close to each other and the gametes are released in very large numbers. Some mollusks lying in beds will undergo a wave of gamete release presumably triggered by a pheromonelike stimulus emanating from nearby mollusks.

Frogs and some fish also release their gametes directly into the water. Here, however, the males and females are very close to each other. In some fish, such as salmon and trout, as the female deposits eggs, the male swims over them and releases sperm (milt).

In frogs the male clasps the female around the trunk in *amp/exus*, and as she releases eggs, he releases sperm. Other adaptations for fertilization involve internal deposition of the sperm. This is achieved in two ways. In many animals a penis is inserted into the genital

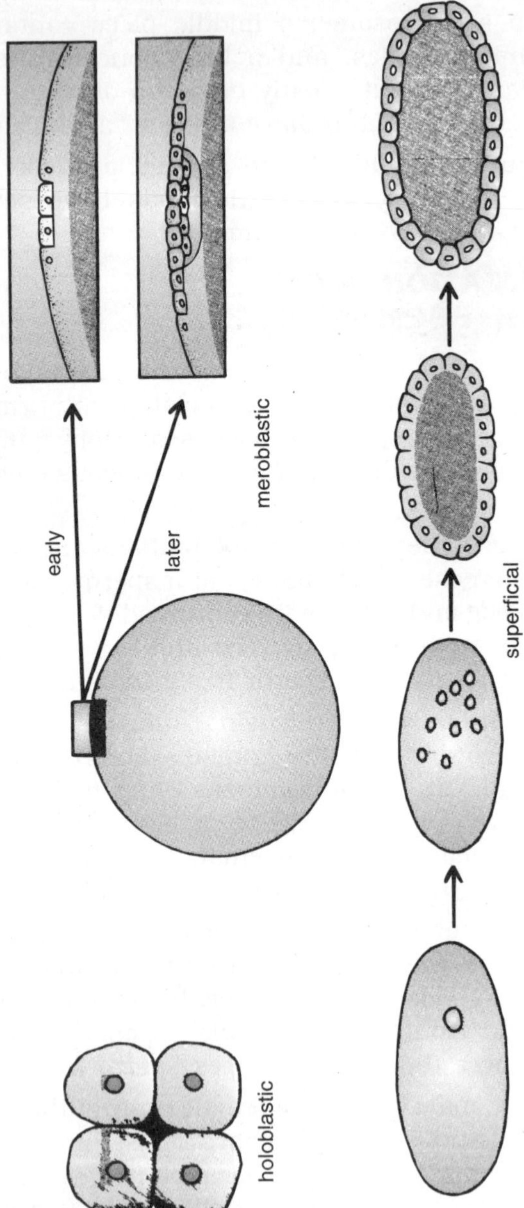

Figure 6.3: Types of cleavage.

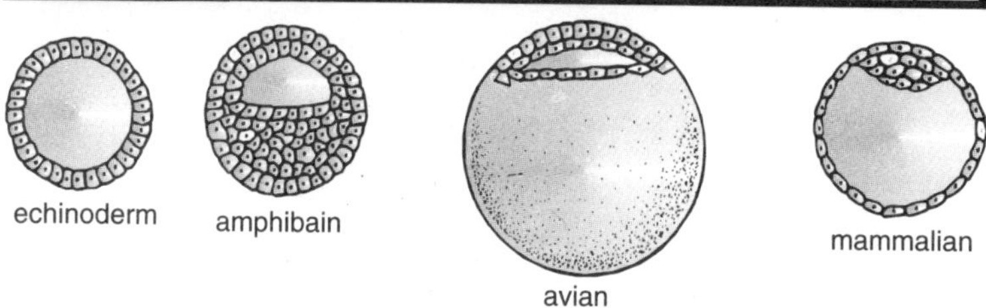

Figure 6.4: Forms in which blastula stages occur in several deuterostomes.

tract of the female and sperm deposited. Other animals, such as some salamanders and squids, produce gelatinous packages of sperm, *spermatophores.*

In the case of salamanders, the male deposits a gelatinous cone topped by packaged sperm onto a leaf or stone in the water. The female passes over the spermatophore and picks sperm up with her cloacal lips.

In squid, the spermatophpre is transferred by specialized tentacles (arms) into the mantle of the female. The process of union of eggs and sperm has been thoroughly studied in only a relatively small number of species of animals. Most of the knowledge about the union of gametes comes from studies on invertebrates.

There is still no major generalization about how sperm are attracted to eggs; random contact on the one hand or *chemotaxis,* chemical attraction, on the other have been proposed. However, there do appear to be cell surface conditions that hold the gametes together once they have met.

In a number of species, for instance, the acorn worm, Saccoglossus, an acrosome on the tip of the sperm's head ruptures to liberate enzymes that lyse jelly coats around eggs.

This is followed by the penetration of the jelly by an acrosomal tubule that contacts and penetrates the vitelline membrane around the egg.

The tubule fuses the sperm plasma membrane with

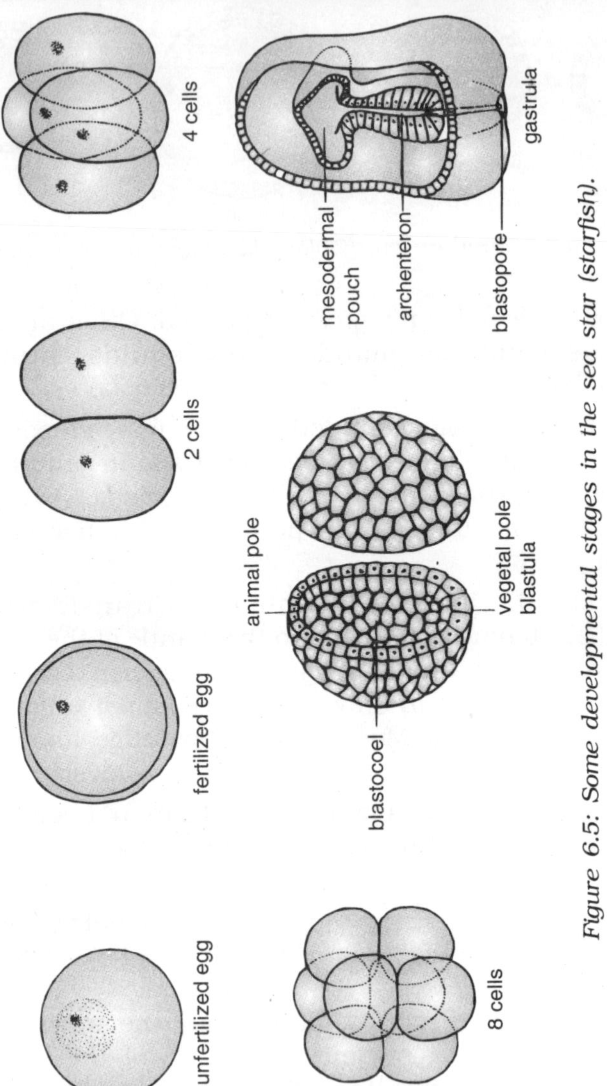

Figure 6.5: Some developmental stages in the sea star (starfish).

that of the egg. The egg's cytoplasm bulges into this point of union, and the sperm nucleus passes into the egg cytoplasm to become the *male pronucleus*. This moves to unite with the egg nucleus, the *female pronucleus*, to create the diploid zygote.

It is conjectured that processes similar to this operate in mammals. For instance, mammalian eggs are surrounded by a mucoprotein and attached cells that are dissolved by an enzyme, hyaluronidase, which is found in the acrosome.

CLEAVAGE

The process of cell division, cleavage, leads to the development of numerous blastomeres. The cleavage process itself occurs in several ways. Zygotes that have little to moderate amounts of yolk start to cleave at the animal pole and the cleavage furrow proceeds to the vegetal pole, interposing plasma membranes between the two progeny cells.

Such complete separation is called *holoblastic* cleavage. There are two kinds of cleavage that do not totally isolate the cytoplasm of individual cells from the surroundings. In bird eggs, for instance, the cleavage furrows extend through the cytoplasm to the yolk and stop, leaving the inner surface of the cell's cytoplasm exposed to the yolk.

This is *meroblastic cleavage.* Later cleavages will isolate cells completely from the yolk to create a small disk of cells, *a blastodisk,* at the animal pole. The central cells of the disk become isolated from the yolk, the peripheral cells are exposed to it.

Continued cleavages are centrifugal, thus expanding the size of the blastodisk. In centrolecithal eggs, found in insects, for example, the zygote nucleus divides many times and the nuclei migrate to the cytoplasm at the periphery of the egg.

This stimulates *a superficial* cleavage in which cytokinesis creates a set of furrows between nuclei that resemble early stages of meroblastic cleavage. Soon the cells become completely separated from the yolk. Many of the invertebrates of the protostome line have a form of holoblastic cleavage that differs from that seen in sea urchins or sea stars, for instance.

This cleavage patttern is called *spiral* cleavage. The cleavage spindles tend to orient at angles to prior blastomere axes. The result is that blastomeres tend to lie in furrows between other blastomeres rather than on top of them. In eggs with this form of cleavage there are often fairly well restricted differences in the cytoplasm; the blastomeres isolate different parts of the cytoplasm from each other.

If a blastomere is lost, a part is usually lost from the developing embryo. This is also called *determinate* cleavage for this reason. It contrasts with *indeterminate* cleavage such as seen in sea urchins and sea stars.

Here the loss of a blastomere does not necessarily mean the loss of a part later. Instead, the remaining blastomeres are said to *regulate* to produce a whole.

THE BLASTULA

Figure elsewhere in this chapter shows some characteristic blastula stages. The important point is that at this time the embryo is about to undergo shifting movements of cells and enter gastrulation.

THE GASTRULA

To understand better the development of the body plan through gastrulation, four examples are used: sea stars, frogs, birds, and humans.

Sea Star

The zygote cleaves into two blastomeres from animal to vegetal pole. The second cleavage is at right angles and produces four cells. The third cleavage is at right angles to the two prior cleavages creating an eight-cell stage of two tiers of four cells.

Subsequent cleavages occur at rather well coordinated intervals to produce 16, 32, 64 cells, and so forth, until a blastula is formed.

An early blastula has rounded blastomeres composing its wall, but as cell division continues, the cells

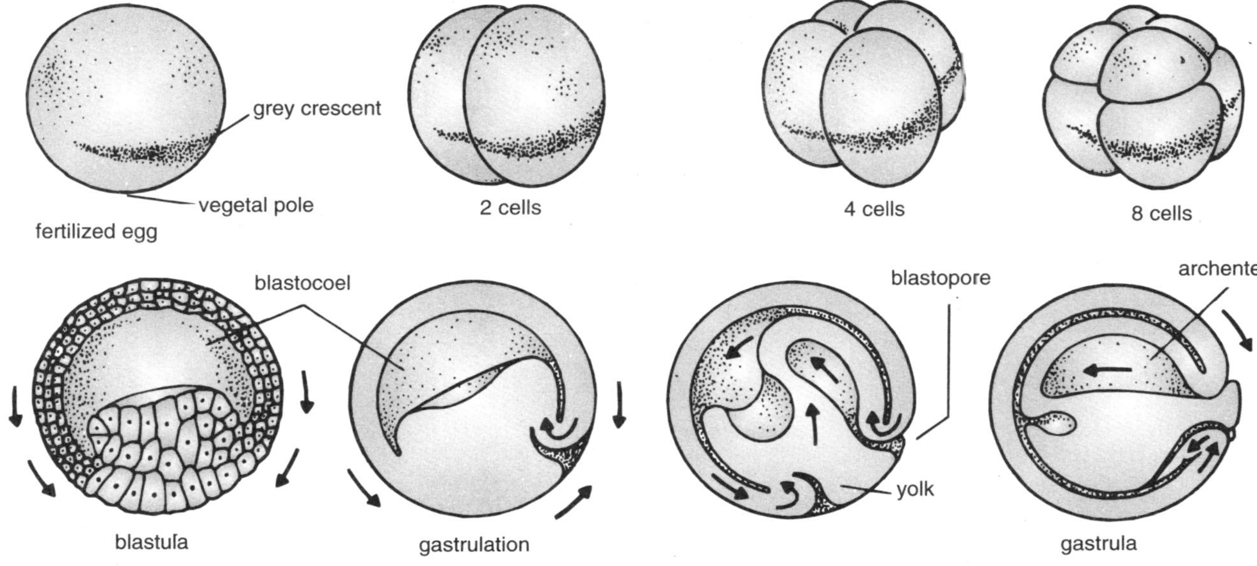

Figure 6.6: Stages in the formation of frog gastrula (gastrulation).

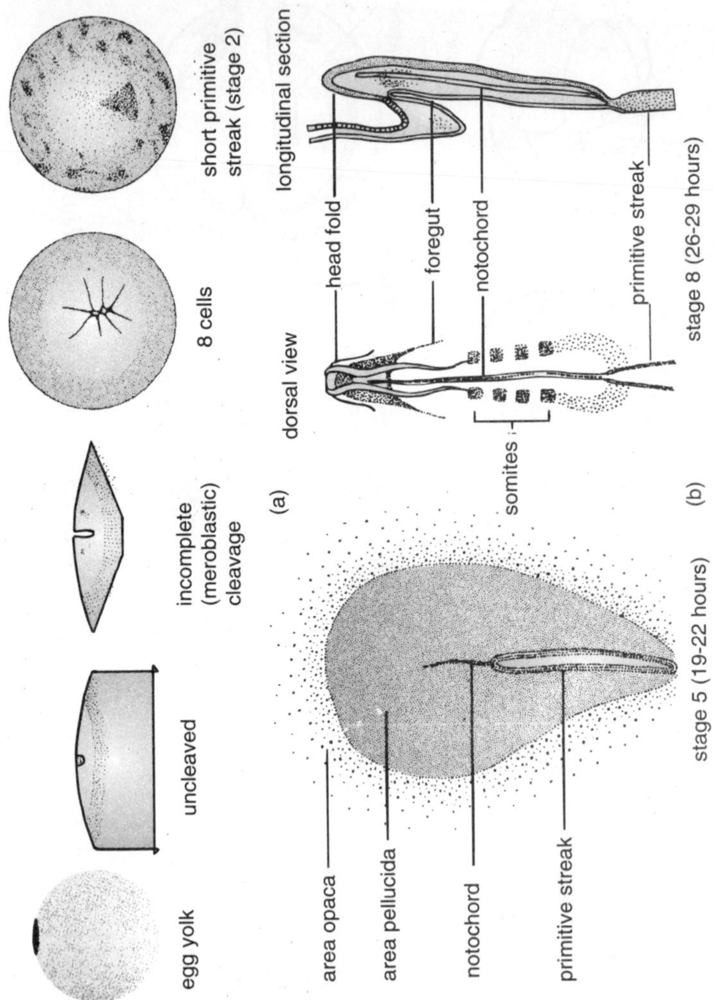

Figure 6.7: Early chick development. (a) Egg showing area of "active cytoplasm" (left), early cleavages (center), and early blastodisk (right). (b) Elongated blastodisk (left), surface view (center), and longitudinal section (right) of a chick after incubation for more than one day.

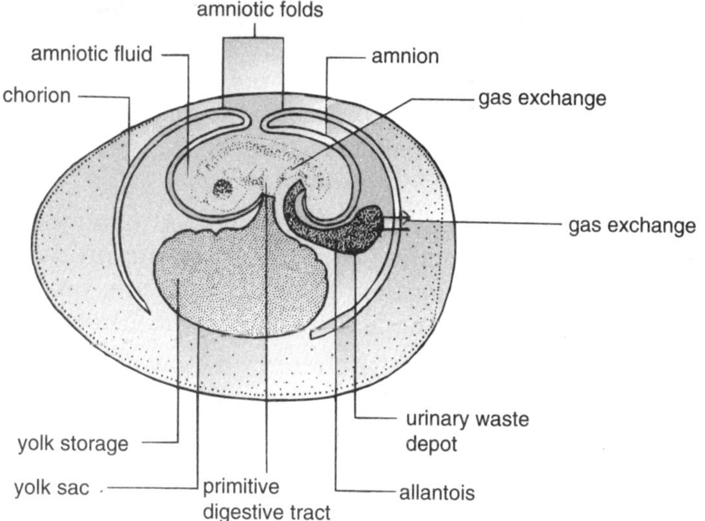

Figure 6.8: Diagram of the four extraembryonic membranes of a bird. All four membranes, chorion, amnion, allantois, and yolk sac, are present in the development of reptiles, birds, and mammals which are called Amniotes. Fish and amphibia are Anamniotes.

become compressed to each other in a single layer of columnar cells.

This emphasizes the great increase in the amount of DNA that is produced for each new nucleus and the large amount of new plasma membrane that develops. The next event, characteristic of echinoderms, is for a group of small cells to separate from the surface at the vegetal pole. These are primary mesenchyme cells.

They assist in the process of gastrulation. Gastrulation is initiated by a sinking in of the vegetal pole region. In association with this, mesenchyme cells develop pseudopodia which extend out as thin processes that explore the inner surface of the animal hemisphere.

These processes establish contact and begin to contract. This assists in the movement of the vegetal area to the interior in the form of a blind tube.

The point of movement to the interior is the blastopore. The invaginated tube is the *archenteron.* The innermost portion of the archenteron is destined to be mesoderm. It bulges outward into pouches that become separated into *mesodermal vesicles.* One or both of these, depending on the echinoderm, expands to line the old blastocoel and form the coelom.

This kind of coelom formation is called enterocoelic because of its outpouching from the archenteron. When the mesoderm has separated from the archenteron, that which remains is the endoderm lining the future gut.

The blind end of the archenteron now grows in a curved fashion to contact the outer wall of the embryo. At the point of contact, the layers break down and a mouth opening is formed. The blastopore is the site of the future anus.

Frog

Frog cleavage is similar to that in the sea star except that cleavage furrows running through the yolk of the vegetal hemisphere are retarded. The result is that the blastula consists of small cells near the animal pole

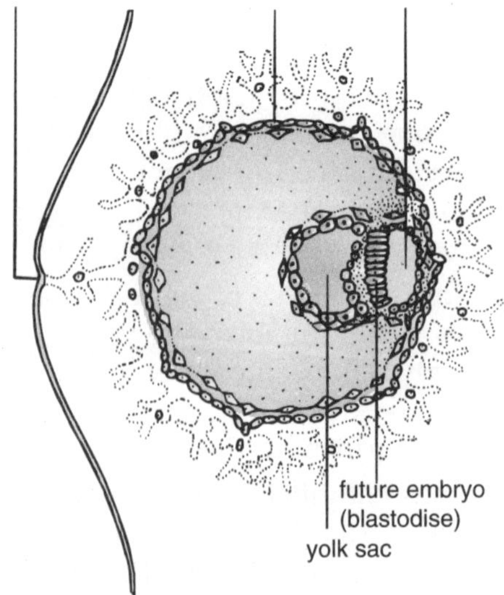

Figure 6.9: Implantation of embryo in wall of uterus.

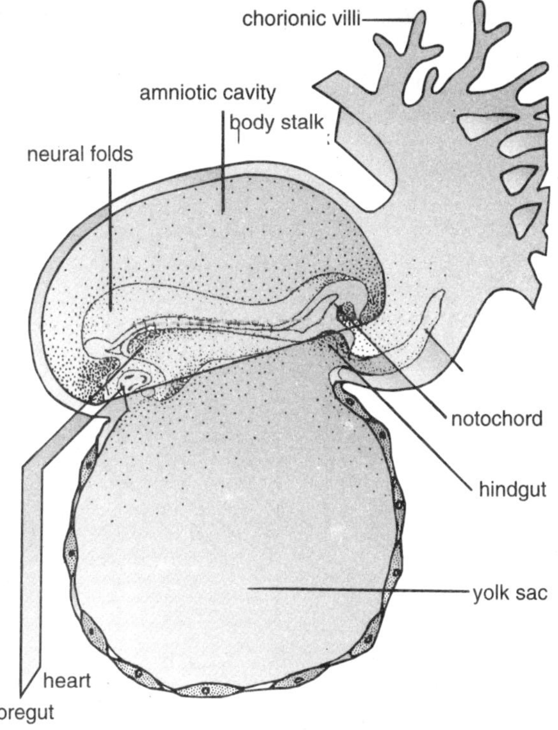

Figure 6.10: Human allantois in relationship to embryo.

grading to larger cells at the vegetal pole and with the blastocoel displaced toward the animal pole.

Gastrulation in frogs also is through a blastopore and with the formation of an archenteron. As with the sea star, the materials coming to line the archenteron are mesodermal and endodermal.

While the pattern of movements from exterior to interior is more complicated than in sea stars and will not be expanded here, it is noteworthy that the blastopore does not lie at the vegetal pole, but is displaced toward the equator where the cells are smaller and more capable of formative movements.

In the frog the mesoderm forms the roof of much of the archenteron. At the lateral edges of the archenteron, where mesoderm and endoderm have been in continuity, they now separate through a loss of tissue affinities. The freed endodermal edges grow upward and complete the lining of gut while the mesoderm grows downward between the outer ectoderm and the endoderm of the archenteron.

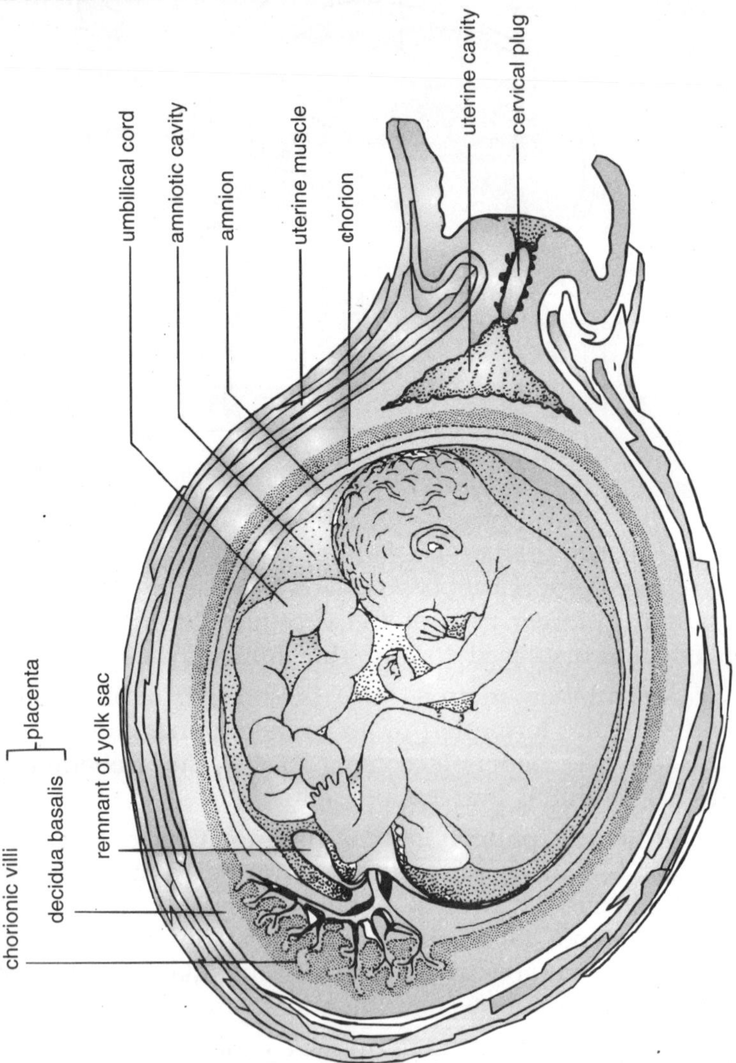

Figure 6.11: Diagram of advanced fetus shows its membranes and their relationship to the uterus.

The flanking mesoderm splits into an inner and outer sheet, and the coelom is formed between them. The forward end of the archenteron meets the outer ectoderm and later perforates to form the mouth.

In the frog and bird, another developmental principle is illustrated, tissue interaction. In these two vertebrates, the mesoderm underlying the ectoderm along the dorsal side of the embryo induces that ectoderm to thicken to become neural ectoderm.

Chick

Recall that through meroblastic cleavage a blastodisk forms. The blastodisk expands and the central part, now free from the underlying yolk, thickens. The inner layer next to the yolk in this region separates away from the cells above to form the *hypoblast,* the endodermal germ layer. The space between the hypoblast and the surface tissues is the *blastocoel.*

On the surface, extending from the center toward the periphery, a thin pair of elevations appear with a depression between them; this is the *primitive streak.* It corresponds to the blastopore. Cells on the surface move in an orderly fashion from each side of the primitive streak, enter the streak, and emerge below the surface on each side as a middle mesodermal germ layer.

This is gastrulation. In the area in front of the primitive streak where this has occurred, the underlying mesoderm also induces the overlying ectoderm to thicken as neural ectoderm in the form of a thickened horseshoe-shaped plate.

The neural plate folds up and closes into a neural tube. This tube is the future brain and spinal cord. Its presence shows that the long axis of the embryo is established. During later stages of development various structures along this axis appear.

Eyes appear near the anterior part of the head, and a series of ridges, the pharyngeal arches, appear along the future neck. Also, in the chick the animal rotates onto its left side and flexures appear in the head and neck region.

Thus gradually the definitive traits of the chick develop in an orderly progression. Birds, along with reptiles and mammals, differ from other vertebrates in developing extra*embryonic membranes*. These are sheets of tissue which function during development but do not persist at hatching or birth.

There is an evolutionary legacy associated with these membranes. Figure elsewhere in this chapter illustrates these membranes. The *chorion* and *amnion* in reptiles and birds arises by common folds that extend from the embryo's body wall.

They provide an outer moist surface at the boundary of the egg with its surrounding albumen and shell. Within the amnion a mildly saline fluid is secreted so that the embryo develops in a watery environment.

The yolk sac and allantois are associated with the primitive gut. The yolk sac of reptiles and birds is large and surrounds the fluid yolk. It is also important in that blood cells and blood vessels first appear in its walls.

The allantois grows into the coelom at the rear of the primitive gut and expands into the extraembryonic coelom between the amnion and the chorion. It makes a close union with the chorion to produce the *chorioallantoic membrane.*

This provides a large surface for the exchange of gases between the blood of the embryo and the exterior. It serves another function as a repository of metabolic waste products such as uric acid.

Human

The basic stages of development described above for the establishment of body form apply to humans but, in addition, we must understand the contributions of *extraembryonic membranes* to establishing relationships with the maternal tissues of the uterus.

An egg fertilized in the human oviduct undergoes cleavages as it moves along and enters the uterus in the equivalent of the blastula stage. It is called *a blastocyst* and differs from blastula stages of nonmammalians by having a solid cluster of cells, the *inner cell* mass, internally pendant from one wall.

The blastocyst invades the uterine wall through lytic activity of its outer cells which also proliferate vigorously in the invasion process. This outer proliferating area of the blastocyst, made up of ectoderm and a lining of mesoderm, is an extraembryonic membrane, the *chorion.*

The chorion will be the site of exchange of materials between the embryo or fetus and the mother. The inner cell mass becomes divided into two small cavities whose linings make up, respectively, the *amnion* which lies closest to the chorion and the hollow *yolk sac* which lies closest to the cavity of the blastocyst.

The amnion is destined to become fluid-filled, to expand, and to bathe the developing fetus that will be suspended in it, just as occurred in reptiles and birds. The yolk sac, while yolkfree in most mammals, is the site of early blood-cell formation.

BODY FORMATION

The formative movements of gastrulation take place in a disk of tissue, the *blastodisk,* at the confluence of the amnion and the yolk sac. Only the blastodisk contributes to the formation of the embryo; for this reason the other tissues are called extraembryonic.

In addition to the formative movements that create the primitive gut, the outer ectoderm thickens, produces the *neural tube,* and becomes the brain and spinal cord.

The formative movements have hardly begun, however, before a thin fingerlike endodermal evagination appears at the rear end of the blastodisk. This projects into the *body stalk* which connects the developing embryo with the chorion.

The outgrowth is the *allantois.* While the allantois itself remains small, it is vitally important because it is the route over which the embryo's blood vessels develop to grow into fingerlike outgrowths of the chorion, called *villi,* to provide for exchange of nutrients, wastes, and gases between the embryo and the mother.

This is the region of the placenta.The embryo grows into a fetus within the amniotic cavity and this is accompanied by great enlargement of the uterus.

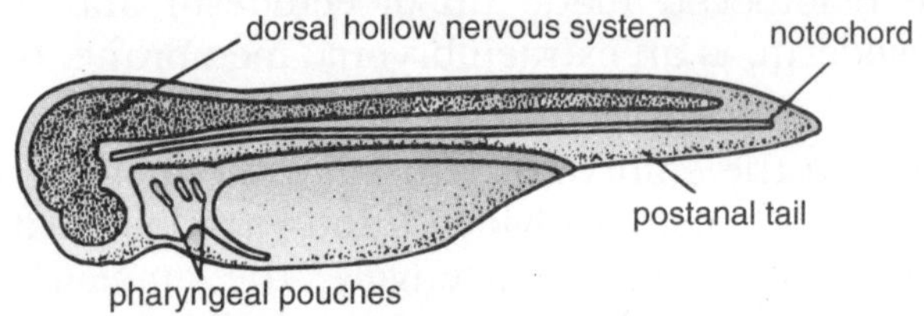

Figure 6.12: Chordate characteristics as seen in an early frog larva, tadpole (median sagittal section).

The Placenta

The placenta is formed by a combination of tissues from the embryo and from the mother. The region of the endometrium of the, uterus into which the chorionic villi grow and to which the definitive unbilical cord is attached is called the *decidua basalis*, the site of the future placenta.

The portion of the endometrium which surrounds the embryo just external to the chorion is the *decidua capsularis* and the remaining endometrium is the *decidua parietalis*.

Placentas vary among different species of mammals. In humans it is a disk about 17.5 cm (7 inches) in diameter and about 2.5-3.5 cm (1-1½ inches) thick.

Some animals, such as cows, have numerous isolated clusters of fetalmaternal associations, while others have diffuse fingerlike projections of the chorion. In carnivores, such as dogs and cats, the placenta forms a broad ring around the fetus.

Placentas also differ in the degree to which the chorion enzymatically erodes the surface of the endometrium. In some animals there is no erosion and the chorionic villi fit into crypts and crevasses of the endometrium.

Other animals only partially erode the endometrium. In humans, however, the chorionic tissue erodes the endometrium until maternal blood pools are created between the chorion and the endometrium.

The chorionic villi project into these pools of blood, making for an efficient exchange of gases, nutrients, and wastes between the blood vessels in the cone of the villi and the maternal blood pools.

Changes at Birth

A number of important changes occur in both the mother and the fetus at the time of birth, usually at nine calendar months from conception.

Some of these changes are hormonal. A hormone *relaxin,* produced by the ovary, placenta, and uterine tissue, prepares the birth canal by relaxing the pelvic region.

The pubic symphysis separates and the pelvic bones become less rigid. Relaxin also influences the condition of the uterus.

The beginning of the birth process is marked by uterine contractions, influenced in part by a hormone of the posterior lobe of the pituitary, *oxytocin.*

As the uterine contractions become stronger, the membranes surrounding the fetus break and the amniotic fluid is discharged.

Eventually, accompanied by distention of the vagina, the uterine contractions, and the force of abdominal muscles, the fetus is expelled through the birth canal.

Of course, the newborn baby still has the umbilical cord attached. This is tied and cut. Further uterine contractions force out the placenta, the remaining extraembryonic membranes, and much of the uterine lining as the *afterbirth.* (Some normally herbivorous animals, such as the cow, eat their afterbirth, presumably benefitting from nutrients and hormones.) The newborn baby fills its lungs and starts breathing. Accompanying this is an increased flow of blood to the freshly expanded lungs.

This change in the amount of blood flowing to the heart is reflected in an increased amount returning to the left atrium. This results in the closure of two flaps that had allowed blood to be exchanged between the right and left atria.

This separates the right and left sides of the heart into a functionally double pump. Also, where the blood used to flow from the right ventricle to a shunt that took the blood to the aorta instead of to the lungs, it now flows to the lungs, and the shunt, known as the *ductus arteriosus,* reduces to a closed *ligamentum arteriosus.*

Failures of the changes in circulation just described can lead to abnormalities creating so-called "blue babies." Another event associated with birth is the release of milk when the baby suckles the breast.

Of course, progesterone had caused enlargement of the breasts during pregnancy. *Prolactin,* from the anterior pituitary, however, causes the onset of the secretion of milk, and its ejection is influenced by oxytocin which is released from the posterior pituitary (though synthesized in the hypothalamus) through reflexive responses to the suckling of the infant.

From the four examples chosen, the following generalizations about early development can be made.

1. A zygote develops through predictable cleavage patterns to the blastula stage.
2. Formative movements shift cells from the surface to the interior in gastrulation.
3. The blastopore or primitive streak through which

the cells migrate is at the future posterior end of the body.

4. The long axis of the embryo is thus created with the neural plate in vertebrates lying dorsally along the axis.
5. Changes in the cells on the surface are induced by underlying cells. This is the result of a tissue interaction.
6. The changed status of the cells that are induced is to move from a more general, less differentiated condition to populations of cells that become progressively specialized. This is a reflection of *differentiation* of cells, presently one of the poorly understood frontiers in biology.

EXPERIMENTS RELATED TO INDUCTION

In the case of induction of tissues, these briefly described experiments focus on some of the problems. When a piece of the dorsal lip of the blastopore is transplanted to a site on a late blastula or early gastrula in frogs, the transplanted lip turns to the interior and causes the surrounding tissues also to become involved.

The result of such an operation can be to produce an embryo with its normal archenteron and a secondary one arising from the transplant.

Furthermore, this new archenteron's roof will induce the overlying ectoderm that normally would only form skin to form neural plate, neural tube, and finally central nervous system.

The embryo then has two, one its own, the second induced. This clearly shows that external influences on the ectoderm have altered the direction of differentiation of the ectoderm.

A second experiment shows that the nature of the response is under the genetic control of the responding cells.

The experiment involves transplanting ectoderm from the oral region between frogs and salamanders. The frog ectoderm normally forms oral suckers; some salamander ectoderm normally forms rodlike projections, called balancers. Both suckers and balancers require the inductive influence of underlying tissues to develop at all.

In this experiment the frog ectoderm lying over the tissue that normally induces balancers is induced by this tissue. But it responds according to its own genetic composition and produces frog suckers on the salamander.

In the reciprocal experiment salamander balancers develop on the frog. A third experiment shows that once the primary induction of the central nervous system is achieved, a succession of inductions follows. After the neural plate becomes a neural tube, at the anterior end a pair of lateral bulges appear.

These are the optic vesicles. Their outer sufaces will fold in· to form optic cups, the future lining of the eye. When these optic cups expand laterally and touch the lateral ectoderm, the ectoderm thickens locally, indents to form a vesicle that pinches from the outer ectoderm, and comes to lie within the rim of the optic cup; this is the future lens of the eye.

By surgically removing only an optic cup without disturbing the outer ectoderm, no lens develops on the side of the operation. From this we can conclude that the optic cup induces the ectoderm to become lens. Since the optic cup came from the original neural plate that was induced from the underlying mesoderm, we see that there is a hierarchy of inductions.

In this case neural plate formation is a primary induction, optic lens formation is a secondary induction. Other experiments can be done to show that the lens induces the differentiation of the cornea, a tertiary induction.

ESTABLISHING CHORDATE CHARACTERISTICS

Four things distinguish chordates from other animals: a dorsal hollow nervous sytem, a notochord, pharyngeal pouches (or clefts), and a postanal tail. It has earlier been shown how a dorsal hollow nervous system is established.

The notochord is a stiff rod of cells derived from mesoderm that develops in thc midline in the roof of the archenteron before the archenteron becomes completely enclosed in endoderm.

This tissue has a capablity for selfdifferentiating, that is, at the time the cells that comprise it move through the blastopore they are determined to differentiate as notochord.

In the vertebrate chordates the notochord is either reinforced or replaced completely by vertebrae that develop from the adjacent mesoderm.

The third characteristic, the pharyngeal clefts, develops on the lateral walls of the anterior end of the archenteron, the area that expands to become the pharynx.

Here a complex set of inductive relationships between outer ectoderm, intermediate mesenchyme (loose mesoderm), and inner endoderm results in endodermal pouches serially extending outward and ectodermal grooves indenting inward to meet the pouches.

In the lower vertebrates, the fishes and amphibia, the tissue between the pouch and the groove breaks down and gill slits are formed.

In higher mammals the perforation normally does not occur, but the endodermal pouches give rise to several pharyngeal derivatives such as the tubotympanic canal and the middle ear chamber, the thymus glands, and the parathyroid glands.

The fourth characteristic, a postanal tail, does not

occur in other animals. In other words, in other animals the anal opening is terminal, although it may be concealed by such outgrowths as a telson in crayfish.

EMBRYONIC GERM LAYER DERIVATIVES

Later development of vertebrates goes beyond the scope of this textbook. However, the three embryonic germ layers contribute predictably to specific parts of the future animal. Table elsewhere in this chapter itemizes these.

Table 6.2: Derivatives of Embryonic Germ Layers.

Derivative	*Ecto-derm*	*Meso-derm*	*Endo-derm*
Skin and skin glands	×	—	—
Hair, feathers, parts of scales, covering of horns	×	—	—
Entire nervous system	×	—	—
Pituitary	×	—	—
Lining of mouth to rear edge of teeth	×	—	—
Part of lining of rectum Adrenal medulla (from neural crest)	×	—	—
Connective tissue	×	—	—
Most cartilage (pharyngeal cartilages probably mainly from neural creast)	—	×	—
Bone	—	×	—
Muscles (a few exceptions)	—	×	—
Kidneys and ducts	—	×	—
Gonads and ducts, including uterus and part of vagina	—	×	—

Blood vessels, heart, lym phatics, blood (at least partly)	—	×	—
Lining of alimentary canal from pharynx to rectum	—	—	×
Thyroid and parathyroids	—	—	×
Thymus	—	—	×
Trachea, lungs, swim blad ders of fish, liver, and pan creas (in the main)	—	—	×
Bladder	—	—	×
Cloaca (most) and perhaps some stem cells of white blood cells	—	—	×

METAMORPHOSIS

It was stated at the beginning of this chapter that development does not stop at birth, or at a free-feeding stage. An outstanding change that illustrates this is seen in the process of metamorphosis.

Metamorphosis occurs in postembryonic stages, and in a limited time morphological and physiological changes occur. In the discussions of development in various invertebrate groups a number of examples will be given. Here, two will suffice.

The tunicate, a urochordate, has a larva superficially resembling the tadpole of a frog. It has the typical chordate characteristics (see above).

At a stage in its life cycle it rapidly resorbs its tail and notochord, most of the nervous system except for a ganglionic mass, and it settles to become sessile and attached. In this form it is difficult to see its chordate affinities.

The frog represents a better known metamorphosing form. From a tailed, totally aquatic form, possessing gills, the frog larva undergoes changes that lead to the resorption of the tail and gills, the development of limbs, and respiration by lungs.

It has been clearly demonstrated, through thyroid or pituitary removal, or thyroid injections, that metamorphosis is under the control of the thyroid gland.

Insects, too, undergo metamorphosis, also under hormonal control, that causes them to pass through a few or several stages where reorganization of the anatomy and physiology occurs.

AGING

There is growing interest in the study of aging as a developmental process. Although there are several theories of aging, one that is noteworthy here is that proposed by Leonard Hayflick of Stanford University.

He proposes that cells have built into them a maximum average number of cell divisions that they can undergo before they cease to divide and perhaps then begin to die. Hayflick developed his hypothesis from the results of tissue culture where he found that some cell lines could not be cultured past a certain number of generations.

While there is much yet to be learned about aging, one observation that is not inconsistent with Hayflick's hypothesis is that central nervous system cells stop dividing after a period of time in an organism's development.

Also the number of living central nervous system cells decreases as the individual ages. This very brief statement about aging perhaps makes it understandable why the United States National Institutes of Health now has an Institute for Aging.

DARWIN S THEORY OF PANGENESIS

Charles Darwin's interest in genetics was a consequence of his studies of evolution. It will be necessary, therefore, to give a brief statement of his evolution theory in order to show its relation to genetics.

Darwin imagined that evolution occurred in this manner: Among the individuals of any species there would be many differences. For., example, some might be slightly larger than the average, or ha e longer legs, or have a thicker coat of fur.

If any of these variations made their possessors better adapted to survive, those with the better characteristics would have a greater chance of leaving offspring ('survival of the fittest,' as Spencer later described it).

With the passage of time the original population would change, its individuals gradually becoming larger, or developing longer legs or a thicker coat of fur, or whatever characteristic was of value for survival.

In this way one species could evolve into another or give rise to two or more differelt species. At a later time we shall discuss in detail Darwin's theory of evolution.

For the present; we should merely note the importance of variations. Evolution cannot occur unless, there are differences among the individuals of the same species.

If all individuals are identical and remain so generation after generation, obviously there is no evolution. So variation is essential and, furthermore, to be of importance in evolution it must be inherited.

A thick coat of fur might be advantageous for a mammal living in the Arctic, but unless this variation is inherited it is unimportant for evoluti Darwin fully realized that his theory of evolution must be based on a sound understanding of the mechanism of inheritance.

In an attempt to provide such a basis, he collected all the data possible on animal and plant breeding, and then developed the first comprehensive theory of heredity, or as we now call it, genetics. This appeared in 1868 as a two-volume work entitled *The Variation of Animals and Plants under Domestication.*

In this he assembled many observations on inheritance, largely of domestic plants and animals, and attempted to provide a theory to explain these observations. Darwin's work in this field was of major interest in the last half of the nineteenth century.

He was, of course, the outstanding biologist of his time, so anything he did attracted attention. In addition to this, for many years his theory was the only one available.

We shall examine his theory briefly, not only for its historical interest but to see how the problems were stated, what data were available, and finally, to what extent the theory contributed to an understanding of natural events.

Let us constantly keep in mind that our purpose is twofold: first, learning genetics, and second, learning how scientific theories develop and change. For this second purpose, it will be important for us to keep an open mind and, if possible, not to be prejudiced by what we may have read or learned before.

It is difficult not to be influenced by what we may know of genetics, but if possible this knowledge should be ignored. If we are discussing the state of genetics in 1868 our approach should be this: Given the data available in 1868, how would we view the problems of inheritance>

First, something of the background for Darwin's work will be given. Knowledge of.cell structure, which in later years was to form a foundation for genetic concepts, was in a rudimentary state. It was known that animals and plants were composed of cells, but little was known about the internal structure of cells.

The nucleus was thought to be a universal cell constituent, although its role in the life of the cell was unknown.

It was generally believed, as we believe today, that cells arise solely from pre-existing cells and not *de novo.* Opinions on heredity were vague and varied.

The crossing of varieties in both animals and plants had been practiced for centuries, but no general laws or rules to explain the results had been discovered. In fact, the data were so confusing that some doubted that they could be scientifically explained.

One type of observation that conviHced Darwin of the 'force of inheritance' was that 'with man and the domestic animals, certain peculiarities have appeared in an individual, at rare intervals, or only one or twice in the history of the world, but have reappeared in several of the children or grandchildren.'

One of the most spectacular instances of this was the porcupine man, whose skin was covered by warty projections.

Six of his children and two of his grandchildren showed this same defect. Another instance was found in some domestic pigs, entirely lacking hind legs, whose abnormality was carried through three generations.

To most biologists of the mid-nineteenth century, such instances seemed to be the result of mere chance, or of environmental influence, but to Darwin they were evidence that 'something' was transmitted from parent to offspring. The following quotation illustrates the way he reasoned.

When we reflect that certain extraordinary peculiarities have thus appeared in a single individual out of many millions, all exposed in the same country to the same general conditions of life, and again, that the same extraordinary peculiarity has sometimes appeared in individuals living under widely different conditions of life, we are driven to conclude that such peculiarites are not directly due to the action of the surrounding conditions, but to unknown laws acting on the organisation or constitution of the individual that their production stands in hardly closer relation to the conditions than does life itself.

If this be so, and the occurrence of the same unusual character in the child and parent cannot be attributed to both having been exposed to the same unusual conditions, then the following problem is worth consideration, as showing that the result cannot be due, as some authors have supposed, to mere coincidence, but must be consequent on the members of the same family inheriting something in common in their constitution.

Let it be assumed that, in a large population, a particular affection occurs on an average in one out of a million, so that the *a priori* chance that an individual taken at random will be so affected is only one in a million. Let the population consist of sixty millions, composed, we will assume, of ten million families, each containing six members.

On these data, Professor Stokes has calculated for me that the odds will be no less than 8333 millions to 1 that in the ten million families there will not be even a single family in which one parent and two children will be affected by the peculiarity in question.

But numerous cases could be given, in which several children have been affected by the same rare peculiarity with one of their parents; and in this case, more especially if the grandchildren be included in the calculation, the odds against mere coincidence become something prodigious, almost beyond enumeration. Even today, it would be hard to supply better reasons for the belief that 'something' was transmitted from the first porcupine man to his son.

Darwin ruled out the possibility of the external environment having any causal relation to the appearance of the defect: If something in the environinent was the stimulus, why did just these few persons and no others have the defect?

Surely if there was some unusual feature of the environment, such as rare climatic conditions or a peculiar substance in the diet, many individuals might be expected to have a 'porcupine skin.' Neither could it be due to chance. It was inconceivable that a defect, so rare as never to be recorded before, should affect a father, son, and grandson merely by chance.

Darwin concluded that the best explanation was that the son had inherited his father's defect. This, in turn, means that something is transmitted from father to son.

If this is the case, it should be possible to obtain information on the laws governing this transmission. If these laws could be formulated, not only would this represent a tremendous advance for genetics, but a firm foundation would be provided for the theory of evolution.

The Data To Be Explained

Darwin's procedure, that is, his 'scientific method,' was as follows: First, he assembled all the information he could find that seemed to have a bearing on heredity. Second, he proposed a theory to account for all of the information he had assembled.

The mass of data contained in his two-volume work is considerable, but it can be combined into a small number of categories. These were the types of data that Darwin felt must be explained by any comprehensive theory of inheritance.

Transmission of Characters from Parent to Offspring

Darwin summarized a tremendous mass of observations on this topic. Most of the characters known to him were morphological, such as differences in body size, type of feathers, or hair and color patterns. Others were physiological; examples are the inheritance of profuse bleeding in than, and peculiar tics or nervous defects.

The inherited characters might be large or small, important or unimportant. He concluded, 'When a new character arises, whatever its nature may be, it generally tends to be inherited, at least in a temporary and sometimes in a most persistent manner.'

It is clear that Darwin had no conception of an orderly or predictable transmission of characters from parent to offspring. Inheritance to him was a capricious phenomenon, sometimes temporary and sometimes persistent.

Mutilations

Some races of man habitually knock out their teeth, cut off parts of their fingers, or perforate their ears or nostrils, yet their children do not show corresponding defects.

There were other cases where mutilations appeared to be inherited and they were given on such good authority that Darwin found it 'difficult not to believe them.'

One of these was 'a cow that had lost a horn from an accident with consequent suppuration, produced three calves which were hornless on the same side of the head.' Once again the situation was complex. Mutilations appeared to be inherited in some instances but not in others.

Atavism (or Reversion)

This is the presence in an individual of some peculiar characteristic not expressed in its immediate parents, but resembling a remote ancestral condition. Children occasionally resemble their grandparents or more remote ancestors more closely than they do their parents.

Domestic animals may have peculiar features not characteristic of their breed, but resembling the wild species from which the domestic forms were derived. Black sheep (it was thought that sheep in early times were dark) occasionally arise in carefully bred flocks of white sheep.

Instances are reported of reversion during the life of a single individual. Darwin crossed white hens with black cocks. Some of the chicks were white the first year and the same individuals became black the second.

Sex

For most characters it appeared that inheritance could be by way of the male or the female, but Darwin knew of a few instances in which the sex of the parent was important in inheritance.

Cases are quoted on traits being transmitted from father to son but never to daughters, or from mother to daughter but never to sons. In color blindness, males are much more commonly affected than females, yet the defect can be transmitted through normal females.

In fact, it seemed probable to Darwin that fathers can never transmit color blindness to their sons. Daughters of color-blind fathers, on the other hand, though normal themselves, transmit color blindness to their sons.

'Thus, the father, grandson, and great-great-grandson will exhibit a peculiarity-the grandmother, daughters, and great-granddaughter having transmitted it in a latent state.' From observation of this sort Darwin states, 'We thus learn, and the fact is an important one, that transmission and development are distinct powers.'

Inbreeding and Inheritance

If two organisms are crossed and their offspring bred

with each other generation after generation, we speak of this as inbreeding. The data available to Darwin suggested that if one began with two types of organisms and inbred them generation after generation, there would result a relatively homogeneous population in which there is a blending of characteristics.

Darwin regarded this as the general rule, but he adds (in small print!) that in other cases "some characte-rs refuse to blend, and are transmitted in an unmodified state either from both parents or from one. When gray and white mice are paired, the young are not piebald nor of an intermediate tint, but are pure white or the ordinary gray color.'

Selection and Inheritance

Selection is a breeding method that has been employed since the early days of agriculture. If a farmer is interested in increasing the size of his chickens, he selects the largest individuals and breeds them. From their offspring he selects the largest and breeds from them. With this procedure, it is usually possible to increase the average size of the descendants in'a few generations.

One of the most puzzling aspects of selection was the fact that frequently it was possible to produce an organism with characteristics, not even remotely suggested in the original stock.

For example, by continued selection it was possible to produce the most bizarre'varicties of pigeons that had characteristics that did not occur in the ancestors. In short, selection could create something new. This will be considered in the, following section.

Origin of Variability

All domestic and wild species familiar to Darwin were variable. Numerous varieties of roses or pigeons were known, for example. Many varieties bred true, indicating the hereditary nature of the special features.

In some cases a variety was known to have originated from a single exceptional individual. In many cases it appeared that the new variety was 'new' in the sense of never having occurred before.

The factors concerned with the origin of variability were important and had to be considered in any comprehensive theory of inheritance.

The cause of variability was 'an obscure one; but it may be useful to probe our ignorance.' Darwin favored the view that 'variations of all kinds and degrees are directly or indirectly caused by the conditions of life to which each being, and more especially its ancestors, have been exposed.'

The great importance of the 'conditions of life' can be brought out by the following quotation: '. . . if it were possible to expose all the individuals of a species during many generations to absolutely uniform conditions of life, there would be no variability,' The actual conditions of life that were thought to cause variability included excess food (probably the most important), climate, hybridization, grafting in plants, and in fact 'a change of almost any kind in the conditions of life.'

Regeneration

When the tail or the legs of a salamander are cut off the lost structures are replaced perfectly by regeneration. The regenerated leg or tail is *a salamander* leg or tail.

The ability to regenerate lost parts is of widespread occurrence and appears to be similar to events occurring in embryonic development.

Darwin felt that both the formation of a structure during the course of normal development and its replacement following injury to the adult were due to the workings of inheritance.

Inheritance and Mode of Reproduction

There are two main types of reproduction, sexual

and asexual. An animal like Hydra is capable of both. Sexual reproduction consists of the fertilization of an ovum by a spermatozoon. Asexual reproduction in Hydra is by budding. A small protuberance forms on the side of the Hydra. This grows and eventually detaches as a small individual.

The Hydra that originates from a fertilized ovum is identical with a Hydra developing from a bud. Inheritance is the same whether by sexual or asexual means, in Darwin's opinion.

Delayed-Action Inheritance

Darwin listed several cases, which he believed to be well substantiated, of the male gametes having an effect on the female organs.

One of these was published by Lord Morton. An Arabian chestnut mare was crossed to a quagga (a wild African species belonging to the horse genus and closely resembling the zebra).

One offspring was obtained and it was intermediate in form and color. The mare was subsequently crossed to a black Arabian horse. One filly and one colt were produced.

In coloration and type of mane these two offspring showed a striking resemblance to the quagga. For example, dark bars were present on the hind part of the body and the mane was stiff and erect.

Darwin concluded, 'Hence, there can be no doubt that the quagga affected the character of the offspring subsequently begot by the black Arabian horse.

He felt that the quagga sperm had acted directly on the reproductive organs of the female in such a way as to affect the characteristics of future offspring sired by other males.

THE THEORY OF PANGENESIS

These ten categories represent the types of data that Darwin felt must be explained by any comprehensive theory of inheritance. After collecting as much of the pertinent data as he could, he set about to formulate a theory. The result was '. . . the hypothesis of Pangenesis, which implies that the whole organization, in the sense of every separate atom or unit, reproduces itself.'

The starting point of this is the postulation of gemmules that determine all characteristics of the organism. The properties that gemmules were assumed to possess were these: Each and every cell of an organism, and even parts of cells, produce gemmules of a specific type corresponding to the cell or part.

These are able to circulate throughout the body and they become aggregated in the gametes. Every sperm and every egg will contain gemmules of all sorts. By the union of egg and sperm they are transmitted to the next generation.

During development they unite with partially formed cells or with other gemmules, and in this way produce new cells of the type from which they were formed. In some instances the gemmules could remain dormant for generations.

We should think of a liver cell as producing gemmules for every part of that cell, enough kinds to produce the identical cell type in the next generation.

All other parts of the body would also be producing their own specific gemmules. These must be present in tremendous numbers, since every sperm and ovum will have some of all types produced in the body.

Today we might wonder about the space problem. If every part of the body produced a specific gemmule, would it not be difficult for all of them to fit into an ovum of microscopic dimensions, or into the even smaller sperm?

If gemmules exist, obviously they must be very small. Darwin did not think this difficulty was fatal to his hypothesis. Biologists at that time, and especially those working on disease or with cells, realized that very small things could be extremely important. The questions of basic importance for his theory concerned the existence of the gemmules and their production by cells. Was there any evidence for their existence?

At the time Darwin wrote we must remember that the 'cell theory' was in the process of being accepted. Darwin reasoned this way: If cells can divide and produce other cells, perhaps they can produce other bodies with the assumed characteristics of gemmules by a similar process.

In his own words, 'The existence of free gemmules is a gratuitous assumption, yet can hardly be considered as very improbable, seeing that cells have the power of multiplication through the self-division of their contents.'

Darwin's whole Theory of Pangenesis depended on the actual existence of gemmules, and it should be realized that he had no direct observational evidence for them. In short, he invented them to account for observed-data in the field of heredity.

This is legitimate scientific procedure. Atoms were invented to account for the data of chemistry. The planet which was later named Pluto was invented to account for certain irregularities in the orbits of known planets. But to postulate is not to prove.

The facts available to Darwin were not sufficient to decide whether his theory was 'right' or 'wrong.' His main contribution was the collection of a tremendous amount of genetic data, and an attempt to provide a theoretical framework for its interpretation.

He was most modest about his efforts: 'I am aware that my view is merely a provisional hypothesis or speculation; but until a better one be advanced, it may be serviceable by bringing together a multitude of facts which are at present left disconnected by any efficient cause.

As Whewell, the historian of the inductive sciences, remarks: "Hypotheses may often be of service to science, when they involve a certain portion of incompleteness, and even of error."

Under this point of view I venture to advance the hypothesis of Pangenesis, which implies that the whole organization, in the sense of every separate atom or unit, reproduces itself.'

THE THEORY EXPLAINS THE DATA

Let us now apply the Theory of Pangenesis to the ten categories of data requiring explanation.

Transmission of Characters from Parent to Offspring

The appearance of the same characters in parent and offspring was made possible by the production of gemmules by all parts of the parent's body.

These entered the ova and sperm and by fertilization were transmitted to the offspring where they caused their specific effects. This was true, as well, for those special characters such as those of the porcupine man.

The skin cells of the porcupine man produced 'porcupine' gemmules. These reached his children by way of the sperm.

Mutilations

Mutilations are usually not inherited because the part to be mutilated would have produced gemmules before its removal. These gemmules would enter the gametes and be passed to the next generation. The few cases in which mutilations appeared to be inherited usually involved diseased parts. Darwin explained this as follows: 'In this case it may be conjectured that the gemmules of the lost part were gradually all attracted by the partially diseased surface, and thus perished.'

Atavism

Atavism, according to the Theory of Pangenesis, was due to the ancestral gemmules remaining in a dormant condition for many generations and then suddenly developing.

Sex

Both sexes transmit inherited characters with equal facility, since both transmit gemmules representing every cell of the body. In the case of color blindness in man, and similar instances of inheritance modified by sex, it was assumed that gemmules were latent in one sex.

A color-blind marl transmits gemmules of color blindness to his daughter (in whose body they are dormant) and she may in turn transmit them to her sons. In the sons they develop and the sons are color-blind.

Inbreeding and Inheritance

The blending in the offspring of characteristics of the parents is due to the mixing of the gemmules of the parental types.

Those cases in which the characteristics of one parent predominate merely indicate that the predominating ones 'have some advantage in number, affinity, or vigour over those derived from the other parent.'

Selection and Inheritance

It is possible to influence the inherited characteristics of organisms through selection in this manner: The farmer choosing the largest chickens from his flock is choosing the ones that will produce gemmules for large size.

If this is repeated every generation, the gemmules for small size will be eliminated and the chickens reach their maximum possible size.

Origin of Variability

According to Darwin, new characteristics appear as a result'.of some environmental influence. The new or changed structure will produce new types of gemmules.

These will be transmitted to the next generation, and thus the new character will reappear.

Regeneration

Regeneration of lost parts is possible because the gemmules for the lost parts were produced prior to the loss and are present in the rest of the body. If, for example, the leg of a salamander has been removed, the leg gemmules, which are present in the body, can migrate to the cut surface and develop into a new limb, identical to the old one.

Inheritance and Mode of Reproduction

Inheritance is the same, whether via sexual or asexual means, since the basis is identical—the transmission of gemmules. In the case of our specific example, Hydra, every cell of the body would produce gemmules. These would move to all parts, including the gametes and the cells that form the buds.

Thus, the new individual would receive the same gemmules irrespective of whether they came from a fertilized ovum or from a bud.

Delayed-Action Inheritance

In those peculiar cases where the male gametes were thought to have a lasting effect on the reproductive organs of the females (as in Lord Morton's mare) a ready explanation was possible. Some of the gemmules from the male ametes entered the reproductive organs of the female and were included in ova produced long afterwards.

Darwin's Theory of Pangenesis, like all great theories, involved a great simplification in man's view of his universe. By assuming the existence of gemmules with definite properties he was able to 'make sense' out of a previously bewildering mass of data. Inheritance was not a nebulous and capricious force, but a precise and orderly transmission of the physical entities that are the basis of development in succeeding generations.

We should now pause to ask a few questions: Did Darwin's Theory of Pangenesis explain the data of heredity? If you are aware of later developments in this field you will probably answer 'no,' but if you can repress the bias of the knowledge of what was to come, you will probably conclude that the answer is 'yes.' If the answer is 'yes,' does this mean that the theory is correct?

Darwin's approach to the study of inheritance was one of two possible methods of attack. He was concerned nearly entirely with the *results* of inheritance, i.e. the kind of offspring obtained when patents of different types were crossed. From the results he attemptedlo reconstruct the basis of inheritance. As we have already seen, he concluded that every cell produces gemmules and that these are the basis of inheritance.

In the thirty years following the presentation of the Theory of Pangenesis little or no advance, based on breeding experiments, was made in our understanding of the mechanism of inheritance.,

The second possible method of investigation involves the study of ova and sperm. The gametes are the sole physical link between the parents and offspring, so presumably they would be responsible for the transmission of any inherited characteristics.

A careful study of the gametes might be expected to throw some light on inheritance. The branch of biology that is concerned with the study of cells, including the ova and sperm of course, is *cytology*.

It was in the field of cytology that the major advances in understanding inheritance were made during the last half of the nineteenth century. In the next few chapters we shall consider these findings.

Chapter 8

THE CELL AND ITS DIVISION

The development of cytology, like that of most fields of science, depends partly on tools. The compound microscope, which is the basic tool in cytology, appears to have been invented about 1590 by two Dutch spectacles makers. The birthday of cytology was postponed, however, for three-quarters of a century.

It was not until 1667 that Hooke first described 'cells' in a piece of cork. This discovery of cells in cork could have been an important advance in knowledge or an unimportant one. If it had turned out subsequently that cells were found only in cork, Hooke would certainly not be widely remembered for his discovery.

But the work of many scientists showed that cells were a general phenomenon and, therefore, of some importance. We might conclude that Hooke did not make a discovery that *was* important but, instead, a discovery that *became* important.

THE CELL THEORY

Following the realization that some cells are present in some organisms, the next conceptual advance was to establish the fact that all organisms are composed solely of cells or cell products.

This took nearly a century and a half. In the early years of the nineteenth century a number of cytologists

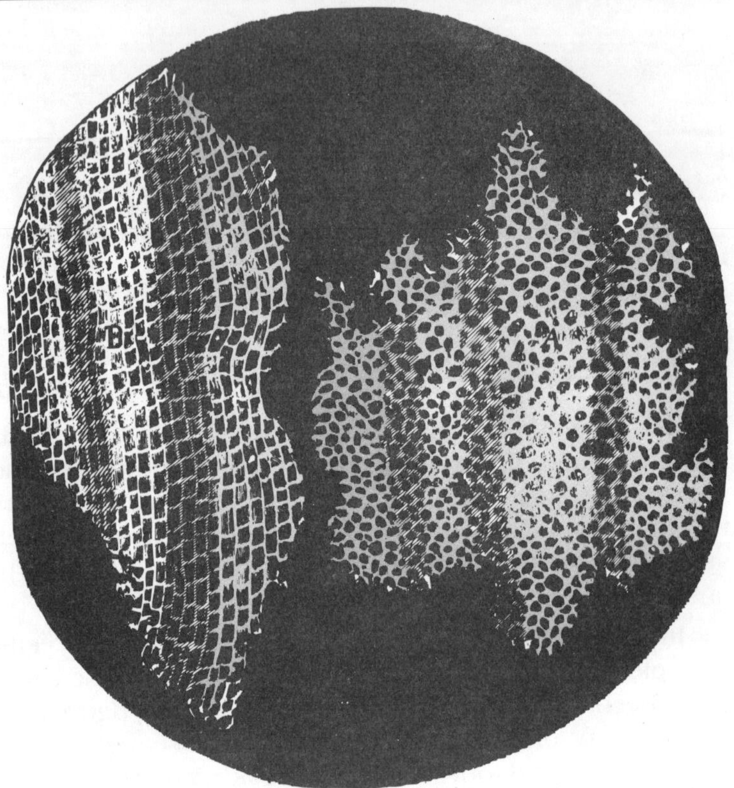

Figure 8.1: The drawing and part of the text from Hooke's observations on cork.

came more and more to adopt this second concept, which we know as the 'cell theory.'

Three names are generally associated with the final formulation of the cell theory. They are Dutrochet, Schleiden, and Schwann.

The lastnamed published his treatise on the microscopic structure of organisms in 1839, when he was 29 years old. In it he summarized his findings on a variety of tissues. His general conclusion was that the bodies of organisms are composed of cells. Figure B2-2 reproduces some of his drawings.

The following quotations from a translation of Schwann's treatise will reveal some of his views:

Though the variety in the external structure of plants is great, their internal structure is very simple. This extraordinary range of form is due only to a variation in the fitting together of elementary structures which, indeed, are subject to modification but are essentially identical-that is, they are cells.

The entire class of cellular plants is composed solely of cells which can readily be recognized as such; some of them are composed merely of a series of similar or even only of a single cell.

Animals being subject to a much greater range of variation in their external form than is found in plants also show (especially in the higher species) a much greater range of structure in their different tissues. A muscle differs greatly from a nerve, the latter from a cellular tissue (which shares only its name with the cellular tissue of plants), or elastic tissue, or horny tissue, etc.

If, however, we go back to the development of these tissues, then it will appear that all these many forms of tissue are constituted solely of cells that are quite analogous to plant cells .. . . The purpose of the present treatise is to prove the foregoing by observations.

Much of Schwann's success was due to the fact that he adopted a definite criterion for the recognition of cells, namely, the presence or absence of a nucleus. The latter structure was apparently first recognized as an important and characteristic cell structure by Robert Brown in 1831.

It had been observed much earlier, however. Schwann took full advantage of this recent (for him) discovery.

The most frequent and important basis for recognizing the existence of a cell is the presence or absence of the nucleus. Its sharp outline and its darker color make it easily recognizable in most cases and its characteristic shape, especially if it contains nucleoli . . . identify the structure as a cell nucleus and make it analogous with the nucleus of the young cells contained in cartilage and plant cells. . . . More than nine-tenths of the structures thought to be cells show such a nucleus and in many of these a distinct cell membrane can be made out and in most it is more or less distinct.

Under these circumstances it is perhaps permissible to conclude that in those spheres where no cell membrane be distinguished, but where a nucleus characteristic of its position and form is encountered, that a cell membrane is actually present but invisible.

Although Schwann's work established the cell as a unit of structure, his views on the origin of cells precluded these elementary bodies from having any importance in inheritance, as the following quotation shows.

The general principles in the formation of cells may be given as follows. At first there is a structureless substance which may be either quite liquid or more or less gelatinous.

This, depending on its chemical constitution and degree of vitality, has the inherent ability to bring about the formation of cells.

It seems that usually the nucleus is formed first and then the cell around it. Cell formation is in the organic world what crystallization represents in the inorganic world.

The cell, once formed, grows through its inherent energy, but in doing so it is guided by the organism as a whole in the way that conforms to the general organization.

This is the phenomenon basic to all animal and plant growth. It is applicable to cases where the young cells originate in the mother cell, as well as those where they are formed outside of them. In both instances the origin of cells occurs in a liquid or in a structureless substance.

We will call this substance, in which cells are formed,

a cell germinative substance or Cytoblastema. It can be compared figuratively, but only figuratively, with a solution from which crystals are precipitated.

The Continuity of Cells

Gradually this view was replaced by the realization that cells are formed solely by the division of pre-existing cells. Even before 1839 cell division had been observed, but it was (luring the following decade that more and more investigators-Remak and Nageli, for example-came to the conclusion that cells never originate from a structureless 'cytoblastema,' but always by cell division.

In 1855 Virchow formulated his well-known statement *omnis cellula e cellula,* which means 'all cells from cells.' The cell then took on a new significance and greater importance.

No longer was it a matter of the organism forming cells *de novo,* but instead cells formed the organism. If existing cells have arisen from pre-existing cells, then there must be a continuity of these elementary structures that goes back to the very beginnings of life.

The connection between generations was shown to be cells. Schwann was of the belief that the ovum was a cell. Therefore a cell produced in the ovary was the link between parent and offspring. (It had been known since 1824 that spermatozoa, and not the fluid in which they are found, were the important agents in fertilization, but the realization that spermatozoa are cells did not come until 1865.)

Nuclear Division

With the gradual accumulation of knowledge, improvement in microscopes, and development of techniques, cytologists,, were able to see more and more detail in cells. The nucleus, being the most characteristic structure within the cell, came in for a good deal of attention. Its role in cell division was not understood at first. Some observers held that the nucleus disappears during cell division and each daughter cell produces a new one.

Using this interpretation, there is no connection between the nuclei of different cell generations. Others believed that during cell division the nucleus was constricted and pinched in two and then one part went into each daughter cell.

The first of these beliefs was held mainly by botanists and the second by zoologists. It goes without saying that the nucleus would be without importance in the transmission of hereditary factors if its existence terminated at each cell division.

It should be kept in mind that when living cells are examined it is frequently difficult to see the nucleus. During cell division this rather indistinct body does disappear, especially if one is looking through a crude microscope. It appears as though a new nucleus forms in each of the daughter cells.

The difficulty in making observations, coupled with the fact that methods of fixation and staining were poorly developed, makes it easy to understand why cytologists believed what their eyes told them: that the nucleus disappears during cell division.

Nevertheless there were many others who *believed* that the nucleus was not completely dissolved, but that in some manner a portion of the original nucleus gave rise to the daughter nuclei.

In the year 1873 three biologists independently described complex nuclear changes which occurred during cell division and which are now termed *mitosis*. (Simultaneous, though independent, discovery is common in science.

We shall have more examples of it.) They were Schneider, Biitschli, and Fol. Schneider's paper appeared first (a 'paper' is an article appearing in a scientific journal). It was not concerned with cell division, but with the morphology of a flatworm called Mesostoma.

The bulk of the paper is taken up with details of the structure but, being a careful observer, he described everything he saw, including cell division in the eggs.

These develop within the uterus. The uncleaved egg has a large fluid-filled nucleus, which contains a nucleolus. Shortly before the first cell division the outline of the nucleus becomes indistinct, but by adding a little acetic acid it again becomes visible, though folded and wrinkled.

Later the nucleolus disappears. All that remains is a mass of delicate, curved fibers, and these arc seen only if acetic acid is added.

Next thick 'strands' appear and become oriented in an equatorial plane. The granules of the egg become arranged in a regular manner. This arrangement is best seen after acetic acid treatment. The 'strands' increase in number and when the cell divides they pass into the daughter cells.

You have probably identified Schneider's 'strands' with chromosomes and that is exactly what they were. The term 'chromosome' did not come into usage until 1888 but from now on we shall use it to avoid confusion.

If Schneider realized the importance of his observations on chromosomes in cell division, he certainly did not stress the point.

The discussion in his paper is concerned with the morphology of the flatworms and the relation of these animals with other groups in the animal kingdom.

It remained for others to interpret and show the importance of the phenomena that Schneider had observed. Schneider was of the opinion that the nucleus persisted during division, though we must remember that he used acetic acid to establish this point.

One could always question Schneider's interpretation, since the acetic acid treatment might have produced artifacts (abnormal structures) and the 'strands' could be so interpreted. Biitschli also published a paper in

1873 describing cell division in a roundworm, Rhabditis. He agreed with Schneider that the nucleus persisted during cell division.

Fol, the third investigator to describe cell division in 1873, thought that the nucleus entirely disappeared during division and was re-formed in the daughter cells. This second view was shared by Flemming and Auerbach who published observations on cell division in 1874.

It should be emphasized that these observers based their descriptions wholly or largely on what they observed in living eggs.

The problem of cell division was immediately recognized as being of considerable importance, and numerous investigators followed Schneider, Biitschli, and Fol.

A review article on cell division and related topics was published by Professor Mark of Harvard in 1881. He quoted 194 papers (by 86 authors) which appeared in the five years from 1874 through 1878. This period was one of more or less blind experimentation and exploration.

The animal and plant kingdoms were combed for favorable material. Some of the investigators observed living cells, and others worked with those that had been chemically treated. Interpretations of the observed phenomena were numerous and varied.

Some order was brought out of chaos by Flemming in 1878 (and more especially in his monograph of 1882). He was outstanding, first in selecting excellent material, namely, the epidermal cells of larval salamanders; second, in being careful to check in living cells all things that he observed in fixed and stained preparations; and third, in employing hitherto unsurpassed technical methods.

Techniques and Instruments

Before Flemming's contribution is considered in detail, we shall digress to discuss the development of techniques for preparing cells for microscopic observation. Many earlier workers used dyes in a more or less haphazard way, but in 1858 Gerlach described an adequate staining method.

He found that the nuclei of preserved cells take up the dye from a dilute solution of carmine, while the rest of the cell remains unstained or becomes only slightly colored.

This became a vastly improved method for observing nuclei, most of which, it must be remembered, are seen with great difficulty in the living state.

Gerlach did not discover carmine; he merely perfected its use in cytology. This dye was well known to the Indians of Mexico long before the coming of the Spanish.

They obtained it from the crushed and dried bodies of cochineal insects reared especially for this purpose. Later the commercial use of carmine spread to Europe.

In all probability Gerlach tried it as a 'hunch.' It happened to work. Another dye, hematoxylin, was first used successfully by Bohmer in 1865.

Commercial preparations were available, derived from a tropical American tree known as logwood. This dye, like carmine, stains the nucleus.

The first synthetic aniline dye was made by Perkin. The date of this discovery is generally given as 1854, when Perkin was a lad of 16 trying to synthesize quinine. Many different aniline dyes were made later, and soon they became the principal ones used commercially.

They were tried by cytologists from time to time, but it was not until the period of 1875-80 that their use was perfected. It was found that some aniline dyes, such as eosin, would stain parts of the cell not affected by carmine or hematoxylin.

It was then possible to use the doublestain methods that are now standard. The nucleus could be stained deep blue with hematoxylin and the cytoplasm a pale pink with eosin. This gave a much improved picture of cell structure.

a b c

d

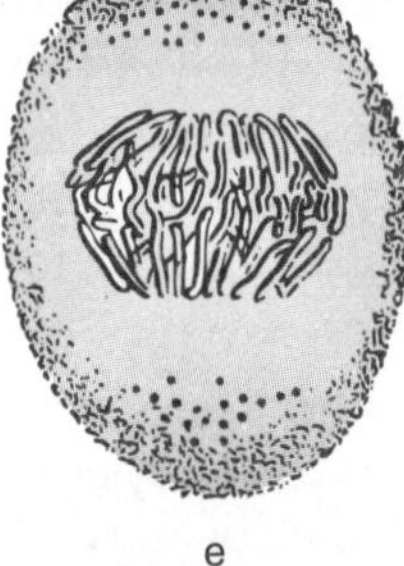

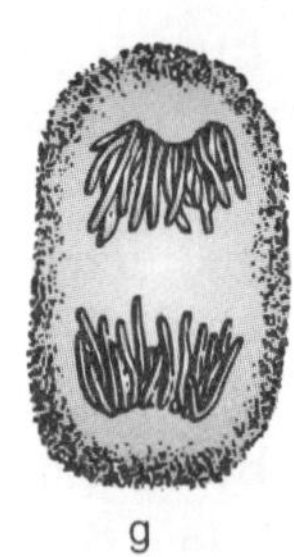

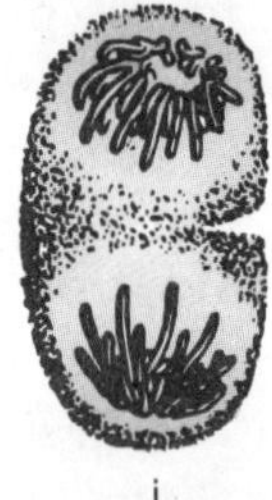

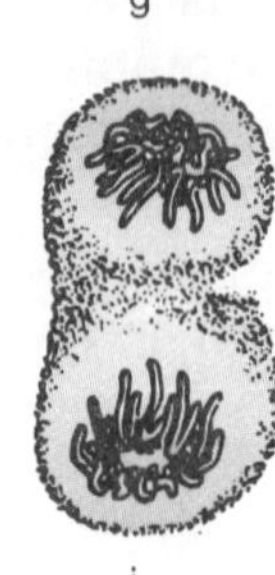

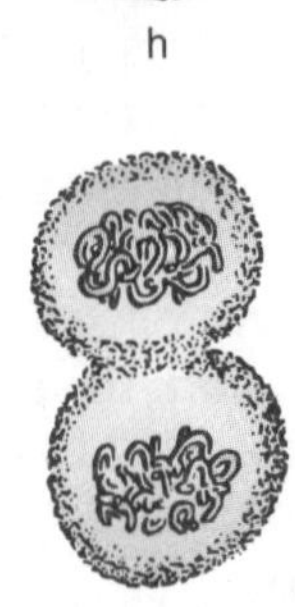

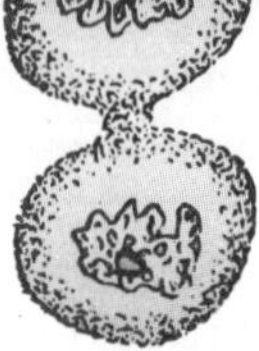

Figure 8.2: Flemming's drawings of mitosis in living epidermal cells of a salamander larva. The drawings are arranged in sequence, beginning with a prophase in a and ending with the two daughter nuclei in 1. The nuclear membrane, asters, spindle, and centrioles are not shown.

Technical advances in still another field were providing an aid to cytologists. Rapid improvement was being made in microscopes. In the 1870s Abbe, the greatest microscope designer of recent times, began his association with the Carl Zeiss optical works and increasingly fine lenses were turned out by this concern.

In 1878 Abbe's oil-immersion objective was first produced (one of the initial users was the famous bacteriologist Koch).

The oil-immersion lens enabled one to obtain a good image of cell structures at magnifications of more than 1,000 diameters.

Technical advances in this field continued with the invention of Abbe's substage condenser, and in 1886 Zeiss produced the apochromatic objective. This is the finest lens so far developed for microscope work.

These advances meant that cytology had reached a point in its development where a person like Flemming could make a culminating advance in our understanding of cell division.

He certainly did not discover mitosis (neither did any single person) but we owe to him more than to any other the concept of mitosis that we hold today. After Flemming, only details were added.

Flemming's Description of Mitosis

It was well known to Flemming and his contemporaries that the structures observed in living cells might be quite different in appearance from those seen in preserved cells.

In some types of living cells no nuclei could be seen, yet after staining typical nuclei were visible. In a situation of this sort the question arises 'Are nuclei present in all normal cells or can they be artifacts resulting from the treatment used in preparing the cells for study?'

Flemming reasoned his answer this way. In some

types of living cells, which we can call type 1, nuclei can be seen. When these cells are fixed and stained, a nucleus of characteristic shape and color appears. In other types of living cells, which we can call type 2, no nucleus can be seen.

Nevertheless when type 2 cells are fixed and stained, a nucleus that in all respects is identical in appearance to the nuclei of fixed and stained cells of type 1, can be seen.

Since the stained nuclei of cell types 1 and 2 have the same appearance, and the treatment is the same in both cases, the most reasonable hypothesis is that a nucleus is present, though invisible, in living cells of type 2.

It seems most unlikely that cells of type 2 could be without a nucleus in the living state and that fixation and staining could produce an artifact that was identical to the nuclei of fixed and stained type I cells.

Flemming made an attempt to apply this type of reasoning to all cell structures, and in every case he tried to use the living cell as the basis of reference. Structures that could never be seen in living cells and that made their appearance only after fixation and staining must be regarded as questionable.

The Resting Stage

Flemming's studies led to this concept of mitosis. A resting stage cell is one not in mitosis. The nucleus is spherical and generally occupies the central region of the cell. A nuclear membrane is present. In living resting stage cells the nucleus does not seem to have any internal structure.

After fixation and staining, an irregular network of strands and granules (chromatin) can be detected. In addition, one or more large spherical granules, the nucleoli, are present. Chromosomes cannot be seen in either the living or the preserved resting stage nucleus.

Prophase

Changes in the nucleus are the first indications that mitosis is under way. Long, delicate threads, the chromosomes, make their appearance. At first they are not easy to see, but with the passage of time they become increasingly distinct. Mitosis is a continuous process, but for descriptive purposes we divide it into a number of stages.

When chromosomes first become visible we say that the prophase stage has begun. If prophase chromosomes are examined carefully, they are seen to be double structures, each chromosome being composed of two long strands, the *chromatids, lying* side by side.

It should be emphasized that only in the very best preparations is it possible to see the chromatids. In most instances, and this is true today, only the entire chromosome is seen.

Flemming was able to see the duplicate prophase chromosomes both in living and preserved salamander cells. During prophase the nucleoli become smaller and smaller and eventually they disappear.

Metaphase

Prophase ends and the next stage, metaphase, begins with the disappearance of the nuclear membrane. By this time the chromosomes have become very distinct. In stained preparations they are prominent cell structures, grouped together in the center of the cell. Early in metaphase the spindle and asters become prominent.

The spindle is given this name because of its shape, which might be compared to that of a chicken's egg that is pointed at both ends. In the living cell the spindle appears as a transparent body. In fixed and stained cells there are one or more tiny granules, the *centrioles,* at each end. One can also see long strands, the *spindle fibers,* connecting the two centriole regions.

At metaphase the chromosomes become arranged in a plate perpendicular to the long axis of the spindle. The *asters* are observed in fixed and stained cells as a series of fibers radiating out from the centrioles.

Anaphase

Metaphase ends and the next stage, anaphase, begins with the separation of the chromosomes into two groups. One group goes to each pole of the spindle. Flemming thought it possible that the double nature of the prophase chromosomes might be of significance in this respect.

Could it be that each chromosome duplicates itself, forming two chromatids, and that at anaphase one chromatid goes to one pole and the other chromatid to the opposite pole of the spindle? (Flemming's belief was found to be true five years later by van Beneden.)

Telophase

The two groups of chromosomes move to the poles of the spindle. When they arrive there the last stage in mitosis, telophase, begins.

The chromosomes become increasingly less distinct and the nuclear membrane is re-formed. The spindle and asters begin to disappear. The cell as a whole now divides into two daughter cells.

The plane of division cuts across the spindle at the equator. As a result, each daughter cell contains a group of chromosomes.

Eventually it becomes impossible to see the chromosomes; the cell has entered the resting stage once more. It should be emphasized that the term 'resting' means that the nucleus is not in mitosis.

It does not signify a lack of metabolic activity. These nuclear changes, known as mitosis, were observed in so many different kinds of animal cells that Flemming believed that they must be a universal feature of living organisms.

The nuclei of plants were found to behave in an almost identical manner. Figure B2-6 shows mitosis in a lily. The chromosome stages are identical with those in the salamander but the lily, like most plants, differs from animals in lacking centrioles and asters.

Our general conclusions based on the work of cytologists up to 1882 are these: cells come from pre-existing cells, nuclei from pre-existing nuclei, and choromosomes from pre-existing chromosomes.

After studying Flemming's illustrations of chromosomes, would you have thought that all of the chromosomes of a cell are more or less alike, or that each was different from every other one in the chromosome set? This is a question that will be of the greatest importance a little later in the story.

A comment on scientific method might be inserted at this point. Flemming's use of living material had the great advantage of allowing him to work out the sequence of stages in mitosis. It was possible to establish that the events in mitosis begin with prophase, pass through metaphase, anaphase, and end with telophase.

If he had studied only fixed and stained material it would have been difficult to establish any such relationship. Put yourself in his position. Would it be necessary to assume any relation between a nucleus in the resting stage and one in metaphase? If you did assume a relation could you prove it from a study of fixed and stained cells?

FERTILIZATION AND GAMETE FORMATION

At the time when some cytologists were studying the chromosomal events during mitosis, others were investigating fertilization and the formation of ova and sperm. These studies were to form the basis of our understanding of heredity, which was to come in the early years of the twentieth century.

FERTILIZATION

The elementary fact of fertilization, namely, that a sperm is required to initiate development of the ovum, was discovered by Prevost and Dumas in 1824. At this time the precise role of the sperm was not understood. In 1854, Newport observed in the frog that the sperm actually penetrates the ovum.

A full understanding of this event had to wait until it was realized that both the ovum and the sperm are cells. Schwann's belief that the ovum was a cell was not shared by many cytologists, but the work of

Gegenbauer in 1861 seemed to convince most workers that this was so. Several years later it was also established that the sperm was a single cell. Inheritance, then, was based on the transmission of cells-an ovum from the mother and a sperm from the father.

Fertilization in the Sea Urchi

In 1873-4 several investigators reported that two

nuclei could be seen in the ovum soon after fertilization and before cell division had begun. It remained for Hertwig (1875) to demonstrate for the sea urchin that one of these nuclei was the nucleus of the ovum and the other was derived from the sperm.

He found that these two nuclei approached each other, made contact, and in a slightly later stage only one nucleus was present. In Hertwig's opinion this single nucleus was the result of fusion of a maternal nucleus of the ovum and a paternal nucleus of the sperm.

Almost immediately other workers came to the same conclusion. Observations were made on eggs of many different species, and it was realized that the formation of the zygote nucleus through the fusion of a *paternal pronucleus* derived from the sperm and a *maternal pronucleus* from the ovum is a general phenomenon.

Two types of material proved of the greatest usefulness in studies of fertilization: the sea urchin (a marine animal related to the starfish) and Ascaris (a parasitic worm found in the intestine of man and other mammals).

The sea urchin was especially suitable because it was easy to obtain the ova and sperm, because fertilization could be carried out under the controlled conditions of the laboratory, and because of the transparency of the ova and early embryos.

The adults were collected in the ocean, usually by dredging, and in the laboratory both males and females could be stimulated to shed their gametes.

The ova could be collected in one dish and the sperm in another. These would number in the millions. When the two were mixed, fertilization occurred in a matter of seconds.

One of the most striking things about fertilization and early development in the sea urchin is the fact that events are synchronous in all the zygotes fertilized at one time.

Thus, if one preserves embryos at successive five-minute intervals after fertilization, the sequence of nuclear events can be worked out with precision. Shortly after fertilization, the paternal pronucleus would be noticed close to the outer membrane of the ovum. At later times it would be found progressively closer to the maternal pronucleus, and eventually fused with it.

Fertilization in Ascaris

As cytological material the sea urchin has one serious defect: its chromosomes are small and numerous. One can observe the general events in fertilization, but the details of chromosome movements and changes could not be determined with ease.

On the other hand, the parasitic worm Ascaris provides excellent material for studying the behavior of chromosomes since it has only four chromosomes and these are large and stain successfully.

As a consequence the detailed nuclear events in fertilization were first observed in Ascaris. The process of fertilization in Ascaris was described by van Beneden in 1883 and by others such as Boveri in 1888.

Boveri's figures, as reproduced in figure elsewhere in this chapter, will be the basis of our account of fertilization. (For the present the reader should ignore the legend for this figure, since it cannot be fully understood until the entire chapter has been read.)

The first figure, a, shows a section of the entire ovum shortly after fertilization. The paternal pronucleus is in the lower right-hand quadrant. It contains two chromosomes.

The structure forming a wrinkled cap immediately above it is the acrosome, which is the portion of the sperm head composed of Golgi material.

In the center of the ovum there is a dark granular area. This is the centrosome, which was formed by a part of the sperm lying immediately behind the sperm nucleus.

There are two structures near the top of the figure. The one within the ovum is the maternal pronucleus. It contains two chromosomes.

The other structure, which is attached to the top of the ovum is a polar body. It can be seen in *b*, c, and *e* as well.

For the present we shall disregard it since it is concerned with meiosis-a subject to be considered in the last part of the chapter. In *b* the maternal and paternal pronuclei have moved somewhat closer and their chromosomes have become indistinct.

In c the chromosomes in both pronuclei have become elongated and coiled. Two centrioles have appeared in the centrosome material. In *d* the centrosome itself has divided, half being centered around each centriole.

The two centrioles, with their associated centrosomes, move farther apart in *e*. In *f* they are on opposite sides of the cell with a spindle between them and an aster radiating out from each.

During this period considerable changes have been occurring in the pronuclei. In *d* the chromosomes have shortened and it can be seen that each pronucleus contains two. A further shortening of the chromosomes is apparent in *e*.

During the interval between *e* and *f* the membranes around both the maternal and paternal pronuclei disappear and in *f* the four choromosomes have entered the spindle. The mitotic stage shown in *f is* an early metaphase.

Somewhat later each of these four chromosomes will become double to make a total of eight, and at anaphase these will separate and four chromosomes will move to each pole of the spindle.

The chromosome number of the zygote, therefore, is four. Half of this total is provided by the paternal pronucleus and half by the maternal pronucleus. The number of chromosomes in a pronucleus is spoken of

OUTLINE OF MEIOSIS AND

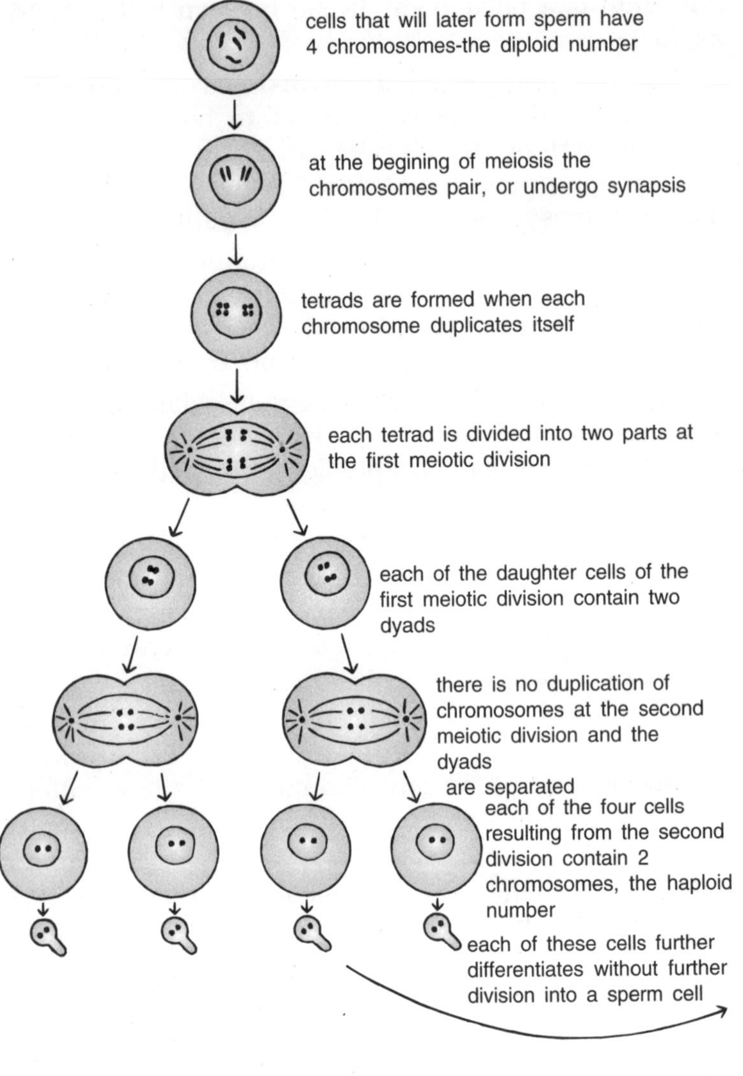

FERTILIZATION IN ASCARIS

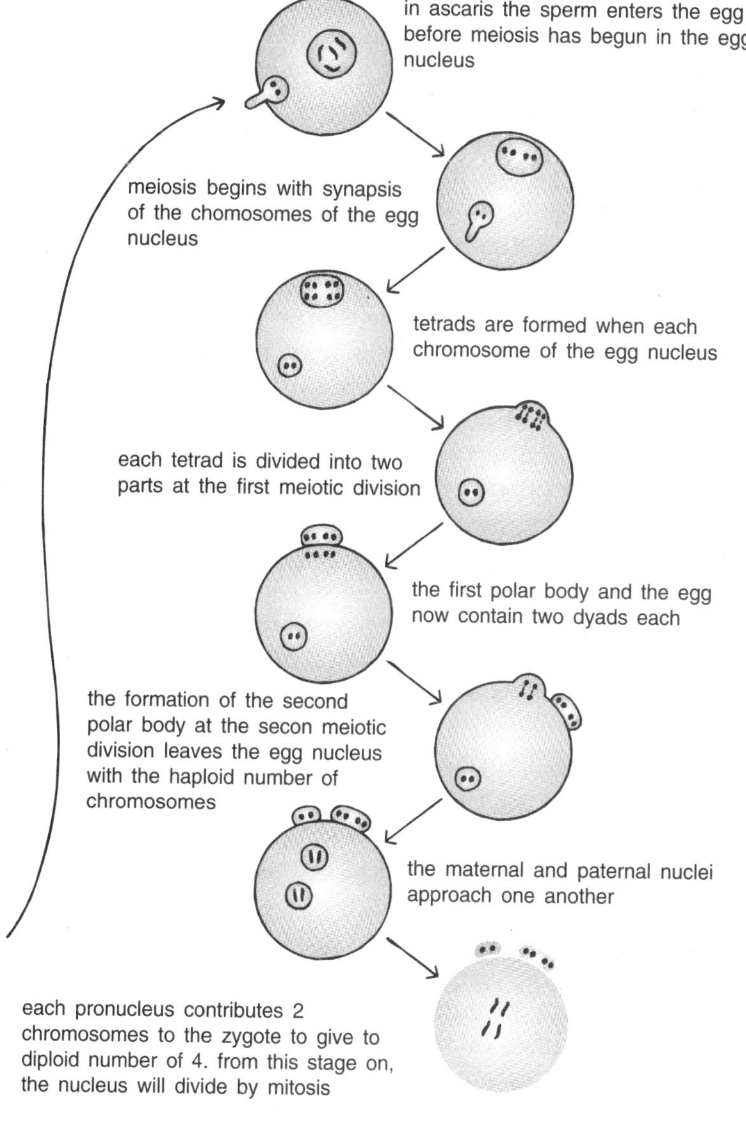

as the *haploid* number and the number in the zygote is the *diploid* number.

It was clear from the work of van Beneden, Boveri, and others that the chromosomal contribution of each parent to the zygote is equal. So far as one could tell the chromosomes in the maternal pronucleus were morphologically equivalent to those in the paternal pronucleus.

Further study revealed that throughout the animal kingdom similar events are observed with only a few exceptions. Fertilization involves the combination of a haploid pronucleus derived from the sperm and a haploid pronucleus derived from the ovum.

Their pooled chromosomes form the diploid number of the zygote. Since the increase in cell number during embryonic development is through mitosis, all the cells of the embryo and adult should be expected to contain the diploid number of chromosomes. Research has shown this to be true with only a few exceptions.

THE FORMATION OF GAMETES

An important problem was raised by these discoveries of the chromosomal events during fertilization: if the nuclei of embryonic and adult cells are diploid, how do the nuclei of ova and sperm become haploid?

Ascaris provided excellent material for the study of this problem and the observations of van Beneden, Boveri, and Hertwig established the essential points during the 1880s, first solving the problem in the ovum and later in the sperm.

They discovered that there are two unusual cell divisions during the formation of gametes. As a result of these divisions diploid cells have their chromosome numbers reduced to the haploid condition.

These two divisions are highly modified mitotic divisions; they are known as the *meiotic divisions*. The

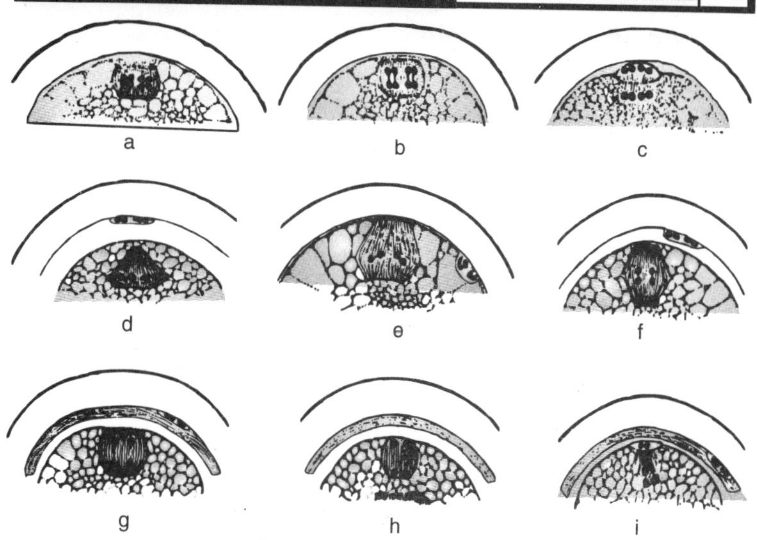

Figure 9.1: Meiosis in Ascaris eggs.

process itself is *meiosis.* The relation between mitosis and meiosis can be brought out by a description of the chromosomal changes during the formation of the ovary and of mature ova.

Mitosis in the Early Ovarian Cells

The ovary of Ascaris begins to form early in development. At first it consists of a few cells and in the course of time these divide to form the tremendous number comprising the ovary of the adult. *This increase in the number of cells is brought about by mitosis.* In mitosis each chromosome duplicates itself at every cell division so the number of chromosomes remains constant from one cell generation to the next.

So far as individual cells are concerned this is what occurs: the Ascaris nucleus contains four chromosomes as the diploid number; before every cell division there is a duplication of each of these four chromosomes to give a total of eight chromatids; at anaphase the chromatids are separated, four going to each daughter cell. This process is repeated with the result that all the cells of the ovary are diploid.

Meiosis in the Female

Many of these ovarian cells become enlarged and form ova. The nuclei of these are diploid. The ovum of Ascaris remains diploid until it has been released from the ovary and entered by a sperm.

The ovum nucleus then undergoes a series of two meiotic divisions that leads to each of the resulting cells having the haploid number of chromosomes. The process of meiosis in the Ascaris ovum is shown in Figure elsewhere in this chapter, which is reproduced from the work of Boveri.

The First Meiotic Division of the Ova

At the onset of meiosis each of the four long chromosomes becomes condensed to form a tiny sphere. Next the chromosomes come together in pairs, a process that is known as *synapsis.*

The chromosomes do not fuse during synapsis, they merely come close to one another. The next event that occurs is that each chromosome becomes duplicate.

Thus, each of the two pairs of chromosomes becomes a group of four, such a group being known as a *tetrad.* The first of Boveri's figures, namely B3-3a, shows an ovum in this condition, which is the metaphase of the first meiotic division.

In it we see the chromosomes grouped into two tetrads. In *b* the tetrads are being divided and in c they have separated completely.

Half of each tetrad, or a *dyad,* goes to each pole of the spindle. It will be noticed that the spindle is not in the center of the cell but instead it is at the periphery. Inasmuch as the cell will divide across the equator of the spindle, the result will be two cells of very unequal sizes.

The large cell resulting from the division is the ovum and the small cell is the *first polar body.* The chromosomes that enter the first polar body are morphologically and numerically equivalent to those that remain in the ovum.

The Second Meiotic Division of the Ova

In *d* the first polar body is well separated from the ovum and the two dyads within the ovum are on the spindle of the second meiotic division. *At this division the chroinosomes do not duplicate themselves.* Consequently the dyads are divided and as a result two chromosomes go to each pole of the spindle.

This second meiotic division divides the cell unequally, as did the first, the result being a large ovum and a tiny second polar body. At the end of the second, and last, meiotic division there are only two chromosomes in the Ascaris ovum.

The nuclear membrane forms around these two chromosomes, the haploid number, and in this manner the maternal pronucleus is produced.

The subsequent history of the maternal pronucleus has been discussed as an aspect of fertilization and Figure elsewhere in this chapter should be re-studied.

Meiosis in the Male

The observation that the paternal pronucleus was haploid, yet the male diploid in its body cells suggested that a process similar to that just described must also occur in the male. A study of sperm formation in Ascaris showed this to be the case.

The last two cell divisions before a sperm forms are meiotic divisions. As in the egg, the four chromosomes form two pairs and each chromosome duplicates itself. The result is two tetrads each composed of four chromatids.

During the first meiotic division the tetrads are divided and half of each goes into each of the daughter cells. Not only is nuclear division equal but cell division is also equal, which is in contrast to the situation in the ova. At the next division the dyads are divided between the two daughter cells, which are again of equal size.

Thus, from one cell with four chromosomes, and by means of two meiotic divisions, we end with four cells each with two chromosomes. Each of these four haploid cells then develops without further division into a sperm cell.

The essential difference between meiosis and mitosis is this: in mitosis there is one duplication of every chromosome for each cell division; in meiosis there is only one duplication of every chromosome for the two meiotic divisions.

As a consequence, in mitosis the chromosome number remains constant from one cell generation to the next; in meiosis the two meiotic divisions form cells with the haploid number of chromosomes.

With full realization that the nuclear events associated with maturation and fertilization were important biological phenomena, cytologists examined many species of animals and plants.

It was found that the reduction divisions leading to haploid pronuclei occur throughout the animal and plant kingdoms.

In short, another principle of almost universal application (a few exceptions were found) had been discovered. The facts as outlined in this section were generally, though not universally, believed by 1890.

Chapter 10

THE NUCLEUS AND HEREDITY

The middle years of the 1880s witnessed several attempts to see if inheritance was controlled by some definite part of the cell. We might have expected this to be the case when we realize that cytologists, in a decade of unparalleled discovery, had worked out the essentials of mitosis, fertilization, and meiosis.

Haeckel's Hypothesis of the Nuclear Control of Inheritance. An effort to find a cytological basis for inherit-ance was made as early as 1866 by Haeckel, who postulated that the nucleus was responsible for the transmission of the inherited features of an organism.

The data available to Haeckel in 1866 were not sufficient to test this hypothesis. As E. B. Wilson, the great American cytologist, was to remark some years later, it was a lucky guess.

If a lucky guess of this sort had been made by some obscure scientist, it is probable that its influence on subsequent events would have been negligible. But Haeckel was a leader in the field of biology in his day.

An idea of his, no matter how slight the factual basis, would have been noticed. It is conceivable, therefore, that Haeckel's hypothesis of nuclear control of inheritance helped to prepare others for thinking and experimenting along these lines.

Nageli's Idioplasm Theory

In 1884 Nageli suggested that a substance which he called the *idioplasm* was responsible for inheritance. The idioplasm was thought to be an invisible chemical network that extended throughout the cell and from cell to cell. Nageli did not observe the idioplasm in cells. He invented it to account for inheritance.

He did not regard it as a highly stable material, but as one that might change during development, or as the result of nutrition or other external conditions. In any event it must return to the original condition in the embryo.

Nageli did considerable theorizing on the subject of inheritance, but his concept of possible mechanisms was extremely vague.

His hypothesis was nearly impossible to test, and hence it could be of no real usefulness in directing efforts to profitable experimentation.

Early Evidence for the Nuclear Control of Inheritance

In 1884-5 four German scientists, working independently, came to the conclusion that the physical basis of inheritance must lie in the chromosomes. They were Hertwig, Strasburger, Kolliker, and Weismann. The first three were primarily laboratory scientists.

For at least a decade they had been leaders in the analysis of problems concerned with the nucleus. Weismann, on the contrary, is remembered largely for his theoretical work.

These four men believed that the chromosomes were the physical basis of inheritance for the following reasons.

1. Even though inheritance was not well understood, it seemed that both parents have an equal share in transmitting their characteristics to the offspring. What is the physical basis of this

equality? It was known, of course, that the only links between parent and offspring are the ovum and sperm.

These two cells are about as different as any two cells could be. Usually the ovum has a mass thousands or millions of times the mass of the sperm. Ova usually contain a large quantity of cytoplasm, whereas sperm contain almost none.

This would suggest that the cytoplasm was not the basis of inheritance because, if it were, it might be expected that the female's contribution would be much greater than the male's.

The only parts of the sperm and ova that seemed to these four scientists to be equivalent were the nuclei. The sperm pronucleus and the egg pronucleus were identical so far as one could tell.

Perhaps this equivalence of structure was the basis of the equivalent importance of the two gametes in inheritance. Van Beneden's description of the pronuclei in Ascaris, each with two chromosomes, seemed most suggestive.

2. During cell division, the cytoplasm and its formed structures seem to be divided passively. The chromosomes, on the other hand, go through a complicated mitosis which results in each of the daughter cells receiving exactly the same number of chromosomes.

   It seemed to Hertwig and the others that the significance of this complicated process might be that the nucleus was the basis of inheritance: why should the chromosomes, alone among the cell structures, be duplicated and then divided equally unless they were of great importance in inheritance?

3. The complex chromosomal changes during meiosis were understandable in terms of keeping the

chromosomes constant from generation to generation. There was no similar phenomenon for any other cell structure.

Since inheritance was an intergeneration phenomenon and the chromosomes seemed to be the only cell structures that were transmitted in an exact way from one generation to another, perhaps the chromosomes were of importance in inheritance.

4. Finally, there was a more direct test of nuclear function in regenerating protozoa. The forms selected for this work were single-celled organisms with one nucleus. It was possible to cut the animals into two parts, one part containing cytoplasm and the other cytoplasm and the nucleus.

   Both parts healed. The part without a nucleus lived for some time, but it was unable to regenerate to form a whole animal, and it was incapable of reproduction. The part with the nucleus could regenerate a whole animal and could reproduce normally.

These observations were suggestive, but they did not 'prove' that the nucleus was the physical basis of inheritance.

The fact that chromosomes appeared to be the only cell structure that remained constant from cell to cell, and from generation to generation, could mean that inheritance was by way of the chromosomes. Many famous cytologists believed that a good working hypothesis was 'The nucleus is important in heredity.'

In the next chapter, we shall learn that in the year 1900 the rediscovery of a scientific paper written much earlier by Mendel put the subject of inheritance in an entirely new light.

It is of interest, therefore, to summarize the advances that those cytologists interested in heredity had made up to the year Mendel's results became generally known. Such a summary was given retrospectively by Wilson in 1914:

The work of cytology in its period of foundation laid a broad and substantial basis for our more general conceptions of heredity and its physical substratum.

It demonstrated the basic fact that heredity is a consequence of the genetic continuity of cells by division, and that the germ-cells are the vehicle of transmission from one generation to another.

It accumulated strong evidence that the cell-nucleus plays an important role in heredity. It made known the significant fact that in all the ordinary forms of cell-division the nucleus does not divide *en masse* but first resolves itself into a definite number of chromosomes; that these bodies, originally formed as long threads, split lengthwise so as to effect a meristic division of the entire nuclear substance.

It proved that fertilization of the egg everywhere involves the union or close association of two nuclei, one of maternal and one of paternal origin. It established the fact, sometimes designated as 'Van Beneden's law' in honor of its discoverer, that these primary germ-nuclei give rise to similar groups of chromosomes, each containing half the number found in the body-cells.

It demonstrated that when new germ-cells are formed each again receives only half the number characteristic of the body-cells. It steadily accumulated evidence, especially through the admirable studies of Boveri, that the chromosomes of successive generations of cells, though commonly lost to view in the resting nucleus, do not really lose their individuality, or that in some less obvious way they conform to the principle of genetic continuity.

From these facts followed the farreaching conclusion that the nuclei of the body-cells are diploid or duplex structures, descended equally from the original maternal and paternal chromosome-groups of the fertilized egg. Continually receiving confirmation by the labours of later years, this result gradually took a central place in cytology; and about it all more specific discoveries relating to the chromosomes naturally group themselves.

All this had been made known at a time when the experimental study of heredity was not yet sufficiently advanced for a full appreciation of its significance; but some very interesting theoretical suggestions had been offered by Roux, Weismann, de Vries, and other writers. While most of these hardly admitted of actual verificat-ion, two nevertheless proved to be of especial importance to later research. One was the pregnant suggestion of Roux (1883), that the formation of chromosomes from long threads brings about an alignment in linear series of different materials or 'qualities.'

By longitudinal splitting of the threads all the 'qualit-ies' are equally divided, or otherwise definitely distrib-uted, between the daughter-nuclei.

The other was Weismann's far-seeing prediction of the reduction division, that is to say, of a form of division involving the separation of undivided whole chromoso-mes instead of the division-products of single chromos-omes.

This fruitful suggestion (1887) pointed out a way that was destined to lead years afterwards to the probable explanation of Mendel's law of heredity. Such, in bird's-eye view, were the most essential conclusions of our science down to the close of the nineteenth century.

Chapter 11 MENDEL

During the entire period from Darwin's attempted synthesis of the facts of inheritance down to 1900, a scientific paper that was to revolutionize our understanding of heredity lay unappreciated on the shelves of many libraries. The article itself had been published in 1866. In it the author, Gregor Mendel, presented some of the results of his experiments in crossing varieties of garden peas.

The Discovery of Mendel's Paper

The 'discovery' and appreciation of the importance of Mendel's paper is a very dramatic incident in the history of science. Three individuals, de Vries, Correns, and Tschermak, independently in the year 1900, realized the great importance of Mendel's work.

During the 1890s there was renewed interest in plant hybridization. The three scientists who 'discovered' Mendel-de Vries, Correns, and Tschermak-were doing breeding experiments of their own.

Each of them independently came to more or less the same conclusions that Mendel had expressed in 1866 *before they knew of Mendel's paper.* This is another example of a frequent happening in science. When the field is 'ready,' the discovery is certain to be made.

If Mendel had never lived, the history of genetics would not have been greatly different. About the year

1900, either he would be rediscovered or, had he never lived, others would reach essentially the same conclusions as he had in 1866.

His work was unappreciated in his own lifetime, for biologists in 1866 did not have the background to understand the significance of what lie had accomplished.

Gregor Mendel's famous article is not a scientific paper in the usual sense, but a lecture presented to the Natural History Society of Briinn in 1865.

The full results of his research were never published, but the portion that he did include, coupled with an extraordinary analysis of the data, make his paper one of the landmarks of science.

Mendel was fully aware that experiments in plant breeding had been conducted by many famous men. It was true, nevertheless, that no general principles had emerged from previous studies.

To Mendel this was a serious affair, since an understanding of inheritance was essential for an understanding of evolution and he was deeply interested in Darwin's work *(The Origin of Species* appeared during the period he was conducting his experiments). He began experiments which were intended to give information on inheritance and evolution.

Peas as Experimental Material

Mendel selected peas for his experiments because they possessed many desirable features:

1. Numerous varieties of peas were available commercially. They provided the material that he studied.
2. The plants were easy to cultivate and the generation time was short.
3. The offspring of the crosses between the varieties were fertile.
4. The structure of the pea flower is such that accid-

ental pollination was thought not to occur. The anthers that produce the pollen and the stigma where the pollen grains germinate, are completely enclosed by the petals. Normally, pollen from a flower falls on the stigma of the same flower and self-fertilization results. In those cases where crosses between varieties are desired, it is possible to remove the anthers before they mature and somewhat later, when the stigma is mature, to cover it with pollen from another flower.

Mendel's approach to the problem of inheritance was different from that of previous workers. His predecessors had concentrated on the whole organism. Usually they had crossed varieties that differed in many characters and the offspring were found to be intermediate or in rare cases more like one parent.

Mendel focused his attention on specific differences and studied how these were inherited generation after generation. Some of his varieties had *round* seeds; others had *wrinkled* seeds. In all he studied seven different characters of the pea, and for each he had two varieties, as shown in the following lists:

Character Affected	***Varieties***
Seed shape	*round or wrinkled*
Seed *color*	*yellow or green*
Seed coat *color*	*colored or white*
Pod shape	*inflated or wrinkled*
Pod *color*	*green or yellow*
Flower position	*axial or terminal*
Stem length	*long or short*

Crosses of Plants with Contrasting Characters

First, he made sure that all of his varieties would breed true. Once this was established he made crosses between all of the pairs just listed. The results were most unexpected in the light of earlier experiments by other plant breeders.

The offspring were never intermediate but were always like one of the parents. When peas with *round* seeds were crossed with peas with *wrinkled* seeds, for example, the offspring were plants with *round* seeds.

Mendel spoke of the form that appeared in the offspring as *dominant* in comparison to the form that (lid not appear, which he called *recessive.* (Dominance can be determined only by making a cross and observing the type of offspring obtained; it could not be predicted before the experiment was performed merely by examining the parent plants.) The varieties that Mendel used were found to have these relationships:

Dominant	**Recessive**
round seed	*wrinkled* seed
yellow seed	*green* seed
colored seed *coat*	*white* seed *coat*
inflated pod	*wrinkled pod*
green pod	*yellow* pod
axial flowers	*terminal* flowers
long stem	*short* stem

Over the course of years, geneticists have introduced some terms that make it easier to discuss crosses. The original parental generation is abbreviated P. The offspring of the P generation is the first filial or F_i generation.

The offspring of the F_3 is the second filial generation or F_0',, the third is the F_3, and so on. It is also customary to describe crosses in terms of the character. Thus, the cross of a plant with round seeds with a plant with wrinkled seeds is shortened to *round X wrinkled.*

The F_2 Generation

Some plant breeders might have stopped the experiments after a single cross had determined dominant and recessive characteristics. The results, after all, were uniform and clear cut. The F_1 plants were always like one of the parents.

Mendel, however, continued his crosses and was careful to realize that although an F_1 of the *round X wrinkled* might be identical with the *round* parent, its parentage was different. Perhaps its genetic behavior would reflect the different origin.

Since peas are self-fertilizing, the F_1 plants pollinated their own ovules and gave the F_2, and when Mendel studied the F_2 plants he found that both dominant and recessive characters were present.

Now he did a simple though revolutionary thing: he counted the number of individuals of each type. In every cross there was a ratio of 3 dominant to 1 recessive. His results can be summarized as follows:

P	***F_1***	***F_2 Counts***	***Ratio***
round X wrinkled	round	5,474 round	
		1,850 wrinkled	2.96:1
yellow X green	yellow	6,022 yellow	
		2,001 green	3.01:1
colored X white	colored	705 colored	
		224 white	3.15:1
inflated X wrinkled	inflated	882 inflated	
		299 wrinkled	2.95:1
green pods X		428 green	
yellow pods	green	152 yellow	2.82:1
axial X terminal	axial	651 axial	
		207 terminal	3.14:1
long X short	long	787 long	
		277 short	2.84:1

These results would suggest that the rules of inheritance were the salve, irrespective of the varieties being crossed. The F_1 plants were always of one type, which resembled one of the parents. In the F_2, two classes appeared and the frequency was 75 per cent dominants and 25 ' per cent recessives, or a ratio of 3: 1.

***The F_3** Generation.* Mendel continued his experiments and obtained an F_3 generation. We may take as an example of his work the *round X wrinkled,* which in the F_2 gave 75 per cent *round* and 25 per cent *wrinkled.* He allowed a number of the *wrinkled* plants to self-fertilize to give an F_3, and found that all bred true, that is, only *wrinkled* plants were obtained in the F_3. The *F_2 round* plants gave two results:

1. One-third (193 of 565 plants) bred true, giving *round* plants in the F_3
2. Two-thirds (372 of 565 plants) gave *round* and *wrinkled* in a ratio of 3: 1. (On the basis of their genetic behavior these were like the F_1 plants.)

Mendel's Hypothesis

Mendel explained these results in this way: Let us assume that the *round* variety is round because it has *a gene R,* and the *wrinkled* variety is wrinkled because it has gene r. (Mendel did not use the term gene but spoke of 'factors' or 'traits.'

It will be simpler for us to use the modern term gene from the very beginning and note the gradual change in its meaning. For the present we shall understand it to be the basis of an inherited character.) If a cross is made between the *round* and *wrinkled* varieties, the gametes of the *round* plant will have R and the gametes of the *wrinkled* plant will have r.

Fertilization will produce an F_1 with both genes, Rr. In appearance this plant is *round,* R being dominant and r recessive. We speak of the appearance of the individual as its *phenotype* and the genetic composition of the individual as its *genotype.* Thus, the phenotype of this F_1 plant is *round* and its genotype is Rr.

Plants of the Rr type will produce gametes and

Mendel assumed that any single gamete would contain either R or r *but never both.* He also assumed that gametes containing R and gametes containing r are produced in equal numbers. If the union of F_1 gametes is at random, then we will obtain a 3:1 ratio of *round* to *wrinkled.*

It is actual'y unnecessary to show two plants in the F_i since both are the same. Two are used in order to make it easier to visualize the cross that gives the F_2.

This scheme provides a formal explanation of the results, namely, the origin of the 3: 1 ratio. It also shows that the F_2 *round* plants are of two types. One in three of the *round* plants is pure *round.* If selffertilized, it would breed true. The remaining %/$_3$ of the *round* plants are Rr.

If these are allowed to self-fertilize there will result an F_3 ratio of 3 *round* to 1 *wrinkled.* It will be recalled that Mendel made these tests of the F_2 and the theoretical and actual results are the same.

This schematic interpretation applies to all of Mendel's crosses involving one pair of genes. Several important conclusions can be reached if the interpretation is correct:

1. Dominant and recessive genes do not affect one another. In the F_1 of the cross discussed, the genotype was **Rr.** There was no visible effect of the r gene, the seeds being just as round as in the pure *round* parent. When the **Rr** plant was allowed to self-fertilize both *round* and *wrinkled* seeds were obtained. These F_2 *wrinkled* seeds were identical in appearance to the P generation *wrinkled* seeds.
2. The gametes produced by an F_1 plant of the Rr constitution will contain either R or r, never both.
3. The R and r types of gametes will be produced in equal numbers by an Rr plant.
4. Combination between gametes is a chance affair,

and the frequency of different classes of offspring will depend on the frequencies of gametes. Since an F_1 plant having the **Rr** constitution will produce 50 per cent gametes of the R type and 50 per cent gametes of the r type the mathematical basis of the F_2 frequencies will be as follows:

		POLLEN	
		50% **R**	R 50% **r**
OVULES	50% **R**	25% **RR**	25% **Rr**
	50% **r**	25% **Rr**	25% **rr**

Crosses Involving Two Pairs of Genes

Mendel's next step was to see if the conceptual scheme devised for crosses involving one pair of genes could be applied to crosses involving two pairs of genes. For this he used *round* and *wrinkled* as one pair and *yellow* and *green* as the other. Previous work had shown that the cross between *yellow* and *green* produced *yellow* in the F_1 and a ratio of *3 yellow* to 1 *green* in the F_2.

When a cross was made between a plant with *round-yellow* seeds and a plant with *wrinkled-green* seeds all of the F_1 plants had *roundyellow* seeds. In the F_2 the following seed types were obtained:

315 round-yellow
108 round-green
101 wrinkled-yellow
32 wrinkled-green

One interesting thing brought out by these data is the appearance of two new seed types that were not present in either the P or the F_1 generation. These new types are *round-green* and *wrinkled-yellow*. This and the other results, however, fit perfectly into the Mendelian scheme, if we assume the complete independence in inheritance of the two pairs of genes.

In the formation of gametes by the F_1 plant, Mendel assumed that a gamete would have only one member of a pair of genes. Thus, a gamete would have either *R or r* and in addition either *Y or y*. Four classes of gametes would be produced and these in equal frequency. The classes would be RY, Ry, *rY*, and *ry*. If an F_1 plant is allowed to self-fertilize there will be these four types of pollen and the same four types of ovules. This will give 16 possible combinations, as shown below:

POLLEN

		RY	**Ry**	**rY**	**ry**
	RY	**RR YY** round-yellow	**RR Yy** round-yellow	**Rr YY** round-yellow	**Rr Yy** round-yellow
Ovules	**Ry**	**RR Yy** *round-yellow*	**RR yy** *round-green*	**Rr Yy** *round yellow*	**Rr yy** *round-green*
	rY	**Rr YY** round-yellow	**Rr Yy** round-yellow	**rr YY** wrinkled yellow	**rr Yy** wrinkled yellow
	ry	**Rr Yy** round-yellow	**Rr yy** round-green	**rr Yy** wrinkled yellow	**rr yy** wrinkled-green

Of the 16 possible F_2 combinations, 9 will be *round-yellow*, 3 will be *round-green*, 3 will be *wrinkled-yellow*, and 1 will be *wrinkled-green*. Here is a comparison of Mendel's data with the theoretical expectation:

	Actual	***Expected***
Round yellow	315	313
Round-green	108	104
Wrinkled-yellow	101	104
Wrinkled-green	32	35
	556	556

The figures given in the 'actual' column are those obtained by counting the seeds. The 'expected' values are computed in this manner: If we have a total of 556 plants and expect $^1/_{16}$ of them to be *wrinkled-green*, we find $^1/_{16}$ of 556, which is 35. The other expected classes are $^9/_{16}$, $^3/_{16}$, and $^3/_6$ of 556.

Testing the Hypothesis

Mendel made a further test of the adequacy of his hypothesis. On the basis of his hypothesis the F_2 plants would have four phenotypic classes and a total of nine genotypic classes (refer to the checkerboard). Genetic tests would allow him to distinguish among plants of the same phenotype but of different genotypes.

His test consisted of allowing all the F_2 plants to self-fertilize to produce an F_3 and then seeing if the actual results of the crosses were the same as were expected on the basis of the hypothesis. This is what he found.

The Breeding Behavior of the F_2 Round-yellow

It can be seen from the checkerboard that $^9/_{16}$ of the F_2 plants are *Round-yellow.* These plants are listed in the first column of the table that follows, grouped according to genotype. These plants are all of the same phenotype but they belong to four different genotypes, namely **RRYY, RRYy, RrYY,** and RrYy.

Although of identical appearance, these four genotypes can be distinguished on the basis of the ratios of the types of offspring they will produce following self-fertilization. These expected ratios are listed in the second column.

The third column gives the number of plants that one would expect to give the ratio listed in column 2, if Mendel's hypothesis is correct. For example, Mendel expected one out of every nine *round-yellow* plants to be RRYY. If a plant of this genotype is self-fertilized, it would give only *round-yellow* offspring in the F_3.

No other genotype will give this result. Mendel planted 315 of the F_2 *round-yellow* plants and of these 301 gave progeny. He would expect therefore $^1/_9$ of these 301 plants, or 33, to be RRYY and give only *roundyellow* seeds. The fourth column gives the actual results. In the example we have been using, Mendel expected that 33 of the plants would be RRYY and he found that 38 were of this genotype.

F_2	Expected F_3 Ratios	Expected	Actual
RRYY	all *round yellow*	33	38
RRYy	*3 round yellow; 1 round-green*	67	65
RRYy			
RrYY	*3 round-yellow; 1 wrinkled yellow*	67	60
RrYY			
RrYy			
RrYy	*9 round-yellow; 3 round-green;*		
RrYy	*3 wrinkled yellow; 1 wrinkled green*	134	138
RrYy			
		301	301

The Breeding Behavior of the F_2 Round-green. Three-sixteenths of the F_2 were of this category. Mendel raised 102 of these plants and these are the results:

F_2	Expected F_3 Ratios	Expected	Actual
RRyy	all *round-green*	34	35
Rryy	*3 round-green; 1 wrinkled-green*	68	67
Rryy			
		102	102

The Breeding Behavior of the F_2 Wrinkled-yellow. The *wrinkledyellow* comprised $^3/_{16}$ of the F_2. Mendel raised 96 of these plants and these are the results:

F_2	Expected F_3 Ratios	Expected	Actual
rrYY	all *wrinkled-yellow*	*32*	*28*
rrYy	*3 wrinkled yellow; I wrinkled-green*	*64*	*68*
rrYy			
		96	96

The Breeding Behavior of the F_2 Wrinkled-green. This category comprised $^1/_{16}$ of the F_2. Mendel raised 30 plants of this type. The results were as follows:

F_2	Expected F_3 Ratios	Expected	Actual
rryy	all *wrinkled-green*	30	30

The fact that the F_2 plants gave an F_3 that did not differ materially from the expected, indicated that Mendel's conceptual scheme of inheritance was in lull accord with his experimental results. In every case the actual values are surprisingly close to those expected.

The expected values are based on the probability of the various types of gametes combining in a certain way. The expected and actual values are rarely identical: we should not expect them to be so any more than we should always expect five heads for every ten tosses of a coin.

Mendel went one step farther and crossed plants differing in three contrasting characters. The results were entirely according to expectation but they will not be discussed.

These are some of the conclusions that may be drawn from Mendel's experiments:

1. The most important conclusion is that inheritance appears to follow definite and rather simple rules. Mendel was able to apply the same type of explanation to the results of all of his crosses.

   He had reached that stage in the development of a scientific theory where results could be predicted with a high degree of accuracy. This is one goal of a scientist.

2. When plants of two different types were crossed, there was no blending of the individual characteristics. Mendel studied seven pairs of contrasting characters. One member of each pair of contrasting characters could be thought of as dominant and the other as recessive.

   In a hybrid formed from crossing a pure-breeding

dominant and a purebreeding recessive, the appearance of the plant was identical with that of the dominant parent.

3. The factors responsible for the dominant and recessive condition were not modified by their occurence together in a hybrid. If two hybrids were crossed, both dominant and recessive offspring would appear.

   Neither the dominant nor the recessive offspring would give any evidence of contamination resulting from hybridization. In short, an F_2 recessive would be identical in genotype and phenotype to the P generation recessive.

4. When a pure-breeding plant exhibiting a dominant characteristic (A) is crossed with a recessive (a) the F_1 (Aa) is like the A plant in appearance. *Segregation* occurs in the F_2, which results in a ratio of three plants having the dominant character (one of which will be pure breeding and the other two like the F_1) to one recessive. Segregation is often called *Mendel's first law.*

5. If two pairs of genes, such as **Aa** and **Bb,** are involved in a cross, each pair acts independently so far as transmission to the next generation is concerned.

   This phenomenon is known as *independent assortment* and it is often spoken of as *Mendel's second law.* Its mode of operation can be understood if we consider the F_2 originating from an F_1 **AaBb** plant. So far as the phenotypes are concerned ¾ of the plants will have the **A** phenotype and ¼ will have the a phenotype.

   The same is true for the other pair of genes: ¾ of the plants will have the **B** phenotype and ¼ will have the b phenotype. It is entirely a matter of chance which combination of genes a given F_2

plant will receive.

Thus of the ¾ that will have the **A** phenotype, ¾ will also have the **B** phenotype and ¼ will have the b phenotype. Of the ¼ that will have the a phenotype, ¼ will have the **B** phenotype and ¼ will have the b phenotype.\

So far as both characters are concerned 9/16 of the F_2 (¾ of ¾) will have both the A and B phenotypes, 1/16 will have the **A** and **b** phenotypes, 3/16 will have the **a** and **B** phenotypes, and 3/16 will have the **a** and **b** phenotypes. The 9:3:3:1 ratio of the F_2 is due to the independent assortment of genes in the gametes of the F_1 plant.

6. The gametes will contain only one type of inherited factor of each contrasting pair. Thus the gametes of an F_1 Aa plant will produce gametes containing either A or a, never both. If two factors are involved, as in an AaBb plant the gametes will be AB, or Ab, or **aB,** or **ab,** never Aa, **Bb, ABb, Aab,** and so on. All possible combinations will be obtained, consisting of one member of each pair of genes. Every type of gamete will be produced in equal frequency.

It must be remembered that, without further work, these conclusions could apply only to the seven pairs of pea genes actually studied by Mendel. The fact that Mendel's rules applied to these would indicate that other genes of peas *might* behave in a similar way.

The discovery that rules of inheritance could be established for peas would suggest that the same or similar rules might also apply to other plants (and possibly animals). This, of course, would have to be tested by experimentation.

The great worth of Mendel's theory was that its clear and definite formulation made testing by experimentation possible. The same could riot be said for any previous theory of inheritance.

Most of the important discoveries in biology turn out in retrospect to be fairly simple. Inevitably we wonder, Why did not that idea occur to someone before? Why had no one discovered these simple relations when varieties were crossed?

Why had no one realized the significance of Mendel's approach during the 34 years between 1866 and 1900? These are unanswerable questions, but the following facts are germane to the last one. Mendel was almost unknown among biologists during his day and his results were published in a journal that attracted little attention.

This is clearly only part of the story. It is perhaps more correct to say that biologists in 1866 were unable to appreciate the significance of Mendel's work. Their minds were not prepared. There is one interesting bit of information in this connection.

Mendel carried on a lengthy correspondence with Nageli, explaining the results of his experiments. It should be remembered that Nageli was greatly interested in heredity, he being the proponent of the idioplasm concept. He, of all people, should have seen Mendel's point but he failed to appreciate the significance of the pea experiments.

Still another fact is that Mendel did not believe for long in the universality of his findings. This was the result of an unfortunate choice of material, the hawkweed, for some additional experiments. In the hawkweed the ovules are capable of parthenogenetic development.

As a result, many of the crosses he believed he was performing were not crosses at all. Mendel did not realize this and was unable to understand why he did not observe the ratios he had previously found in peas. He probably came to believe that his results held for peas alone.

The three biologists who made the theoretical import

of Mendel's paper known to their contemporaries supplied data of their own that could be explained in Mendelian terms, and in the few years after 1900 the results of much more genetic work became available.

Most of it could be understood in Mendelian terms, but some could not. Many of the exceptions could not be explained until the physical basis of inheritance was established by cytologists. We should, therefore, now examine what students of the cell were discovering during the first years of the present century.

Chapter 12: BOVERI AND SUTTON

In other chatper of this book, we learned that in 1900 the hypothesis that 'chromosomes are the physical basis of inheritance' seemed to be reasonable. It was far from being established as true and, in fact, there was a real difficulty in knowing how to test such a hypothesis. Until 1902 no one had a clue as to how this might be done.

In that year, *Boveri* carried out an ingenious experiment demonstrating that a complete set of chromosomes was necessary for normal development. Since development is one aspect of *inheritance*, the relation between chromosomes and inheritance was established.

The significance of Boveri's experiment will be more apparent if we give something of the background from which he worked. At the time of his experiment, most cytologists believed that within any single species one chromosome was about the same as another.

Thus, in the sea urchin each cell of the embryo has 36 chromosomes. They were all very small and looked identical in shape; they reacted alike to fixation and staining; and when things look alike there is a natural tendency to believe that they are alike in other respects as well.

Boveri thought otherwise. He believed that chromosomes differed from one another, and that a complete set of 36 was necessary for normal development in the sea urchin.

He believed that not just any 36 would suffice: but the very 36 which were present in each cell of the normal embryo were the necessary ones.

DOUBLE FERTILIZATION OF SEA URCHIN OVA

Boveri tested this hypothesis in a clever way. Hertwig and others had observed previously that if one used a highly concentrated sperm suspension, it was possible to get two sperm to enter one egg of the sea urchin. *Mitosis* becomes most confused in these double *fertilizations*, but it is possible by this method to vary the number of chromosomes distributed to the cells.

In order to understand the complications we should first review normal fertilization. In the case of an embryo entered by a single sperm, the sperm brings in a *centrosome*, which is the region containing the centriole. (In the sea urchin the centriole is composed of several granules surrounded by an area, the centrosome, which stains differently from the rest of the *cytoplasm*.)

The centrosome divides into two and the spindle forms between the two *centrosomes*. The paternal and maternal nuclei fuse, and then their chromosomes go on the spindle. Each *pronucleus* of the sea urchin has 18 chromosomes so the fusion nucleus will have 36. Each of these 36 duplicates itself, thus forming a total of 72 chromosomes.

These are divided equally at the first cleavage division, and each daughter cell receives 36. When two sperm enter, not only will there be an additional 18 chromosomes to make a total of *54* but there will be an extra centrosome as well. Boveri observed that one of two things happened:

1. In some embryos the centrosomes of both sperm divided. This resulted in four centrosomes in the

single cell. At the time of first cleavage these embryos divided into four instead of into two cells.

2. In the remaining embryos, the centrosome of one sperm divided and the other remained single. This gave three centrosomes for the single cell and at the time of first *cleavage* this type of embryo divided into three cells.

In both classes of double-fertilization embryos, there would be 54 chromosomes (18 from the maternal nucleus and 18 from each of the two *paternal nuclei*). These 54 will duplicate themselves during the first mitotic division of the embryo to give a total of 108 chromosomes.

In those embryos with four centrosomes, the chromosomes will be divided among four cells. Boveri found this division very unequal. Some cells would get many chromosomes and others only a few. If the apportionment was strictly equal, each cell would receive 27 chromosomes (108/4 = 27). This is far from the normal complement of 36 per cell, which Boveri believed necessary for regular development.

In fact, there is no way in which each of the four cells could get the normal complement of 36. Abnormal development was to be expected, and this Boveri observed in 1,499 out of 1,500 *embryos*. The embryos with three centrosomes that divided into three cells at the first division also showed very abnormal distributions of chromosomes.

One would expect, however, that they would have a better chance of getting *36* chromosomes in each cell than would the group that formed four cells. The reason is this: We have seen that there is no way of apportioning 108 chromosomes among four cells so each will receive a normal complement of 36.

If the 108 chromosomes are divided equally among three cells, however, the result is 36. The experimental results validated this reasoning. In the group that divided into three cells, 58 in a total of 719 developed normally. We have already seen that only one embryo in 1,500 developed normally among the embryos that divided into four cells at first cleavage.

According to Boveri, these data correspond fairly well with the chance expectation that normal larvae will come from embryos that begin development with a normal set of chromosomes in each of the cells formed at the first division.

He interpreted the data to mean that for normal development every cell of the embryo must have the regular set of *36* chromosomes. He believed that every single chromosome in the set must be endowed with a different quality, and that all are necessary for normal development.

These experiments emphasized the importance of chromosomes for normal development, which is one aspect of inheritance. It was a direct approach to the study of the role of chromosomes in inheritance.

SUTTON AND GRASSHOPPER CHROMOSOMES

In the sane year that Boveri published the results of his work, a second and much more *fruitful* approach was made by Sutton. At the time, he was a graduate student working at Columbia University with the cytologist Wilson. He published two papers on the chromosomal basis of inheritance, the first in 1902 and the second in 1903.

Individuality of the Chromosomes

Sutton's 1902 paper was a study of the chromosomes in the testis of a *grasshopper* of the genus *Brachystola.* The chromosomes of this form

> exhibit a chromosome group, the members of which show distinct differences in size. Accordingly one feature of this study has been a critical examination of large numbers of dividing cells (mainly from the

testis) in order to determine whether, as has usually been taken for granted, these differences are merely a matter of chance, or whether in accordance with the view recently expressed by *Montgomery*.... characteristic size relations are a constant attribute of the chromosomes individually considered. With the aid of camera drawings of the chromosome group in the various *cell-generations*, I will give below a brief account of the evidence which has led me to adopt the latter conclusion.

The cells in the testis undergo a series of mitotic divisions before they begin meiosis. These cells are known as *spermatogonia* and they have the *diploid* number of chromosomes. The youngest *spermatogonia* that Sutton could find possessed 23 chromosomes.

One of these, the 'accessory' chromosome, had a peculiar behavior and it will be considered separately. The other 22 were of various sizes. When these were measured carefully it was found that there were not 22 different sizes, but only 11.

In other words there were two chromosomes of each size class. In addition to the minor size variation, the chromosomes could be divided into two groups that differed strikingly in size. Three of the pairs were very small and the other eight were large.

Sutton found that these early spermatogonia went through eight mitotic divisions. At each *metaphase* the same 11 pairs of chromosomes were observed. Of these, eight pairs were large and three small. He concluded that constant size was an attribute of the individual chromosomes.

After these eight mitotic divisions, the cells undergo the usual two meiotic divisions. The chromosomes synapse in pairs, each member of the pair being of the same size. As a result, 11 tetrads form; eight are large and three are small. Then the two meiotic divisions occur and each sperm receives one chromosome of each of the 11 sizes.

Sutton found that the diploid number in the female was 22. Further, these had the same size relations as were present in the male, consisting of eight large and three small pairs. (Sutton made an error in this count. Later workers found 24 chromosomes.) He postulated that every ovum after meiosis would contain one chromosome of each of the 11 sizes.

Fertilization of an *ovum* containing 11 chromosomes with a sperm containing 11 would restore the diploid number of 22. Some of the sperm will have an accessory chromosome in addition to the regular 11. Fertilization with a sperm of this type will result in a zygote with 22 chromosomes plus an accessory. (In 1901 McClung suggested that the accessory chromosome is in some way concerned with sex determination.) Sutton continues:

> Taken as a whole, the evidence presented by the cells of Brachystola is such as to lend great weight to the conclusion that a chromosome may exist only by virtue of direct descent by longitudinal division from a preexisting chromosome and that the members of the daughter group bear to one another the same respective relations as did those of the mother group-in other words, that the chromosome in Brachystola is a distinct morphological individual.
>
> This conclusion inevitably raises the question whether there is also a physiological individuality, i.e., whether the chromosomes represent respectively different series or groups of qualities or whether they are merely different-sized aggregations of the same material and, therefore, qualitatively alike.
>
> On this question my observations do not furnish direct evidence. But it is a *priori* improbable that the constant morphological differences we have seen should exist except by virtue of more fundamental differences of which they are an expression; and, further, by the unequal distribution of the accessory chromosome we are enabled to compare the develop-

mental possibilities of cells containing it with those of cells which do not.

Granting the normal constitution of the female cells examined and the similarity of the reduction process in the two sexes, such a comparison must show that this particular chromosome does possess a power not inherent in any of the others-the power of impressing on the containing cell the stamp of maleness, in accordance with McClung's hypothesis.

The evidence advanced in the case of the ordinary chromosomes is obviously more in the nature of suggestion than of proof, but it is offered in this connection as a morphological complement to the beautiful experimental researches of Boveri already referred to.

In this paper Boveri shows how he has artificially accomplished for the various chromosomes of the sea-urchin, the same result that nature is constantly giving us in the case of the accessory chromosome of the Orthoptera.

He has been able to produce and to study the development of blastomeres lacking certain of the chromosomes of the normal series. If, as the facts in Brachystola so strongly suggest, the chromosomes are persistent individuals in the sense that each bears a genetic relation to one only of the previous generation, the probability must be accepted that each represents the same qualities as its parent element.

A given relative size may, therefore, be taken as characteristic of the physical basis of a certain definite set of qualities. But each element of the chromosome series of the spermatozoon has a morphological counterpart in that of the mature egg and from this it follows that the two cover the same field in development.

When the two copulate, therefore, in synapsis the entire chromatin basis of a certain set of qualities

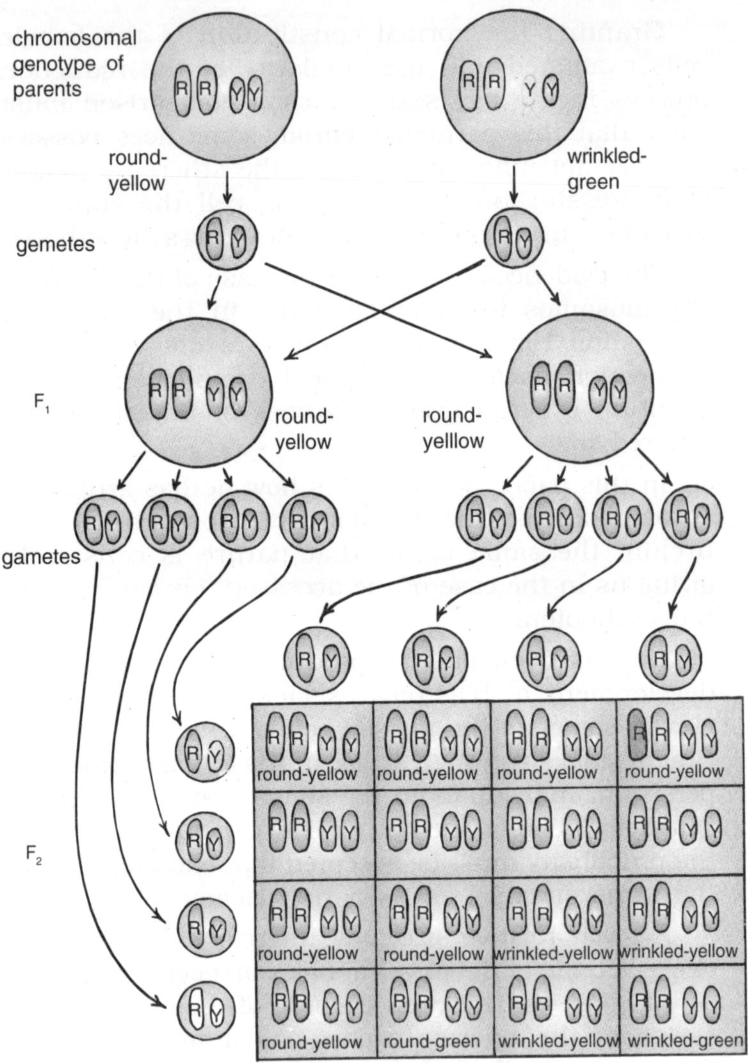

Figure 12.1: Diagram of chromosome distributions in Mendel's cross of a round-yellow X wrinkled-green pea on the basis of Sutton's hypothesis.

inherited from the two parents is localized for the first and only time in a single continuous chromatin mass; and when in the second spermatocyte division, the two parts are again separated, one goes entire to each pole contributing to the daughter cells the corresponding group of qualities from the paternal or the maternal stock as the case may be.

There is, therefore, in Brachystola no qualitative division of chromosomes but only a separation of the two members of a pair which, while coexisting in a single nucleus, may be regarded as jointly controlling certain restricted portions of the development of the individual.

By the light of this conception we are enabled to see an explanation of that hitherto problematical process, synapsis, in the provision which it makes that the two chromosomes representing the same specific characters shall in no case enter the nucleus of a single spermatid or mature egg.

I may finally call attention to the probability that the association of paternal and maternal chromosomes in pairs and their subsequent separation during the reducing division as indicated above may constitute the physical basis of the Mendelian law of heredity. To this subject I hope soon to return in another place.

The Chromosomes in Heredity

The far-reaching suggestion made in the last paragraph was developed in Sutton's 1903 paper entitled 'The Chromosomes in Heredity.' In this he pointed out that the segregation and recombination of genes as studied by the geneticists showed a striking parallel to the behavior of chromosomes as revealed by the cytologists. The pertinent cytological data, according to Sutton, were as follows:

1. The diploid chromosome group consists of two morphologically similar chromosome sets. Every

chromosome type is represented twice. Expressed another way, chromosomes exist in homologous pairs. Strong grounds exist for the belief that one set was derived from the father and one set from the mother at the time of fertilization.

2. Synapsis consists of the pairing of homologous chromosomes.
3. As a result of meiosis every gamete receives only one chromosome of each homologous pair.
4. The chromosomes retain their morphological individuality throughout the various cell divisions.
5. The distribution in meiosis of the members of each homologous pair of chromosomes is independent of that of each other pair. As a result, each gamete receives a random assortment of chromosomes so far as the members of each pair are concerned.

Sutton then made the point that Mendel's results could be explained on the assumption that genes were parts of the chromosomes. The following example will show how this is possible:

Let us assume that the *round* and *wrinkled* genes in peas are carried on a certain pair of chromosomes. If a chromosome has the *round* gene, we shall call it **R** and if it has the *wrinkled* gene, we shall call it r. Let us further assume that the *yellow* and *green* genes are carried by a different pair of chromosomes.

If the chromosome has the *yellow* gene, we shall designate it **Y** and if it carries the *green* gene, we shall call it y. A pure-breeding *round-yellow* plant would be symbolized as **RRYY** indicating that it had a pair of chromosomes carrying the *round* gene and another pair with the *yellow* gene. Similarly, a *wrinkled-green* plant would be rryy.

When the reduction divisions occur the *round-yellow* plant would produce haploid gametes with one **R** and one **Y** chromosome—or **RY**. This alone could result, since a gamete receives only one chromosome of every kind. A **RR** or a **YY** gamete would be impossible in normal meiosis.

The *wrinkled-green* plant would produce gametes solely of the ry type. A union of gametes of the two plants would result in one type of offspring, namely, RrYy. This F_1 individual would be diploid and would have received one member of each chromosome type from the male gamete and one from the female gamete.

The gametes of the F_1 plant would be of four possible types. The R and the r would go to different cells during meiosis. The Y and y chromosomes would likewise be separated and *their separation would not affect the separation of R and r.* Thus, all possible combinations, namely, **RY, Ry, rY,** and ry would be produced, and in approximately equal numbers. If you will re-examine Mendel's description of this cross, you will note the exact parallel between the scheme for Mendel's breeding experiments and the chromosome movements just described. The F_2 chromosomes would be of the type shown in the genetic checkerboard.

The sole difference to be noted is that Mendel characterized his pure-breeding peas o' the parental generation as **RY** and ry, while we have used a diploid chromosome designation **RRYY** and **rryy**. Mendel could have used **RRYY** and **rryy** just as well.

Sutton's Hypothesis

We may conclude, therefore, that genes of a type postulated by Mendel could be

1. parts of the chromosomes, or
2. parts of some other cell structures that behave in the same way as chromosomes in mitosis, meiosis, and fertilization.

When a scientist is confronted with two hypotheses, one involving known factors and the other invoking unknown factors, the first is usually chosen. In the case under consideration, such a choice would have a great practical advantage: It would be easier to make observations and design experiments to test the role of chromosomes in Mendelian heredity than it would be to investigate the role of some unknown cell structures.

Sutton's general hypothesis was not new. As we have already seen, some cytologists believed, at least as early as 1884, that the chromosomes were involved in inheritance. Sutton pointed out additional reasons for so thinking and, even more important, made a definite link between genetic data and cytological data.

If we continue to use the genes-are-parts-of-chromosomes hypothesis, it will be necessary to find a parallel between all types of genetic behavior and chromosome behavior. Any variations in chromosomal phenomena from the usual condition must be reflected in the genetic results.

Similarly, if genetic ratios are obtained that cannot be explained in Mendelian terms, one must find a chromosomal basis for the deviation. Sutton indicated one type of genetic behavior that could be expected if his hypothesis was correct.

We have seen reason, in the foregoing considerations, to believe that there is a definite relation between chromosomes and allelomorphs or unit characters, but we have not before inquired whether an entire chromosome or only a part of one is to be regarded as the basis of a single allelomorph.

The answer must unquestionably be in favor of the latter possibility, for otherwise the number of distinct characters possessed by an individual could not exceed the number of chromosomes in the germ-products; which is undoubtedly contrary to fact.

We must, therefore, assume that some chromosomes at least are related to a number of different allelomorphs. If then, the chromosomes permanently retain their in(iv uality, it follows that all the allelomorphs represented by any one chromosome must be inherited together. If Sutton's reasoning is correct, the Mendelian principle of independent assortment could apply only to cases where the two pairs of contrasting factors were carried on separate chromosomes.

The importance of Sutton's theoretical considerations can scarcely be overemphasized. Two completely different disciplines were found to have an area in common: cytology and genetics became mutually supporting and stimulating fields. Theories of inheritance could be 'double-checked.'

Chapter 13 GENETICS AND DEVELOPMENTAL BIOLOGY

In other chapters of this book explored the maturation of sperm and eggs, fertilization, germ layer formation, organ formation, and, finally, the acquisition of the form of the organism. The mature sperm and egg, the genetic bridges between generations, are highly differentiated cells, specialized for their specific functions in fertilization.

Zygote formation and restoration of the diploid number signal the beginning of a train of events which must be controlled by a fastidious set of mechanisms if a healthy mature organism is to be the result. The zygote, a single cell, contains all the genetic information required for the program of development, that is, all development ultimately is specified by genes, whether they be nuclear, cytoplasmic, or organellar genes.

Since the mechanism of gene action is through specification of proteins, all cells derived from a zygote would be the same if differentiar gene activity did not occur among cells. The potential of a cell is related to the structure of that cell at a particular time and the protein population (including enzymes) which it contains.

A human erythrocyte contains about 95 percent of one protein, hemoglobin, while the cells of the iris of the eye are characterized by specific pigments. Likewise, in muscle cells the genes for myoglobin, actin, and myosin are turned on while in fibroblasts the gene for collagen is expressed.

Erythrocytes and iris cells are traceable back to their origins from the zygote and its genetic endowment. As development and differentiation proceeded, the iris cells and erythrocytes had some genes turned on and other (most) genes turned off. The levels of regulation of genetic and developmental control may be identified at three general points on a hierarchy of complexity:

1. *Intracellular,* within the cell
2. *Intercellular,* among cells
3. *Environmental,* through factors coming from the surroundings of the developing organism

INTRACELLULAR FACTORS IN DEVELOPMENT

The modern theory of animal development at the cellular level relies on two principal components: the nucleus and the cytoplasm. The general theme of transport of information (mRNA) and materials (tRNA, rRNA) as well as regulation of transcription according to the operon model were detailed in other chapter of this book.

Various cytoplasmic events and factors (accumulation of maternal ribosomes in the egg, the role of the grey crescent and nuclear transplantation) were discussed in other chapter.

Intracellular Processes and Their Controls

During interphase a eukaryotic cell does not show definite chromosomes since the chromosomal material or *chromatin* is in a diffuse or relaxed state. This chromatin can be isolated and has been shown to contain DNA, RNA, and proteins. The proteins are of two major classes, basic histones and nonhistones.

If these proteins are removed (with proteolytic enzymes, for example), the deproteinized chromatin is more active in RNA synthesis than is the intact, "native" chromatin. Presumably deproteinization unmasks the DNA so that more of it is free to be transcribed by RNA polymerase.

For example, using rat liver chromatin, a deproteinized sample provided with the enzyme RNA polymerase and the four ribonucleoside triphosphates (ATP, UTP, GTP, CTP) will produce five times more RNA than the native chromatin.

When "native" chromatin is isolated from different tissues and used as a template for transcription *in vitro*, each chromatin preparation produces RNA that is similar to the RNA produced by the corresponding tissue *in vivo*. This fact suggests that regulatory elements reside in the structures of the chromosomes (native chromatin) themselves.

This conclusion came from experiments in which RNA produced *in vivo* in a given tissue competed with RNA transcribed *in vitro* for hybridization with DNA. Competition was greater when the two RNAs came from the same tissue type as compared to different tissues.

Since many more genes exist than types of histones, a one (or few) histone to one gene ratio is probably an untenable hypothesis. Some workers have suggested that chromosomal RNA (RNA found in chromosomes) may be involved with histones in repression of chromosomal expression.

Some evidence exists that chromosomal RNA is associated with the histones. If the chromosomal RNA recognized specific sites on the DNA by base pairing and the basic groups (positively charged) on the histones were attracted to the negative charges of the phosphates in the sugar-phosphate backbone, then specific interactions for repression and derepression of genes could be accounted for.

On the other hand, the histones seem to be equally spaced over active and inactive regions of the chromosomes, a point consistent with a role as structural components of chromosomes rather than as genetic regulators. Recent evidence from experiments involving the cleavage of chromatin with certain nucleases (DNA hydrolyzing enzymes) suggests a repeating unit of 200 nucleotide pairs that is associated with six histone molecules.

The extended length of 200 nucleotide pairs would be 68 nm, but the actual length is only 10 nm. Thus the complex of histones and DNA is wound into a ball. Chromatin fibers must be able to coil or fold extensively (as in metaphase chromosomes) and accordingly must be flexible. Electron micrographs of chromatin fibers show a structure that resemble beads on a string.

This suggests a flexibly jointed chromatin chain. This model has been called the "kinky helix." In the search for regulator proteins attention has been turned to nonhistone proteins, which are simply defined as chromosomal proteins other than the histones.

Unlike the histones, there is no constant relationship between the amount of DNA and the amount of nonhistones in the chromatin. Like the histones, these proteins are synthesized outside of the nucleus.

The histones are transported into the nucleus immediately after synthesis, but some of the nonhistones are transported immediately into the nucleus where they associate with DNA while others are transported more slowly.

Thus the differential rate of transport of nonhistone proteins into the nucleus possibly could contribute to their specific regulatory function. Whereas histones and DNA occur in about a 1:1 constant ratio, at least part of the nonhistone proteins vary greatly.

While the histones fall into only five clearly defined types, the nonhistones show a great structural and functional diversity. The number of nonhistones is not known, but it is certainly large. They range in molecular weight from under 10,000 to over 150,000 daltons and include a variety of enzymes such as DNA and RNA polymerases, proteases, and DNA modification enzymes (addition and removal of acetate, methyl, and phosphate groups).

Further, different tissues possess a different complement of nonhistones and these proteins recognize specific nucleotide sequences in DNA. Such specific interactions between regulatory proteins and DNA is what would be expected.

The mechanism of action of nonhistones in gene regulation may involve the *inhibition of the inhibition* of RNA synthesis (transcription) by the histones. R. Stewart Gilmour and John Paul isolated chromatin from rabbit thymus and bone marrow and dissociated the DNA, histone, and nonhistone components.

Then these components were put back together; when all components were derived from the thymus, the transcribed RNA hybridized normally to thymus DNA. When the chromatin was reconstituted from bone marrow DNA and histone and thymus nonhistones, the transcribed RNA hybridized more efficiently to thymus DNA than to marrow DNA.

Likewise, chromatin reconstituted from thymus DNA and histone and marrow nonhistone transcribed RNA that was bone marrow RNA: it hybridized more efficiently to marrow DNA than to thymus DNA. These experiments indicate that the presence of tissue specific nonhistones determines which genes will be transcribed in various tissues.

Heterochromatin and Euchromatin in Chromosomes

By staining technique chromatin may be divided into *heterochromatin* and *euchromatin*. Heterochromatin is highly compacted and does not disperse into highly diffuse interphase material as does euchromatin.

The heterochromatic regions that maintain their compactness all the time are called *constituitive heterochromatin* and generally are considered to be inert genetically. Other chromosomal regions may be condensed (heterochromatic) only in certain situations.

Such *facultative* or *functional heterochromatin* is thus sometimes inert and sometimes active (diffuse or relaxed); therefore, facultative heterochromatin often is thought to be associated with gene regulation.

Constitutive heterochromatin is found as whole late-replicating chromosomes of Barr bodies (sex chromatin) and in the centromeres which are known to serve as sites of attachment for mitotic spindle proteins.

The differences afforded by the heterochromatic (constitutive and facultative) and euchromatic regions suggest possibilities for differential gene activity and the basis of cellular differentiation.

The ratio of histone to DNA is the same in heterochromatin and euchromatin, but in heterochromatin there are considerably fewer nonhistones than in active extended euchromatin. Here again, the presence of nonhistones is correlated with gene expression or active RNA synthesis.

Further Examples of Gene Regulation in Eukaryotes

Puffs and Polytene Chromosomes

The giant polytene chromosomes of *Drosophila* and other dipteran flies have been used in important work on differential gene activity. These polytene chromosomes have distinctive banding patterns, and the experienced cytologist can recognize even parts of chromosomes on the basis of the bands.

At certain positions, puffs replace the sharp bands. Studies of the puffing pattern have revealed that the locations of puffs are different in different tissues at any one time, are different in the same tissues at different stages of development, and are the same in all cells of a given tissue type at any one time.

Wolfgang Beerman studied the puffs in salivary

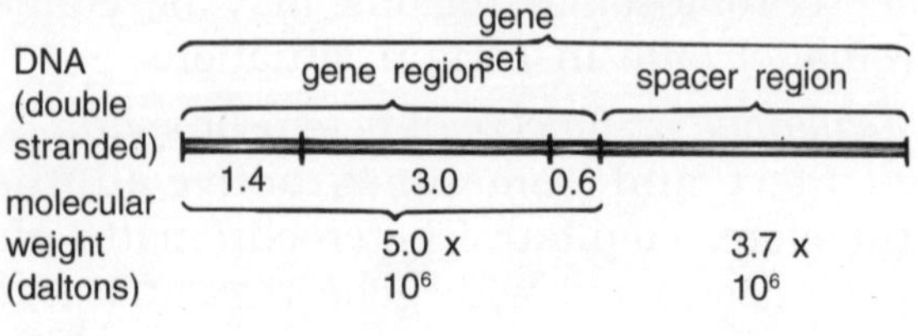

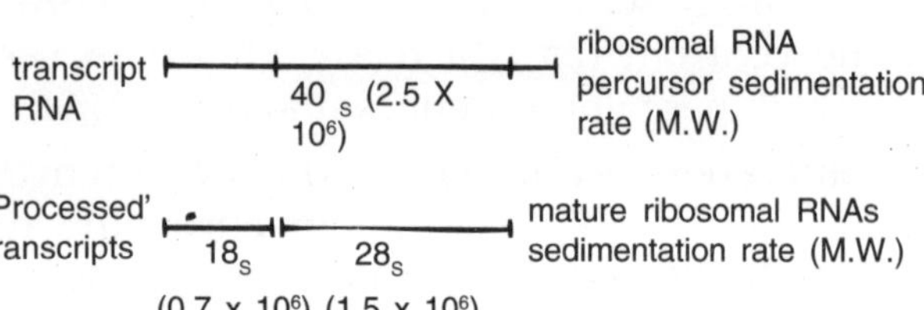

Figure 18.2 Diagram of a ribosomal gene set. The gene set includes DNA which codes for 18s and 28s rRNA as well as an untranscribed "spacer" region.

glands of two species of a dipteran fly, *Chironomus*. In one species, *C. pallidivitatus*, four cells of the salivary gland produce a granular secretion while the rest of the cells produce a clear secretion.

One chromosome in the granule-secreting cells has a puff not present in the cells that produce the clear secretion. In another species, *C. tentans*, the four cells mentioned above are the same as all other cells and no differences in the puffing pattern exists. Hybrids between the two species possess the granule-secreting cells, but the amount of secreted granules is reduced.

The hybrid chromosomes in the four cells have the puff inherited from *C. pallidivitatus*. Thus this work correlates a gene product (the granular secretion) with the presence of a specific puff. Studies with radioactive nucleobases have shown that the puffs are the sites of rapid RNA synthesis and thus of very active genes.

Puffing can be prevented by actinomycin D, an antibiotic known to inhibit the synthesis of RNA. In 1973 evidence was obtained that RNA synthesized in a particular puff is transported to the cytoplasm (and therefore presumably functions as mRNA) and is translated into proteins.

Other recent work in attempting to correlate puffing patterns with specific protein products has been carried out in the laboratory of Herschel Mitchell at the California Institute of Technology. Salivary glands of *Drosophila* larvae and early pupae were dissected out and incubated in a buffer containing ^{35}S-methionine.

After labeling with this radioactive amino acid, the proteins of the glands were separatcd by electrophoresis. The changes in the kinds of proteins at different times between the larval and pupal stages could be correlated with the changes in patterns of chromosome puffs at the corresponding times.

Heat shock of the salivary glands changes the puffing pattern and likewise changes the kinds of proteins that are synthesized. Furthermore, modifications of puffs can be induced by the hormone ecdysone, and the protein patterns of ecdysone-treated salivary glands is changed also.

Gene Amplification

An equal increase of all genes in a genome, such as occur in polyploidy, is not likely to alter the balance of gene expression greatly. Gene amplification refers to an increase in the number of one or more genes in a genome without a corresponding increase in other genes.

Proof of specific gene amplification was provided in 1968 with the isolation of ribosomal genes by Brown and coworkers. In the South African clawed toad, *Xenopus laevis*, each haploid genome contains about 450 adjacent sets of ribosomal genes.

Early in oogenesis these gene sets are increased selectively so that each mature egg contains about 2 million ribosomal gene sets. The extra sets of ribosomal genes are accommodated in 1000-1500 extra chromosomal nucleoli.

Amplification seems to be peculiar to rRNA genes

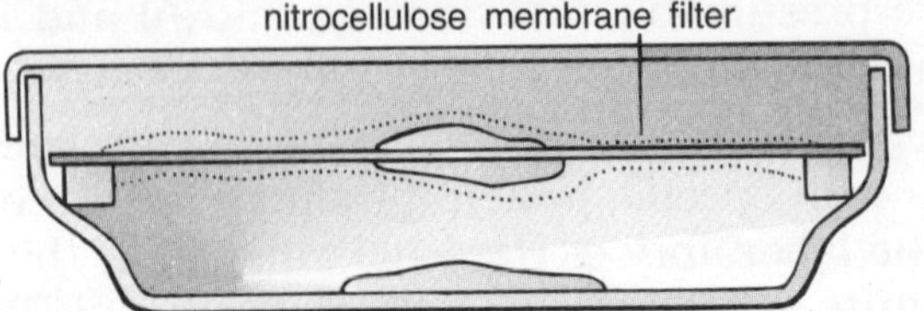

Figure 13.2 Transfilter technique of tissue culture. In covered dish, cellulose filter with pores of known size is supported on Plexiglass ring. Mesenchyme is placed on one side of the filter and epithelium on the other. Both tissues are covered by a plasma clot (dotted). Drying is prevented by providing moisture in the bottom of the dish. Differentiation of epithelium under such conditions occurs in predictable patterns.

where the function is the production of maternal ribosomes that sustain early development of the animal. In three well-studied cases, where a specialized cell produces a majority of one kind of protein, no gene amplification of the respective genes occurs:

1. Posterior silkgland of the silkmoth—silk fibroin
2. Duck erythrocytes—hemoglobin
3. Chick oviduct cells—ovalbumin

Nuclear Transplantation

The constancy of DNA in most cells of a given organism was first established in 1948 (haploid gametes and euploid liver cells have concomitant or corresponding decreases or increases in nuclear DNA content).

This deduction is based on biochemical and cytological techniques and has been confirmed by nuclear transplantation experiments. J. B. Gurdon of Oxford University transplanted nuclei from differentiated intestinal cells of the clawed toad, *Xenopus laevis*, into eggs from which the original nucleus had been removed. (The technique of nuclear transplantation was first carried out successfully in Amoeba in 1939 and has been successful with the leopard frog, *Rana pipiens*, the Mexican salamander, the fruit fly, and the honey bee.)

Using the O-nu (anucleolate) marker, Gurdon was

able to show that eggs containing transplanted nuclei grew into adult frogs wholly derived from the donor nucleus from differentiated cells. An excellent review of gene expression in animal development, with emphasis on nuclear transplantation experiments, is given in Gurdon.

INTERCELLULAR FACTORS IN DEVELOPMENT

As other chapters elsewhere in this book clearly show, developmental processes are affected by specific signals coming from other cells; this section gives some examples.

Clonal Myogenesis

Embryonic muscle starts out as single undifferentiated cells, *myoblasts.* In skeletal muscle the myoblasts fuse to form myotubes and lose their cellular identities (a syncytium is formed). Myotubes ultimately show the typical cross striations characteristic of mature muscles.

Because of the sequence of cellular interactions that produce the syncytium, some experiments were designed to determine if a single isolated myoblast can give rise to a colony of differentiated skeletal muscle tissue.

Muscle from the leg of an embryonic chick was dissociated into individual cells, and single cells were transferred into isolated culture chambers. Cell division over a four-day period produced clusters of cells, about four dozen in number.

At about this time many of the cells would fuse into myotubes and there would be a reduction in the rate of cell division. Continued division was confined to isolated unfused cells. Successful development of differentiated striated fibers was, however, meager, without an added condition being taken into account.

Normal muscle not only has muscle fibers, but it also has fibroblasts, connective tissue cells. Fibroblasts are secretors of collagen, the important fibrous protein

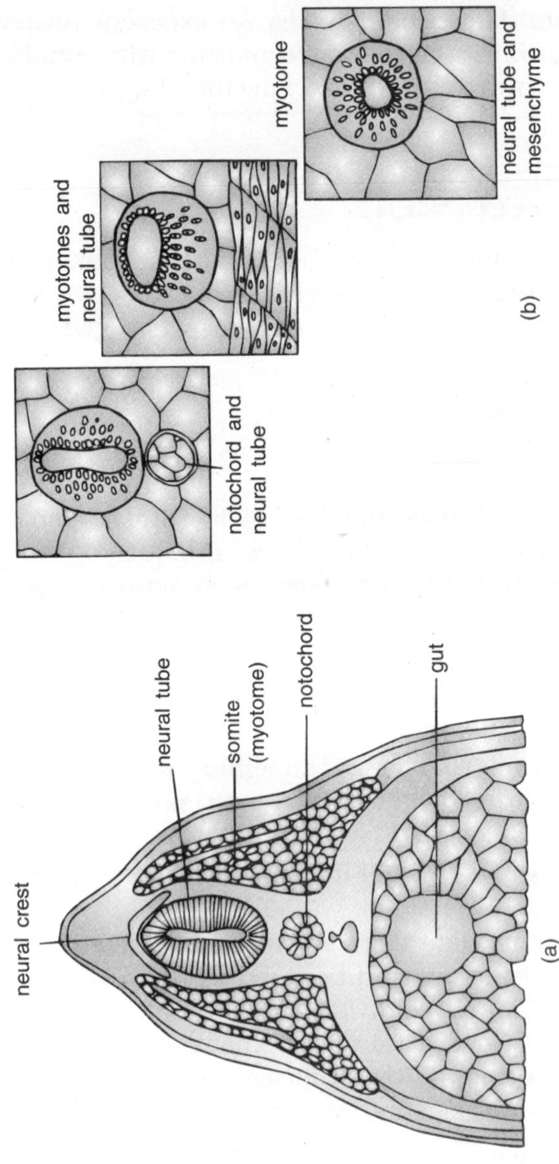

Figure 13.3: Influence of surrounding tissues on differentiation of neural tube. (a) Cross section through dorsal trunk of normal frog tadpole. (b) Effect of specific tissues on differentiation of neural tube under experimental conditions.

of connective tissue. 1. Konigsberg found that the most success in getting truly differentiated striated muscles to grow in tissue culture involved putting isolated clones of myoblasts into old culture medium which had supported the growth of fibroblasts.

This *conditioned* old medium was carefully filtered to remove the old cells before the clones of myoblasts were cultured in it. Therefore the fibroblasts had left something in the medium that signaled the myoblasts to differentiate into striated muscles.

That collagen had been left in the medium by the fibroblasts seemed to be a reasonable hypothesis. Konigsberg finally obtained good development of myoblasts to the level of striated muscle fibers by coating the culture dishes with pure collagen.

When this was done, fresh and unconditioned medium served to support differentiation of striated muscle from a single cell.

The inferences from these experiments for conditions in normal development are obvious. However, a definitive identification that collagen is the necessary factor for normal *in vivo* differentiation of muscle has not been established.

Transfilter Technique of Tissue Culture

This experiment involves the culture of pancreatic mesenchyme, a loosely organized mesoderm, on one side of a thin nitrocellulose membrane filter with micropores of a size known to exclude the passage of cells. Pancreatic endoderm is placed on the other side of the filter.

In this arrangement molecules from the mesenchyme migrate through the pores, and the endoderm is induced to form the characteristic secretory clusters of pancreatic cells, *acini*, that would form in normal pancreatic development. In the absence of the mesenchyme on the other side of the filter, no such differentiation occurs.

An amino acid (*proline*) is found in its hydroxylated

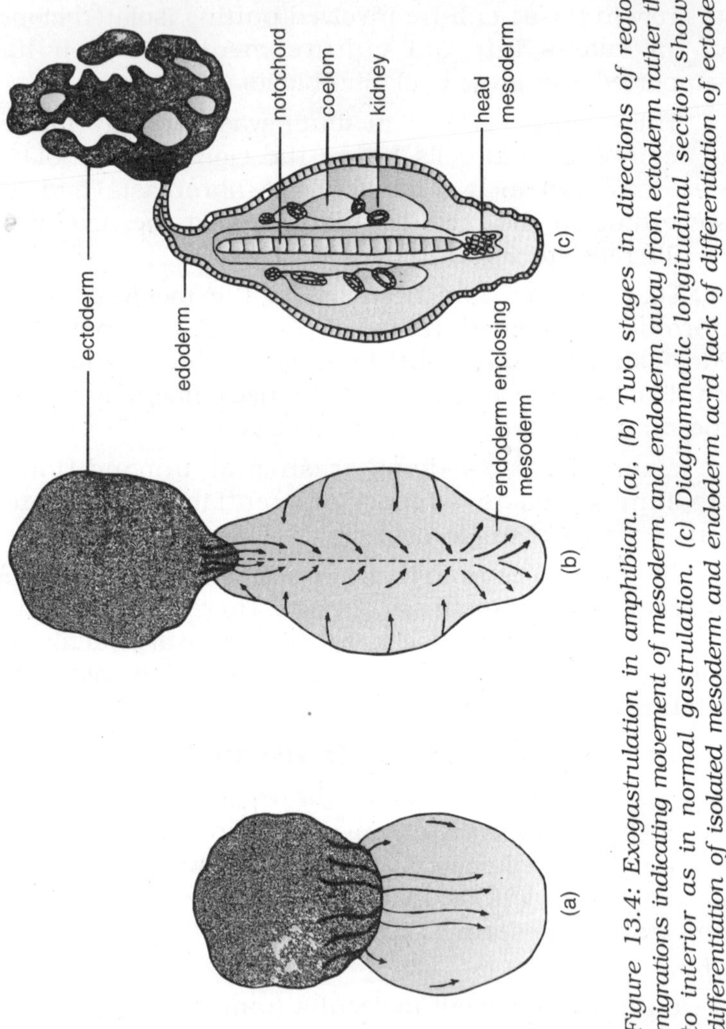

Figure 13.4: Exogastrulation in amphibian. (a), (b) Two stages in directions of regional migrations indicating movement of mesoderm and endoderm away from ectoderm rather than to interior as in normal gastrulation. (c) Diagrammatic longitudinal section showing differentiation of isolated mesoderm and endoderm acrd lack of differentiation of ectoderm.

form *(hydroxyproline)* in molecules of collagen. When the mesenchyme on one side of the filter is labeled with radioactive proline, the label appears later on the opposite side of the filter in a pattern characteristic of the collagen matrix, which lies around the differentiated acini. If the endoderm is labeled with the radioactive proline, the pattern of radioactivity does not correspond to the pattern of the collagen.

This experiment produces strong evidence that the soluble tropocollagen, a precursor of collagen, is synthesized in the fibroblasts on the mesenchyme side, moves across the filter, and is aggregated under the influence of the epithelial cells of the acini into insoluble collagen fibers.

Here, then, is a form of organization of molecules that involves two kinds of tissues. This organization does not occur with either tissue alone.

Figure anywhere else in this chapter illustrates the differentiation of another organ composed of epithelium and mesenchyme, whose differentiation is dependent on interactions of the tissues. This is the salivary gland of the mouse.

Molecular Changes During Development

The proteins of an adult organism are not necessarily identical to the proteins that perform similar functions during earlier stages of development. For example, the enzyme lactase in infants and adults is controlled by different genes, and this is the basis for the galactosemic child outgrowing its intolerance of milk sugar (lactose). 'Another example is fetal and adult hemoglobins, these hemoglobins differ in their amino acid sequences of one pair of chains.

The alpha chains of fetal and adult hemoglobins are identical but fetal hemoglobin contains gamma chains instead of beta chains. The gamma and beta chains are governed by separate genes. There are also multiple forms of enzymes called *isozymes*. For example, lactate dehydrogenase (LDH) contains four polypeptide subunits that may be either the A or B type.

Therefore five forms of the enzyme may exist: AAAA, AAAB, AABB, ABBB, and BBBB. When several kinds of tissues of one adult animal are examined, they are seen to vary in their pattern of isozymes. Also, when a single tissue is analyzed alyzed through several stages of development, the patterns or relative proportions of the isozymes shift.

The study of isozymes is of increasing importance since some developmental abnormalities can be identified with specific mutations, and shifts in enzymatic patterns associated with these mutations have been shown.

Also the isozyme zyme pattern of the blood changes with certain physical traumas; for example, the LDH isozyme pattern of the blood may be used to detect myo- ; cardial infarction (heart attack) in hospital laboratories.

Tissue Affinities

Johannes Holtfreter showed that the form of j the neural tube could be influenced by orientations of tissue associated with the neural tissue. Figure elsewhere in this chapter shows how isolated neural tube, lying on a somite bed, thickens on the side adjacent to the somites and not on the side away from the somites.

With the development of the nervous system as an introduction, consider the great variety of inter relatio-nships that exist in a developing embryo and how they may influence each other.

The pancreas, for instance, begins as a pair of precisely located tubular outgrowths from the developing embryonic gut, and the filter separation experiments discussed previously show that the pancreas will develop normally only if there is an association between the endodermal duct tissue and the mesoderm into which it penetrates.

Pouches grow out from the pharynx into mesoderm and form various organs, such as the thymus and parathyroids. A normal adult mammalian kidney is produced by an outgrowth of a mesodermal duct from another and transient (mesonephric) kidney in the embryo and only develops normal nephrons if the outgrowing duct penetrates into a small region of mesoderm that responds to the inductive influences of the duct. These are but a few common examples where tissues establish spatial relationships with each other.

In order to understand some of the spatial relationships, some developmental biologists have combined various tissues *in vitro,* have observed the affinities of these tissues for each other, and have noted whether one tissue tends to surround another or whether it is surrounded by another, and so forth.

These studies have established hierarchies of differentiated cells that show selective associations among themselves. One procedure is to dissociate cells of selected embryonic tissues by gentle enzymatic digestion or by using a calcium and/or magnesiumfree medium. Cells from two kinds of disaggregated tissue, when grown together in culture, will sort out with one kind of tissue covered by the other tissue.

Thus when chick heart and chick cartilage cells are grown together, the cartilage cells sort to the interior, the heart cells sort to the exterior. Heart and liver cell combinations result in the heart cells to the interior and the liver cells to the exterior.

From these two experiments, using only two tissues in each, it would be reasonable to predict that there is a hierarchy with cartilage cells having stronger association forces for themselves than do heart cells, and, in turn, heart cells have stronger association forces than do liver cells.

A combination of the three kinds of disaggregates confirms this: The liver envelops the heart that envelops the cartilage. The ramifications of such studies raise questions in the realm of biochemistry and biophysics. For instance, are the differences between cells only differences in numbers of binding sites in different tissues or are there qualitative differences as well?

Are there differences in the developmental period in

which the tissues change their ranks in the hierarchy of selective associations? Questions such as these are being tackled by developmental biologists, biochemists, and biophysicists.

ENVIRONMENTAL FACTORS IN DEVELOPMENT

The environmental factors which affect developmental processes are many and the course of animal evolution has produced a remarkable set of mechanisms for protecting the embryo, particularly in the transition of vertebrates from an aqueous to a terrestrial habitat. For the concerted developmental processes to occur properly, extreme variations of environmental factors must be minimized.

The pinnacle of protective barriers is seen in the mammalian uterus and the amniotic cavity. If the protective barriers fail, gross abnormalities may result. Proper development depends on proper nutrition.

If essential amino acids or fatty acids, calories, vitamins, or gases are not supplied in the proper range of concentrations, damage to the developing embryo will be permanent. Like wise, a hormonal imbalance will seriously affect developmental processes.

If the membranes of an amphibian blastula are removed and the embryo is grown in a hypertonic solution, normal gastrulation does not occur. The prospective chordamesoderm and other mesodermal and endodermal cells do not invaginate, but grow outward instead. This *exogastrulation* is shown in Figure anywhere else in this chapter.

Under these conditions, endodermal and mesodermal structures develop to a great extent, but the ectoderm fails to form neural structures. This is a dramatic example of a physical' factor which affects the relationships between tissues, thereby inducing the abnormality.

Another example of an environmental factor affecting development is the rubella (German measles) virus. Rubella is a relatively mild disease for children or adults. However, if a pregnant woman develops rubella during the first 2-3 months of pregnancy, the rubella virus can cross the placenta and damage seriously the developing embryo with resultant abnormalities such as eye and heart defects.

On the other hand, more severe viruses for children and adults such as mumps or measles are not teratogenic (literally, monster producing). A third category of an outside factor which may affect development is drugs.

Some years ago in Germany many babies with abnormally short and malformed aims and legs were noted to have been born of mothers who had used a mild tranquilizing drug, *thalidomide.*

The mother need not have used the drug for long. But if she used it during a critical period of her pregnancy, it affected the growth of the infant's limbs. In this case the drug was removed from the market, but society is left with many deformed individuals who are dependent on others for their care.

HUMAN AND APPLIED GENETICS

How does genetics relate to the college student, the college graduate, or any involved citizen living in the latter part of the twentieth century? Human and agricultural genetics were set aside for this chapter to emphasize that *genetics* affects all people to a substantial degree, both directly and indirectly.

A missing bit of a *chromosome* can mean the difference between mental deficiency, anatomical and physiological abnormalities, or a general inability to live a productive life-and a *healthy*, relatively happy existence.

Much of the agricultural wealth of North America is the result of scientific breeding programs. *Cattle, swine, wheat, corn,* and many other animal *stocks* and *plant* crops are the results of genetic programs conducted by universities, governmental agencies, and private organizations or individuals.

Human and agricultural genetics as "*applied*" or relevant genetics clearly demopstrate how this subject relates to all citizens of the twentieth century. Furthermore, these topics provide excellent review and teaching exercises for the genetics discussed up to this point. The fact that genetics pervades many areas of biology is emphasized by previous discussions of *heredity* in earlier chapters.

More genetics is considered in *conjunction* with the topics of *evolution*, *behaviour*, and ecology in succeeding chapters.

HUMAN INHERITANCE

Human Chromosomes

The normal diploid chromosome number of humans is 46. For many years this number was thought to be 48, but in 1956 workers who used cultured *fibroblasts* of human *embryonic* lung tissues found that the earlier reports had been in error.

These unexpected findings were quickly confirmed by other investigators. This is a good example of how the "*facts*" sometimes change rapidly and how the workers in the field must be receptive to new data and new *ideas*.

As discussed in other chapter of this book, the karyotype of the human female shows 23 homologous pairs of chromosomes; the male has 22 pairs plus an X and a Y chromsome.

The human is usually not thought of as a good organism for the study of genetics—the life cycle is long, controlled matings are not made, and the number of offspring is rather small for *statistical* treatments. Such organisms should be well studied biologically, or they should be of "*simple*" structure and function.

Nevertheless in the past few years there has been an increase in appreciation of humans as organisms for genetic study. *Medical histories* and research have provided much knowledge about the anatomy and physiology of humans.

Chromosome Abnormalities

Two syndromes will illustrate X-chromosome abnormalities that are fairly well understood in humans. The *Turner's syndrome* individual has only one sex chromosome, an X. Such individuals are said to have an XO-sex chromosome constitution; they have only 45 chromo-

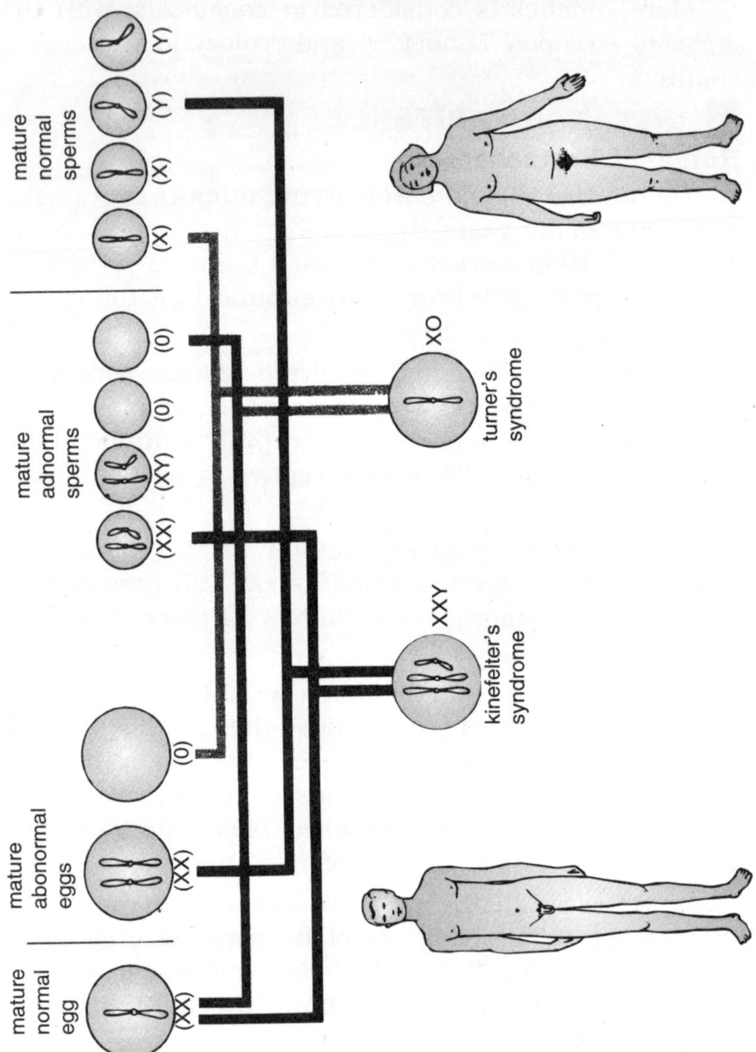

Figure 14.1: Formation of Klinefelter's and Turner's syndromes. Klinefelter's syndrome (XXY) results in a phenotypic male with reduced body hair, female-like breast development, and unusually long legs. Turner's syndrome (XO) results in a phenotypic female with short stature, webbed neck, and underdeveloped breasts. Only the X and Y chromosomes are shown; each individual has 22 pairs of autosomes. The total chromosome number for Klinefelter's and Turner's syndrome is 47 and 45, respectively.

somes. The Turner's syndrome individual has external female genitalia, but the breasts are underdeveloped, the ovaries are small fibrous streaks, and the uterus is small. Thus the Turner's syndrome individual is *a phenotypic female.*

The *Klinefelter's syndrome* results from an extra X chromosome in a regular male chromosomal consitution. Thus the Klinefelter's syndrome individual is XXY and has 47 chromosomes. In the Klinefelter's individual the external genitalia are malc, but the testes are small and the body hair is sparse.

Although Klinefelter's individuals are *phenotypic* males, most have a femalelike breast development. Both Turner's and Klinefelter's individuals are sterile. These two *syndromes* indicate that the loss or gain of chromosomes has great effects on the development and well-being of the individual. Figure elsewhere in this chapter shows how abnormal *gametes* may arise and lead to the two syndromes.

The Turner's and Klinefelter's syndromes are related to the presence of *sex chromatin* in the *interphase* nuclei. In 1949 Murray L. Barr discovered that the nuclei of most females have a deeply staining body attached to the inside of the nuclear *membrane.*

The *nuclei* of most males lack this structure, which is known as the Barr body, or sex chromatin. This sex chromatin is thought to represent an inactive X chromosome. Normal females have one of the two X chromosomes inactivated and are *sex chromatin* positive.

On the other hand normal males have only one X chromosome, which is not inactivated, and the male is sex chromatin negative. Turner's individuals have only one X chromosome and are sex chromatin negative; Klinefelter's individuals have two X chromosomes and are sex chromatin positive.

Thus the sex chromatin in these syndromes is reversed with respect to the *apparent* sex. There is

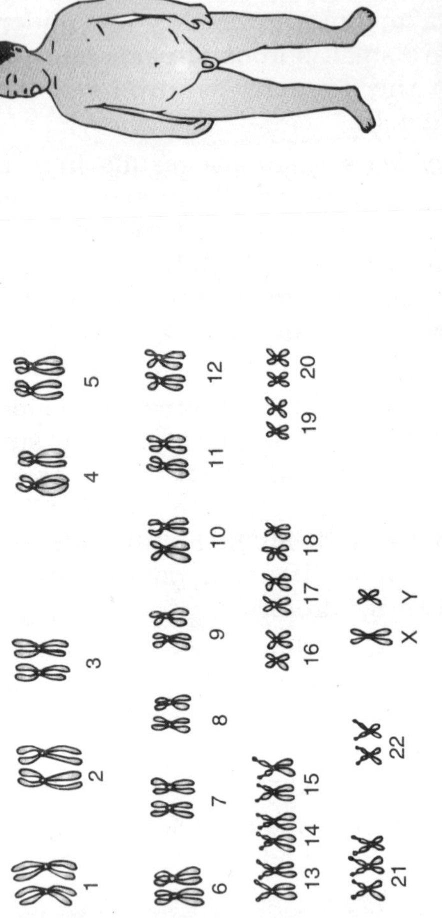

Figure 14.2: Down's syndrome. The individual possesses a third chromosome 21, is of low intelligence, short stature, and "mongoloid" due to the fold of the upper eyelid.

evidence that the number of Barr bodies always is one less than the number of X chromosomes. XYY individuals are known also and they may be produced by *fertilization* of a normal egg by a YY-bearing sperm produced by *nondisjunction.*

The *XYY syndrome* was associated with criminal tendencies in the 1960s and has come to be called the criminal syndrome. Studies on aggressive behaviour of patients in *mental institutions* and *prisons* showed that a relatively large percentage of inmates (3 percent) were

XYY. In the general population about 1 in 1000 (0.1 percent) males is XYY.

The correlation studies of aggressive or antisocial behaviour and the XYY condition were used as legal defense in some courts, and some reduced sentences resulted.

Now the fact that a man is genetically XYY is no longer acceptable as a legal reason for acquittal since many nonviolent XYY in dividuals exist, and whether specific behaviour patterns are due to genetic constitution or *environmental* factors is difficult or impossible to determine.

In 1973 a report of studies in Denmark reported that 22 XYY syndrome males had greater *truancy*, *vagabondage*, *impulsiveness*, school difficulties, and *antisocial* behaviour than a group of 42 male criminals with more or less similar behaviour characteristics.

Other abnormal sex chromosome constitutions are known. XXX individuals are called *triplo-X* and may or may not show phenotypic *abnormalities*. The most common abnormality of the triplo-X person is low *intelligence* and *sterility*. The tetra-X (XXXX) syndrome is also known.

The following additional sex chromosome abnormalities have been found, and they are all classified as Klinefelter's syndromes: XXXY, XXXXY, XXYY, and XXXYY.

Abnormal numbers of autosomes exist also. *Down's syndrome* results from an extra chromosome 21 (or a small chromosome in the same group as 21 according to the Denver classification system of 1960; possibly chromosome 22).

It is also known as *trisomy 21 syndrome*, or *mongolian idiocy*, the former term being preferred. The individuals usually are mentally deficient and have short stature, a round face with epicanthal folds (a heavy skin fold above the eye), and a protruding tongue. Chromoso-

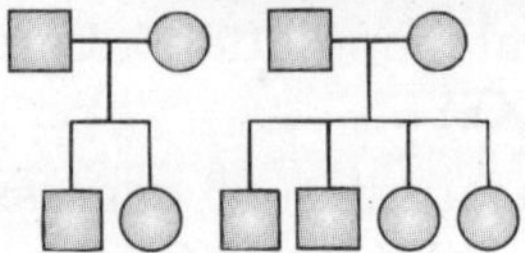

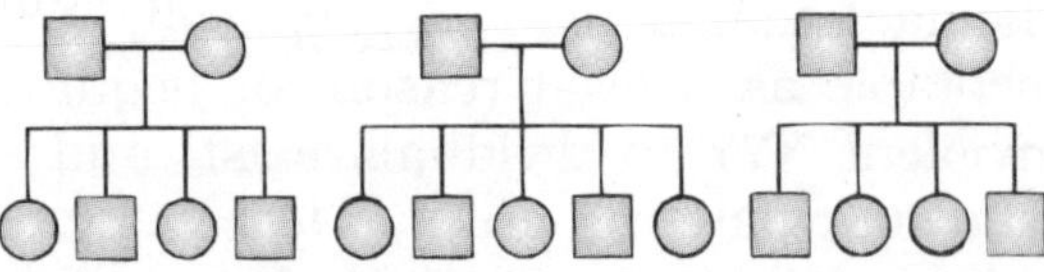

Figure 14.3: Five pedigrees of taste deficiency in man. Individuals represented by the shaded symbols are unable to taste crystals of phenylthiocarbamide. Those represented by the unshaded symbols find the crystals to be very bitter. Males are represented by squares, females by circles.

mal *nondisjunction* appears to be the basis for Down's syndrome. Older mothers are much more likely to have children with this condition than are younger mothers.

Also, Down's syndrome occurs by a mechanism other than nondisjunction of chromosome 21. This mechanism is translocation. The translocation involves chromosome 21 and chromosome 14 or 15. Such individuals have 46 chromosomes, which include two normal chromosomes 21, one normal 14 (or 15), and a large chromosome that is the translocated or fused chromosome 21 and 14 (or 15).

Such cases are known as *translocation Down's syndrome.* As with the Down's syndrome resulting from nondisjunction, the genetic material of chromosome 21 is present in triplicate. Persons with translocation Down's syndrome are *phenotypically* indistinguishable from those with the more common trisomy 21 resulting from nondisjunction.

Down's syndrome of all types occurs in 1 of 500 or 600 births. *This is not a rare or infrequent event.* The incidence of Down's syndrome is much influenced by maternal age. For mothers of 25 the risk of having an *affected* child is about one in 2000-3000, but for mothers of 45 it rises to one in 40-50.

Since ova reach the prophase stage of meiosis I in the fetus and may remain in that stage for 40-45 years before ovulation, aging of the ova might predispose them to nondisjunction. The incidence of Down's syndrome appears to be unrelated to the age of the father.

It is significant that trisomy of chromosome 21, a very small chromosome, has been found often, and trisomy of large chromsomes has, not been found at all. Trisomies of chromosomes 13 and 18, slightly larger than number 21, have been found, but they lead to an early death. Many *trisomies* are probably not detected because their effects lead to an early death *in utero.*

The large chromosomes apparently contain so much genetic information that overdosage is always lethal. Autosomal monosomy is rare, even for the smallest *autosomes*. Besides additions and deletions of whole chromosomes and translocations, other human chromosomal abnormalities are known.

The best known example of a visible deletion of a chromosomal part (believed to belong to chromosome 5) was described in 1963. The individuals who lack the part have severe mental deficiency, a small head, wide spacing of the eyes, and a "*moon face*" appearance. Another feature of the condition is an abnormal larynx, which results in a plaintive cry, described as similar to the cry of a cat.

The syndrome has been called the cri *du chat syndrome* for this reason. Figure elsewhere in this chpater shows a photograph of an infant with the cri du chat syndrome.

Human Pedigrees

Since it has not been a practice to make controlled matings with humans, inbred strains and pure lines are not available. Students of human genetics have used the *pedigree method* for studying certain traits.

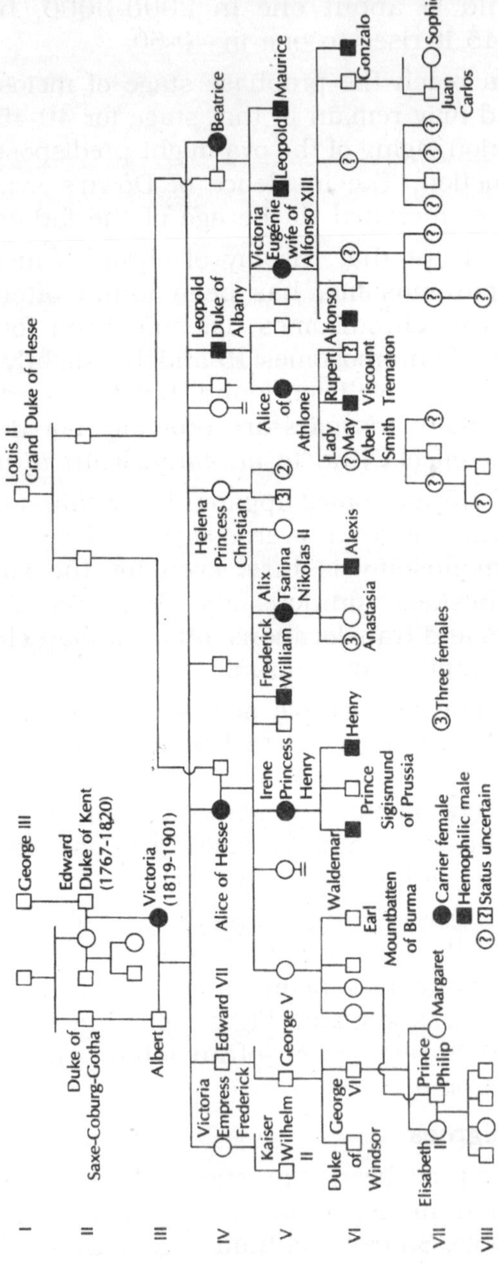

Figure 14.4: Pedigree of Queen Victoria and her descendants. The mutation for hemophilia, an X-linked recessive trait, probably occurred in Queen Victoria or in her father, Edward, Duke of Kent.

Table 14.2: Some Human Traits Thought to Be Controlled by Genes on the X Chromosome.

1. Partial color blindness, deutan series
2. Partial color blindness, protan series
3. Total color blindness; most cases are autosomal, however
4. Glucose-6-phosphate dehydrogenase structure
5. Xg blood group system
6. Hemophilia A (AHG deficiency)
7. Hemophilia B (Christmas disease)
8. Agammaglobulinemia
9. Diabetes insipidus, nephrogenic type
10. Diabetes insipidus, neurohypophyseal type
11. Absence of central incisors
12. Congenital deafness; there are autosomal forms also y
13. Progressive deafness
14. Mental deficiency; a small portion of cases show X linkage
15. Hydrocephalus; most cases are not X linked
16. Ocular albinism
17. Congenital cataract with microcornea

A pedigree is a record of the distribution of one or more traits in a group of related individuals. Figure elsewhere in this chapter shows five pedigrees with the distribution of *tasters* and *nontasters* for *phenylthiocarbamide* (PTC).

About 70 percent of the general population find that PTC has a definite taste, usually bitter, whereas the remaining 30 percent find it tasteless. From these and many other pedigrees that have been studied, it has been determined that the *inability* to taste PTC depends on a recessive gene.

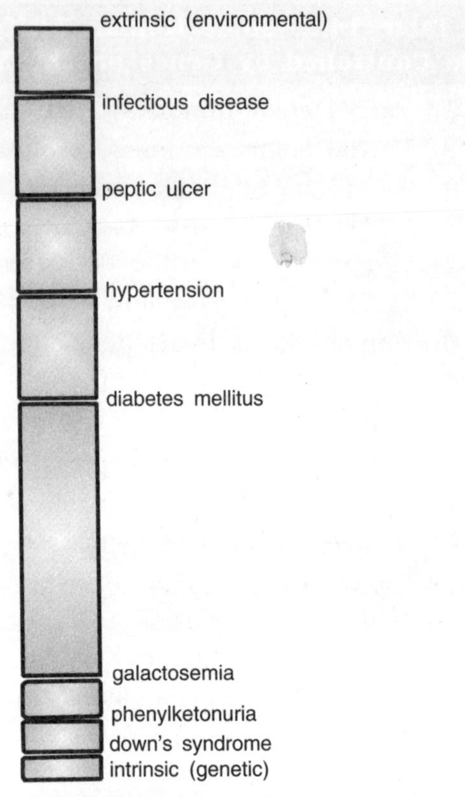

Figure 14.5: Relative contribution of genetic and environmental factors to various human diseases.

Although the nature of the inheritance of many human traits is now understood, the study of human inheritance, when compared to that of corn or *Drosophila*, is still in its infancy.

Table elsewhere in this chapter lists a few human traits and the mode of inheritance. In general the traits listed in Table elsewhere in this chapter are determined by genes that behave according to the simple dominant-recessive pattern.

Other modes of human inheritance are known. Like autosomal traits, those determined by Xlinked genes may either be dominant or recessive.

Table 14.1: Human Traits Inherited as Autosomal Characters.

Dominant	*Recessive*
Brown eyes	Blue or gray eyes
Farsightedness	Normal
Normal	Nearsightedness
Dark hair	Blond hair
Nonred hair	Red hair
Curly hair	Straight hair
Scaly skin	Normal
Thickened skin	Normal
Broad lips	Thin lips
"Roman" nose	Straight nose
Extra digits	Normal
Short digits	Normal
Allergy	Normal
Huntington's chorea	Normal
Normal	Congenital deafness
Normal	Tay-Sachs disease
Normal	Phenylketonuria

In X-linked dominant inheritance both males and females are affected and both transmit the disorder to their offspring. One of the best studied X-linked dominant traits is vitamin-D resistant *rickets*. The genes for hemophilia and colour blindness are sex-linked recessives. *Hemophilia* is a particularly interesting case, both *biologically* and *historically*.

The royal houses of Europe have been afflicted with hemophilia since the days of *Queen Victoria's* children. Queen Victoria herself was a carrier, and since none of her ancestors and relatives were affected, the mutation *probably* occurred in one of her parents or in one of her own *germ cells*.

Figure elsewhere in this chaptrer shows the pedigree of Queen Victoria and her descendants for the hemophiliac trait. Leopold, Duke of Albany, died of hemophilia at the age of 31. Prince Albert, Victoria's consort, did not possess the trait. (If the argument is made that Albert possessed hemophilia in a mild undiscovered form, how does the pedigree disprove this possibility and exonerate Albert?)

Two of Victoria's daughters were carriers, and several of their male *descendants* were "bleeders." The histories of Russia and Spain have been affected considerably by these genetic situations. Table elsewhere in this chapter lists some of the traits thought to be controlled by genes on the X chromosome.

Other patterns of inheritance known in humans include multiple alleles (*blood groups*) and multiple factors (*skin colour*, *height*, and *intelligence*).

Many of the known hereditary traits that are not listed in Tables elsewhere in this chapter involve abnormalities that are of particular interest to the medical profession. As more and more is learned about human inheritance, it becomes necessary for people entering the practice of *medicine* to have a sound training in human genetics.

GENES AND DISEASES

Usually only rare diseases are inherited along simple genetic lines. But genetic factors are involved in many diseases. About 2000 human diseases are now considered to have a strong genetic component. Approximately 25 percent of all hospital beds and extended care facilities in the United States are occupied by persons who suffer from a "*genetic disease.*"

The relative contribution of intrinsic (*genetic*) *factors* and *extrinsic* (environmental) factors varies from disease to disease. Figure elsewhere in this chapter represents this range for several human diseases. At one end of the scale there are diseases such as Down's *syndrome*, *hemophilia*, and so forth, which are exclusively genetic in origin and where the environment plays no direct role.

The intermediate diseases, such as diabetes *mellitus*, *hypertension*, and *peptic ulcer*, have significant contributions from both sides. The far extreme of infectious diseases is almost entirely the result of the environment. Ease of treatment of the diseases is probably inversely proportional to their *genetic factor*.

Infectious disease is relatively easy to control with modern medicine. *Smallpox*, *polio*, and *scarlet* fever are usually rare diseases in technolo-gically advanced countries today. Genetic diseases, on the other hand, may be completely *untreatable* by modern medicine.

Hemophilia and sickle-cell anemia' are good examples of "*incurable*" genetic diseases. Other genetic diseases may be controlled completely or to a large degree in some affected individuals. In galactosemia and phenylketonuria, where galactose and phenylalanine respectively, cannot be metabolized properly, elimination of *galactose* and reduction of *phenylalanine* in the diet at an early age can prevent irreversible damage.

Certain individuals are sensitive or allergic to various drugs or chemicals. These "*genetic diseases*" can be controlled or avoided with proper medical attention. Thus as with environmental diseases, genetic diseases range over varying difficulties in treatment. The question is sometimes asked, "Which is more important in the formation of traits in an organism, heredity or environment?"

This question is actually unanswerable because an organism in its development always has an environment; a gene or a whole group of genes always has an environment. Many studies have shown that a particular genotype develops one way in one environment and another way in another environment (*phenocopies*).

The common Chinese primula, when grown at

temperatures of 13-18° C (55-65° F) will produce red flowers, generation after generation. The same plant, when grown at a temperature of 35°C (95° F) will produce white flowers as long as it is kept at this high temperature. However, if such plants are restored to low temperatures, they will produce red flowers.

A mutant strain of *Drosophila* has been discovered with branched legs; this occurs only at low temperatures. This same strain, when grown at normal temperatures, has normal legs. Many similar examples have been reported. Such studies clearly indicate that what is inherited is the ability to react in a certain way to a certain environment.

But the question may be asked, "Is it possible to set up an experiment in which it may be determined in a particular situation that heredity is more important than environment, or vice versa?" In human society there are certain situations that, when combined, approach such an experimental setup. Human twins constitute the materials for this natural experiment.

Ordinarily twins occur about once in 88 births in the United States, but the number has increased since the use of oral contraceptives became widespread. (Oral contraceptives, "*the pill*," have increased the frequency of multiple births by increasing the number of eggs released from the ovary when the *pill* is discontinued.)

Human twins are of two kinds: one-egg (*monozygotic*), or *identical*, twins that originate from the division of a single fertilized egg, and thus have the same genotype; and two-egg (*dizygotic*), or *fraternal*, twins that, because they result from two different *fertilized* eggs, have different *genotypes*.

Therefore fraternal twins are no more alike genetically than are ordinary brothers and sisters. Identical twins are always of the same sex, whereas fraternal twins may be of either the same or opposite sexes. A number of investigators have realized the value of studying human twins in analyzing human heredity.

One extensive study used 50 pairs of identical twins that had been reared together, 52 pairs of fraternal twins that had been reared together, and 19 pairs of identical twins that had been reared apart.

Identical twins, whether reared together or apart, are very much alike in many *physical traits*, such as *facial* features, hair and *skin colour* and *texture*, eye colour, tooth characteristics, height, head length, and head width.

With regard to these physical traits, differences in the environment have little effect. An extensive consideration of twin studies is not feasible, but some reference should be made to an analysis of the relative effects of heredity and environment on intelligence in twins. Human intelligence should not be considered a single well-defined characteristic.

However, intelligence tests have been devised; the results of these tests are expressed by an intelligence quotient, known as the IQ. This measure is a useful tool in discussing intelligence. A score of 90 to 110 is average, and *theoretipally* denotes an individual who can make normal adjustments in everyday life.

A score-of 140 indicates a genius; one of 120 indicates a superior intellect; and one of 70 to 0 places the individual in the feeble-minded category.

No one suggests that the IQ, as used generally, measures only innate intelligence. *Psychologists* subdivide human mental abilities into distinct primary abilities, such as an ability to visualize objects in space, to memorize, or to reason inductively.

It has been found that two individuals with the same IQ may vary considerably with respect to their primary abilities. Studies in the future undoubtedly will make more use of this new, approach.

As mentioned earlier, the distribution of the IQs in the whole population would seem to *indicate* that intelligence is determined by multiple factors. But the number of these factors, and *precisely* how each works, remain to be determined.

Of course, IQ tests have been criticized because they do not take cultural backgrounds and experiences into account. The inadequacies of IQ tests are being brought to public attention more frequently than a few years ago.

One study found that the average pair difference for 10 scores of the 50 pairs of identical twins reared together was 5.9, the average pair difference for the 52 pairs of fraternal twins reared together was 9.9, and the average pair difference for the 19 pairs of identical twins reared apart was 8.2.

The identical twins reared apart show a greater average difference than identical twins reared together, suggesting an environmental influence on IQ. The identical twins reared together show a smaller average pair difference than that found in the fraternal twins, suggesting that heredity is also important.

It should be pointed out that the average difference between identical twins reared together is no greater than that obtained when the same individual takes the test twice. Furthermore the greater average pair difference for the identical twins reared apart was caused by four of these pairs.

In the majority of the 19 separated pairs the individual differences were about the same as those found for the unseparated twins. In these cases the environments of the separated twins were not greatly different.

However, in a few of the pairs the opportunities for schooling and the amount of formal education varied greatly. A consideration of the case history of a pair of identical twins will illustrate the effects of great environmental differences.

Gladys and Helen were separated at 18 months and did not meet again until they were 28 years old. Helen lived on a farm in Michigan, obtained a college education, and was then employed as a teacher. Gladys attended school for 2 years in Ontario, spent the next 2 years in the Canadian Rockies where there was no school, and when her family returned to Ontario, she never resumed her formal education.

Prior to the time she was examined, she had worked at several occupations. Helen scored 116 on the IQ test and Gladys scored 92.

This is thc greatest difference found in any of the pairs studied, and this correlated with the greatest difference in *educational* experience of all the twins studied. Any conclusions about the relative effects of heredity and environment from the twin studies must be tentative.

Much more study is needed on the identification of these genes and factors and their specific roles in determining intelligence. However, it does seem fair to state that the hereditary components can be modified by the environment.

Heredity seems to provide the individual with upper and lower limits between which some level of intelligence is realized.

If this concept is correct, then it must follow accordingly that it is very important for each individual to have a favourable environment in which to develop.

Without a favourable environment, a person with relatively favourable heredity for intelligence may fall short, in the achievement of intelligent behaviour, of a person with relatively unfavourable heredity.

EUGENICS

Francis Galton coined the term *eugenics,* which means being well born. Galton used the term to cover the whole study of agencies under social control that may result in improving the hereditary qualities of future human generations.

Since Galton's time many people have become interested in the eugenics movement, several eugenics societies have been formed, and many states have passed eugenics laws. Several studies have pointed up the fact that there is a differential birth rate in the United States.

In general these studies show that college graduates have fewer children than those who have finished only high school; these in turn have fewer children than those who finished only grade school; and the largest number of children is found in those families where the parents had less than seven years of formal education.

Many people see a cause for alarm in our djfferential birth rates because they feel that the result will be a slow but continuous downward trend in the average intelligence. Professional *geneticists*, in the main, are a bit wary of drawing any definite conclusions at the present time because they still do not have adequate information about the many factors, both *hereditary* and *environmental*, that determine intelligence.

The approach of the eugenicists to the general problem of improving human heredity has been along two lines: negative eugenics and positive eugenics. The negative approach involves segregation or sterilization of individuals with undesirable traits. In either case the

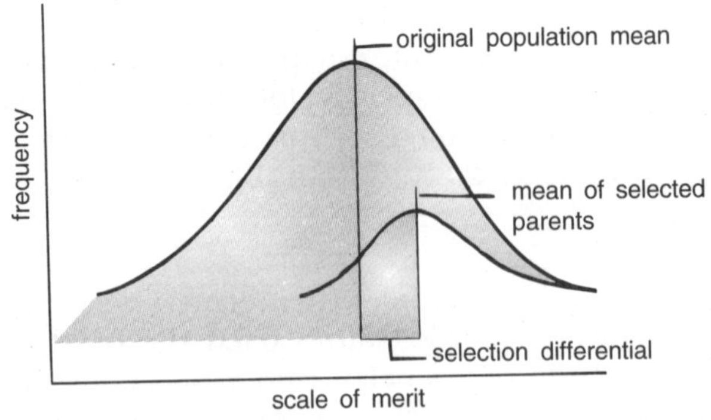

Figure 14.6: Hypothetical record of trait being selected.

reproduction of such individuals would be prevented. The various state laws that have been passed provide for segregation or sterilization, dr both.

Most of the sterilization laws have pertained primarily to the *feeble-minded* and the *insane*. The sterilization operation is rather simple. In the male it involves cutting the sperm ducts; in the female the *Fallopian tubes* are tied.

Such operations do not affect the endocrine functions; they only prevent the transport of gametes. *Vasectomy*, the cutting of the sperm ducts, is beginning to be a fairly popular means of birth control among couples who have the number of children that they desire.

However, there are great difficulties in such a negative program of eugenics. Not all feeblemindedness is hereditary; some is environmentally produced. Also not all insanity is hereditary. Thus such a program must be in the hands of very competent people.

The other aspect of the *eugenics* program, positive eugenics, aims to raise the average intelligence of the population by encouraging those with desirable traits and talents to have more children.

With the present state of knowledge of human genetics, great caution must be followed in connection with specific eugenic measures. However desirable it may be to eliminate undesirable traits from the human population, this cannot be done until the exact nature and mode of operation of the defective genes are known.

And in cases involving recessive genes and multiple genes, it must be realized that the prcblem of their elimination is enormous and that the time required may be many hundreds of years. Genetics cannot be applied to humans as it is applied to livestock, for very obvious reasons.

And in the case of humans, who is to say what the desirable type is? In the human population there are many desirable types, and society would not function for long if all people had the same talents and interests. Human diversity is needed for a society with many goals. This, however, does not mean that a sane program of eugenics based on practical and scientific methods should not be adopted.

Genetic Engineering

Another approach to the problem of human welfare may be made possible by altering the developmental processes of an individual destined to be afflicted with genetic defect. Joshua Lederberg, a Nobel Prize winner for his studies in microbial genetics, has proposed the term *euphenics* for such experimental *modification* of human development by *physiological* and *embryological* methods.

Euphenics would have its effects only on the individual and not on future generations, since the germ cells would not be affected by such "*developmental engineering.*" *Eugenics* and *euphenics* are complementary; some traits may be best modified developmentally; others may be more readily changed by selection.

Eugenics and Genetic Counseling

Presently eugenics does not have a united group presenting its perceived merits. Instead, a growing field of professional activity is that of *genetic counseling.* In brief, a genetic counselor lays the evidence before individuals either contemplating childbearing or already pregnant so that they may make reasonable decisions about conceiving a child or aborting a fetus.

The genetic counselor meets with the prospective parents, gathers as much information as possible for a pedigree analysis, and then discusses the probabilities (figures the odds) that certain traits will or will not appear in the offspring.

For instance, if one parent has a single faulty dominant gene, there is a 50 percent probability that any child will also be faulty; if both parents have a single

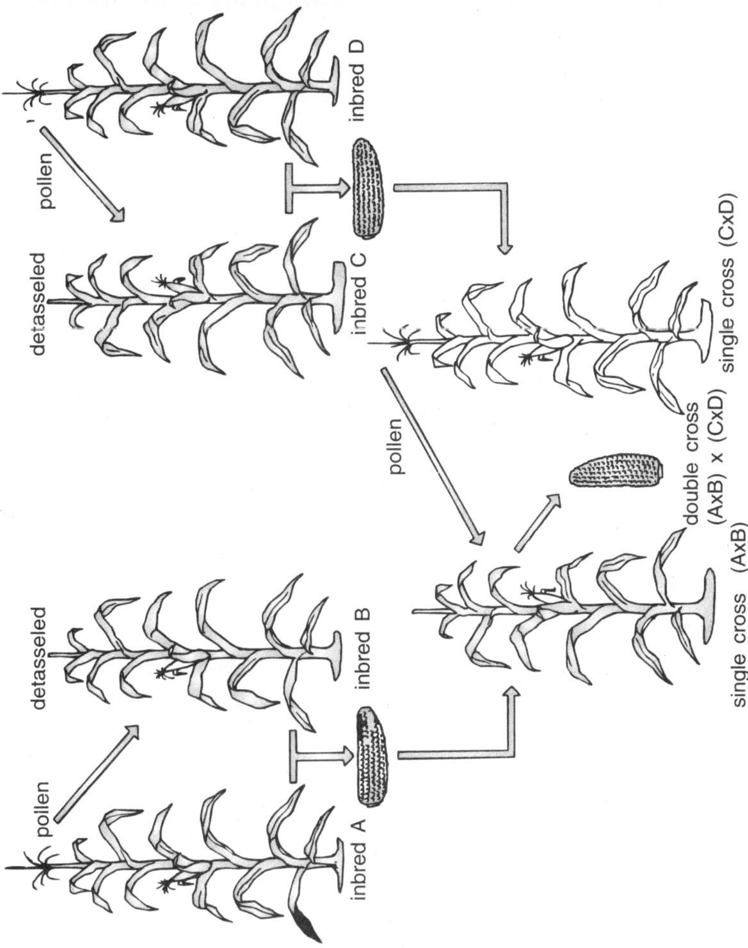

Figure 14.7: Production of hybrid corn. Plants from four inbred strains of corn are crossed pairwise: A x B, C x D. The Progeny of these two crosses are then used to produce the hybrid corn that is used in commercial planting. [Double cross: (A × B) × (C × D).]

faulty recessive gene, the child has a 25 percent chance of showing the faulty trait; or if the genes appear to be sex linked, expectancies for the offspring can be worked out for the child just as they could be for *Drosophila* in other chapter.

Sometimes in the case of multifactorial inheritance, the transmission pattern may be less defined and the genetic counsellor tries to make this obvious to the potential parents. There are several positive things that can be done besides taking family histories. Sometimes carriers of traits can be tested quite simply.

This is true, for instance, for carriers of sickle-cell genes. Sometimes a few cells from a potential carrier can be subjected to short-term tissue culture and these cells used to measure enzyme levels; over 60 metabolic diseases can now bee identified by such procedures.

In cases where the woman is already pregnant, it is possible to obtain cells produced by the fetus through a technique called *amniocentesis.* Here, after the 14th week of pregnancy, amniotic fluid can be taken by hypodermic syringe through the abdominal wall of the woman.

The fluid has cells from the fetus. These can be cultured and tested as above. The procedure also allows prenatal determination of sex by the presence or absence of Barr bodies. Of course there are two principal alternatives after receiving genetic counseling. Either conception can be avoided or terminated, or the decision can be made to have the child.

This often is a case of calculated risk that the child will not show the abnormal trait. There is, however, another aspect to this problem that should not be ignored. The decision to have or not to have a child is a shortterm decision. For instance, parents both of whom are heterozygous for a recessive trait have a 75 percent probability of producing children that appear normal.

However, 66 percent or two thirds of those' that do appear normal will be heterozygous. If the recessive phenotype is not as successful in reproduction and if given sufficient time, the human population will have a growing number of heterozygous persons.

Conception from two heterozygotes will increase in frequency and the number of abnormal children appearing in the population will increase. The significance of this in terms of species survival will be considered apparent again in other chapter of this book where the Hardy-Weinberg concept and genetic drift are considered.

Thus prospective parents who receive counseling have a threefold concern: concern for themselves, concern for the child, concern for society and the human species.

AGRICULTURAL GENETICS

The objective of agricultural genetics is the application of genetic knowledge to agricultural practice. The most economically important organisms to which this has been applied are the vertebrate animals and the flowering plants.

Genetic manipulation with these organisms has shown that inherited traits that are agriculturally useful can be located, transferred, and utilized. In a world where the majority of people have too little food, only a few of the species that are used for food have been improved by genetic breeding programs.

Proper breeding has produced disease-resistant varieties as well as varieties that give greatly increased yields. In general, three procedures are commonly practiced by plant and animal breeders: selection, inbreeding, and outbreeding and hybridization. In modern breeding programs of agricultural genetics the principles of selection are used in various ways.

Two main selection techniques used in plant-breeding practice are mass selection and pedigree selection. In mass selection the undesirable plants are destroyed, and the desirable ones are used for seed. In general, mass selection brings about a rather slow change. In the selection of offspring of naturally (somewhat at random) cross-pollinated plants there is no control over the pollen source. In pedigree selection individual plants and their progeny are maintained as separate lines.

Such pedigree lines enable the plant breeder to follow closely the genetic behaviour of his material. This technique reduces the amount of variability that might be attributed to environmental influences.

Pedigree selection is often used to produce lines that do not have great agricultural or economic value in themselves, but when crossed to another pedigree line, produce superior offspring.

The animal breeder usually considers the individual characteristics and the characteristics of its genetic relatives-ancestral, collateral, and offspring.

The selection of individuals to be parents of the next generation of a herd or flock, and so forth, usually requires some sort of measurement-the opinion of experienced breeders in the case of pedigreed dogs, for example.

The ribbons and trophies won by the dog would-be an index to its breeding potential, or data in the case of quantitative characteristics such as the number of eggs, pounds of meat, amount and quality of wool, and so on. Figure elsewhere in this chpater shows a hypothetical record of a trait being selected.

Sometimes the individuals of a generation will be closer to the original population mean than their parent; such a phenomenon is called re*gression*. This emphasizes the complexities involved in studying traits that may be controlled by many genes.

The nature of gene action in multiple-gene (quantitative inheritance) systems remains rather obscure presently. It is clear that multiple genes usually do not operate through simple additive effects. The systems of mating in natural populations are usually considered to be random (HardyWeinberg equilibrium and population changes).

Other systems of mating are found in nature and in human-controlled populations. Inbreeding is the mating of closely related individuals. Extreme inbreeding occurs naturally in self-fertilizing plants, such as beans and peas. (Mendel's experiments with pure lines of the garden pea depended on this system of mating.)

The effect of prolonged inbreeding is to greatly reduce the number of heterozygous individuals. It is doubtful whether complete homozygosity is ever achieved, but for practical breeding purposes, lines subjected to inbreeding for long periods of time are pure lines.

Self-fertilization occurs only among a few plant types and does not occur at all among higher animals. In animals homozygosity can be approached quickly by brother-sister coatings. Sometimes progeny are backcrossed to their parents.

Inbreeding combined with selection over the years has resulted in many valuable breeds of domestic animals. Thomas Jefferson was an early proponent of genetic improvement of agricultural stocks in the United States. Jefferson was influential in bringing the merino sheep to this country.

The merino sheep themselves make an interesting story. The strain was developed in Spain during the seventeenth century. The original stock had two coats of wool fibers-long coarse ones and short fine ones. Intensive selection for fine wool and inbreeding produced the merino sheep which have a more uniform production of short-fibered wool.

For a time, Spain had a monoply on these sheep, but when France invaded Spain, some of the breed was taken back to France, from where these sheep were distributed to many parts of the world. Intensive inbreeding has led to some unfortunate genetic situations.

For example, inbreeding of Hereford beef cattle has brought together recessive genes for dwarfism. Dwarfs are of little economic value. The dwarf gene has been brought out also in the breeding of the Angus and Shorthorn cattle lines.

Some dog breeders have so selectively inbred their lines that undesir-able traits have been established; for example, hip dysplasia is a rather common disease in pedigreed boxers.

Hybridization is performed in two ways: outbreeding and cross-breeding. Outbreeding is the crossing of unrelated individuals, whereas crossbreeding involves mating of individuals of different races or even different species.

Corn is a good example of a plant that has been improved by the techniques of outbreeding to produce hybridization. In the case of corn it has not been possible up to the present time to produce inbred lines that have all the desired characteristics. In 1968, 99 percent of the corn planted in the United States was hybrid corn. It is produced as shown in Figure elsewhere in this chapter.

The four lines used in the production of the commercial hybrid corn seed are maintained by inbreeding. The final product obtained greatly increases the quality and yield. This phenomenon, which is frequently associated with hybridization, is called heterosis, or hybrid vigor. Heterosis, in general, may be explained on this basis.

Each of two inbred lines is homozygous for certain desirable traits and also for some undesirable recessive traits, but the two lines are homozygous for different genes, and each has dominant genes to mask the undesirable recessive genes of the other.

In the case of corn double crosses are used to produce commercial seed. Here when two inbred lines are crossed, the maternal parent, as is characteristic of most inbred corn lines, is small and produces small low-yielding ears. Double crosses result in the production of seed on large uniform ears of single-cross plants.

It is not possible, however, to obtain good results by using the seed produced by plants grown from hybrid corn grains. Such grains result in a large variety of different kinds of plants and ears as a result of independent assortment, that is, such hybrids will not breed true to type, and continual crossing is practiced to produce the commercial seed.

As is readily seen, both inbreeding and outbreeding are involved in the production of hybrid corn. Several plant species other than corn have shown considerable hybrid vigor when two or more lines were crossed. Sorghum, onions, and sugar beets-all important agricultural cropsare good examples.

Outbreeding has been used in animal husbandry, also. Poultry, rabbits, cattle, and sheep are such cases. Crossbreeding is much more common with animals than with plants for agricultural purposes. The mule is the result of a successful cross between the horse and the donkey. The mule is superior in many ways to either parent.

It is faster, stronger, and larger than the donkey and, at the same time, is more durable and more resistant to disease than the horse. The mule is usually sterile since the chromosomes do not have homologs for pairing in meiosis. Strictly speaking, *a mule* is the offspring of a male donkey (a jackass) and a mare.

The offspring of a stallion and a female donkey is a *hinny*. Successful crosses between zebus, the native cattle of India, and European cattle have produced hybrids that are adaptable to warm humid climates, with good production of milk and meat. Probably a great potential exists for breeding other desirable hybrids for food and work in many areas of the world.

In summary, selection, inbreeding, and hybridization are powerful techniques for improving stocks of plants and animals for agricultural and other purposes.

Although corn is a staple in the diet of large numbers

of people and has been improved by genetic techniques, it is deficient in the amino acid lysine. A strain of corn that is high in lysine has been studied at Purdue University. When corn is the sole or major source of protein in the diet, such as in Latin America, this *opaque-2* strain is superior in support of growth.

The discovery of the high lysine content of opaque-2 corn has stimulated a search for other highlysine mutants in corn and other cereal grains. An example of application of basic biology to food production by animal is the egg of.the domestic fowl.

The egg that you may have had for breakfast this morning probably was laid by a Single Comb White Leghorn hen, which had 13 vitamins and 13 minerals added to its soybean meal-corn-wheat diet, has spent all of its life in a windowless building, produces about 20 eggs per month from age 5 to 25 months, and will be in the soup can after its peak of egg production is past.

The Single Comb White Leghorn has more traits desired by the egg rancher than any other breed: good egg production, large eggs with sound shells and high interior quality, resistance to disease, and it starts laying at a young age.

The genetic rr takeup of the modern Leghorn strain is the result of many poultry breeding experiments. In the 1920s vitamin D was discovered; it became possible to raise chickens in confinement without sunshine.

The minerals and other vitamins are added to the diet in the proper amounts for optimum growth, health, and productivity of the chicken. In addition protein and caloric (energy) requirements were determined. Soybeans are good sources of protein, but raw soybeans contain a protein which inhibits the action of trypsin, a digestive enzyme; therefore raw soybeans interfere with digestion.

The tryspin inhibitor is destroyed by heating, so heated soybean meal is now the bulk of the protein source in chicken feed. Chickens have biological clocks which are set by the intensity and duration of light. Normally chickens lay more eggs in the spring than during any other time of the year.

The modern chicken ranch uses artificial light cycles to influence the biological clock and thereby maximize hen development and egg production. Maturing pullets (young hens) are exposed to 8-hour (short) days to prevent them from laying until their bodies and oviducts have reached the proper size.

If the pullet starts laying too soon, permanent damage to the oviduct may occur. At the proper age and size the light regimen is switched to 16 hours on and 8 hours off, a schedule which induces maximum egg production.

In this one example of food production by animals, biological principles of several disciplines are used: genetics, development, nutrition, biochemistry, and behaviour.

RECOMBINANT DNA

In closing this chapter on human and applied genetics, we turn to a technique that has been discussed increasingly since 1972 when a new class of enzymes, *restriction endonucleases*, was discovered.

The technique, joining of unrelated DNAs by enzymatic methods, involves the cleavage of one kind of DNA with restriction endonucleases and then joining the fragments to the ends of other DNAs (cleaved with the same endonuclease) with *DNA ligase*, the "joining enzyme".

The restriction endonucleases cut both strands of the DNA double helix at points of specific base sequences in such a way that a short, single-stranded region is left at each end of the DNA fragments. Often called "sticky" because they can form hydrogenbonded associations with the ends of other pieces, these ends are covalently joined when the DNA ligase is added. This technique is basically powerful and simple because, in many cases, the two types of DNA may be mixed, digested and added to specially treated bacteria that take up the fragments.

Once inside a bacterium which contains the DNA ligase, the fragments are joined and the cells carrying recombinant DNA only need to be isolated with standard culture techniques of microbiology to obtain strains which are "factories for manufacturing" the recombinant DNA.

Some of the events of the continuing discussion have been

1. In 1974 several scientists called for a moratorium on recomb-inant gene research.
2. A conference in February, 1975 at Asilomar, California-attended by persons from several countries besides the United States-produced temporary guidelines to govern this type of research.
3. Several guidelines meetings were held and the last one, a public input session at Bethesda, Maryland, where the National Institutes of Health (sponsors of much recombinant DNA research) are located was climaxed with long and boisterous public response in February, 1976.
4. The NIH guidelines were released in June, 1976. Designed to ensure that recombinant DNA research can proceed without harm to laboratory workers, the general public or the environ-ment, the guidelines ban certain types of experiments, require justification that the same knowledge cannot be obtained with traditional techniques, establish levels of safety precautions commensurate with potential hazards and set responsibilities for investigators, institutions and the NIH.

This topic has come to national attention in several

specific instances: The city council of Cambridge, Massachusetts, voted to ban these experiments at Harvard University and the Massachusetts Institute of Technology; the attorney general of the state of New York held a hearing in the fall of 1976 for the purpose of deciding what action to recommend to the state legislature; and the University of Michigan and Indiana University have felt the impact of public concern over establishment of recombinant gene laboratories on their campuses.

Succinctly, the possible dangers of recombinant DNA research involve the fact that with "synthetic biology" we leave the web of natural; evolution, and the production of new strains of microorganisms might break down the existing barriers against genetic exchange between prokaryotes and eukaryotes.

The possible beneficial applications include transfer of genes for nitrogen fixation into common food plants, facilitation of gene therapy for diseases in which specific gene functions are lacking, creation of energy crops which offer alternatives to fossil fuels and nuclear fusion, and understanding (cure for?) cancer.

Science magazine has followed the recombinant DNA debate and the following issues provide an initial bibliography for the interested student who wishes to pursue the developments of what has been analogized as the "atomic bomb of biology:" September 21, 1973 (p. 1114); July 26, 1974 (p. 303); and the 1976 issues, February 27 (p. 834), March 19 (p. 1160), April 16 (p. 237), June 4 (p.938), July 2 (p. 6), July 16 (p. 215), July 23 (p. 300), October 1 (p. 44), October 15 (p. 303), November 12 (p. 705).

EVIDENCES OF EVOLUTION

According to the concept of organic evolution, the various kinds of living things in the world today have been (and are being) derived from previously existing ancestral forms by descent with modification. Although the studies thus far made in this field do not reveal the exact nature of the origin of life, they do indicate that once simple forms of life appeared on the earth, there followed, during millions and millions of years, a gradual development of many kinds of organisms with increasing complexity of structure.

Numerous references have been made to this process in other sections of the text. It is now time to examine the concept in some detail. Although the idea of evolution is a very old one, it has had widespread acceptance only in the past hundred or so years.

All aspects of biological study contribute to an understanding of evolution, and the concept is certainly one of the most important unifying principles in the whole field.

In a study of organic evolution it is necessary to distinguish between two aspects of the study: *fact* and *explanation*. The many evidences of evolution constitute the fact; ideas about the mechanisms involved in the process, which include the various theories of evolution, constitute the explanation, or attempted explanation.

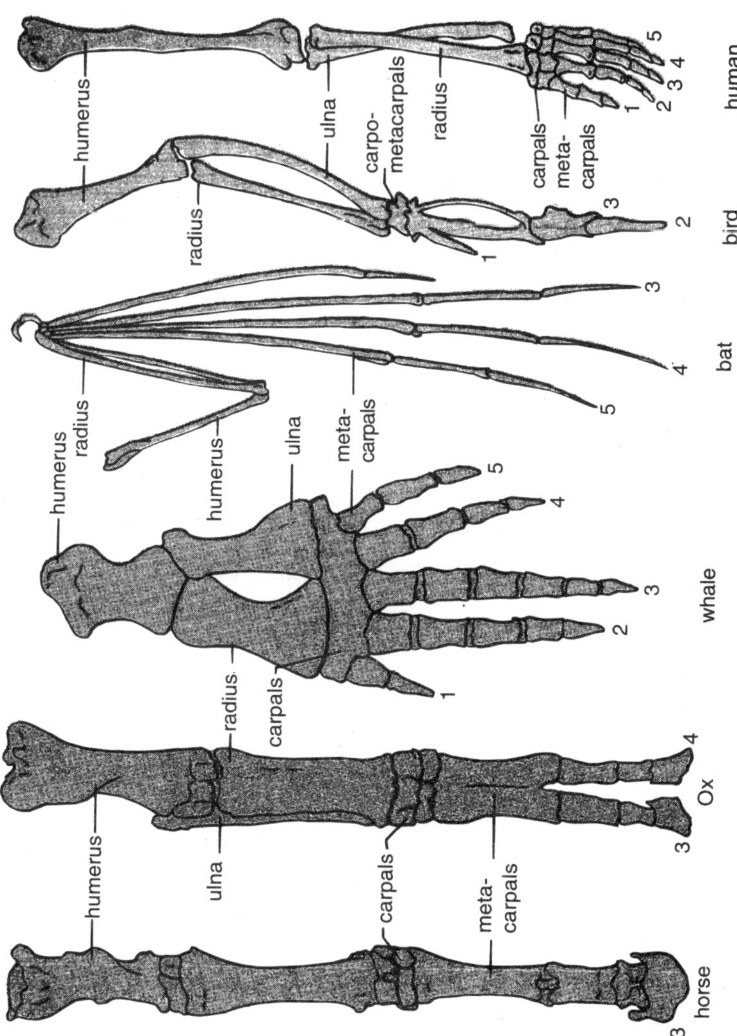

Figure 15.1: Comparison of vertebrate forelimbs.

After considering some of the more important sources of evidence of evolution, some of the interpretations of the causal mechanisms will be discussed.

EVIDENCE FROM COMPARATIVE ANATOMY

Studies in comparative anatomy provide many evidences of evolution. In such a study we are concerned with *homologous structures*—structures that have the same general arrangement of parts and which arise in a similar way from similar embryonic structures. Homologous structures may be quite diverse in function.

The skeletal parts of vertebrate appendages may be used to illustrate homologous structures. The forelimbs of vertebrates will be used to illustrate the point, but the hind limbs would serve equally well. An examination of Figure elsewhere in this chapter shows that all the different forelimbs have the same general arrangement of parts.

The primitive vertebrate forelimb is a five-fingered (pentadactyl) appendage having *a humerus, radius* and *ulna, carpals, metacarpals,* and *phalanges.* All vertebrate forelimbs are modifications of this primitive type. In the bat the metacarpals and phalanges have been greatly elongated for the support of the membranous wing.

In the whale, the whole structure is greatly shortened and thickened to serve as a flipper. The great modifications in the bird are found in the metacarpals and phalanges. The only digit left in the forelimb of the adult horse is the third. The enlarged nail forms the hoof, the radius and ulna are fused together, and the metacarpal of the single digit is enlarged and elongated to form the *cannon bone.*

Closely attached to this bone are the two *splint bones,* which are the reduced metacarpals of the second and fourth digits. In the course of vertebrate evolution, many modifications have occurred which represent adaptations for special modes of existence. Some vertebrate

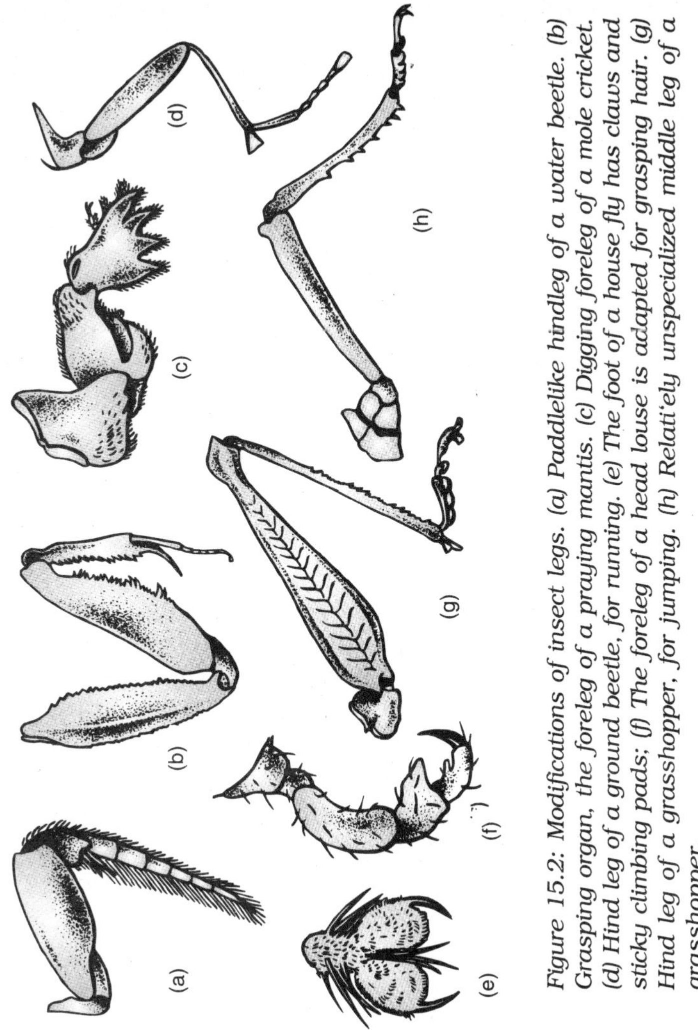

Figure 15.2: Modifications of insect legs. (a) Paddlelike hindleg of a water beetle. (b) Grasping organ, the foreleg of a praying mantis. (c) Digging foreleg of a mole cricket. (d) Hind leg of a ground beetle, for running. (e) The foot of a house fly has claws and sticky climbing pads; (f) The foreleg of a head louse is adapted for grasping hair. (g) Hind leg of a grasshopper, for jumping. (h) Relati'ely unspecialized middle leg of a grasshopper.

forelimbs are adapted for grasping, some for running, some for flying, and some for swimming, but all are constructed upon the same basic pattern.

To the biologist these homologous structures indicate relationship. All vertebrates have this basic limb pattern because they inherited it from an ancestor that had pentadactyl (five-digit) limbs. All insect legs are composed of five parts that always occur in the same order. Starting at their attachment on the thorax, these parts are coxa, trochanter, femur, tibia, and tarsus.

These parts are single segments except the tarsus, which varies from one to five segments. There have been many adaptive changes in insect legs during the evolution of the group. Many insects have a simple type of walking legs, such as the first and second legs of the grasshopper.

Figure elsewhere in this chapter shows the middle leg of a grasshopper. The hind leg of the grasshopper, however, is modified for jumping. The forelimbs of a mole cricket are modified for digging; the legs of a hog louse are adapted for clinging to hairs; the legs of a diving beetle are constructed for swimming; and the claws, pulvilli, and hairs of the tarsi of the common housefly make it possible for the fly to walk upside down.

There are many other modifications of the primitive-type insect leg, but perhaps the most interesting series of special adaptations is that found on the legs of the worker honey bee. The series of special adaptations found, on these legs functions in the collection of pollen.

This material serves as a source of protein for both adults and larvae. The undersurface of the body and the basal segments of the legs are covered with plumose hairs that become covered with pollen as the bee collects nectar from flowers.

The special modifications of the legs serve to concentrate the scattered pollen into a compact mass. Each *foreleg* has a fringe of short stiff hairs on one edge of the inner surface of the tibia that serves as an *eye brush* for cleaning the compound eyes.

The first segment of the tarsus of all of the legs is enlarged, and this segment of the forelegs is covered with long hairs that serve as *pollen brushes* for the removal of the pollen from the plumose hairs on the forepart of the body.

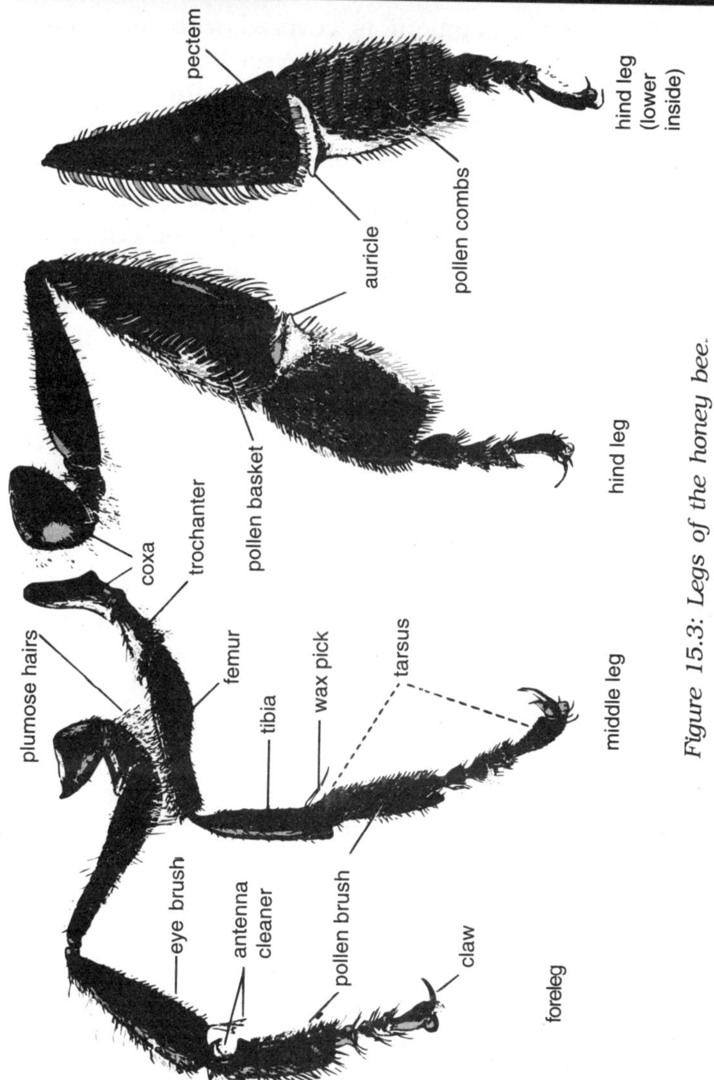

Figure 15.3: Legs of the honey bee.

A notch in this first segment of the tarsus, together with a spur on the end of the tibia, constitutes the *antenna cleaner*. The bee removes the pollen that adheres to the antennae by pulling them through these notches. The *middle* leg is less specialized than the foreleg.

The first tarsal segment is covered with long hairs that serve as *a pollen brush* for removing pollen from the forelegs and the thorax. The *spine* on the end of the tibia functions in the removal of wax from the wax glands on the ventral region of the abdomen.

The most specialized legs in the series are the *hind* legs. The inner surface of the first tarsal segment bears several rows of *pollen combs* that are used to comb out the pollen from the middle legs and the posterior part of the abdomen.

A single stout comb, the *pecten,* is located at the end of the tibia. This is used to remove the pollen from the combs of the opposite leg. The pollen so removed falls on the flattened upper end of the first tarsal segment.

This flattened region is called the *auricle.* When the leg is flexed, the auricle is pressed against the end of the tibia; this action compresses the pollen and pushes it into the *pollen basket* on the outer surface of the tibia.

A concavity in the outer surface of the tibia forms the bottom of the basket and long curved hairs form its sides. Any interested person, in a place where honey bees are active, can easily find a worker bee with a large lump of pollen in each of its baskets.

When the baskets are filled, the bee returns to the hive and places the pollen in special cells. This complex series of special adaptations is one of the most remarkable to be found anywhere in the animal kingdom.

Not only have the legs of insects undergone many modifications in their evolution, but so also have the mouth parts. During arthropod evolution the mouth parts have been derived from the primitive type of appendage.

The more primitive insects, such as the grasshopper, have *chewing* mouth parts. Three pairs of head appendages form the mouth parts: the *mandibles*, the *maxillae*, and the second maxillae fused to form the *labium*. Many variations of the primitive chewing mouth parts are found in the different insect groups.

The honey bee has a chewing-lapping type of mouth parts. The mandibles are similar to the chewing type, but the maxillae and labium are elongated to form a sort of lapping tongue. A variety of forms, including lice, mosquitoes, and aphids, have *piercingsucking* mouth parts. There are several structural variations of this type, but they all follow the same general pattern.

The labium forms a long protective tube for the other parts. The mandibles and maxillae are long slender structures that serve in piercing the skin of an animal or the epidermis of a plant, and also serve as the food channel up which the liquid is drawn.

In the strictly *sucking* type of mouth part, found in butterflies and moths, the mandibles are usually absent and the labium is represented only by the labial palps. The functional structure is formed by the two elongated maxillae.

Each maxilla forms a half tube, and when the two are-together, they form a long sucking proboscis. This proboscis is coiled under the head except when feeding. There are other modifications of insect mouth parts, but these will suffice to indicate that many adaptive changes have occurred.

Throughout the evolution of the arthropods, many modifications of the basic biramous appendage have occurred. Each of these modifications which persisted enabled its possessor to inhabit a different habitat and to lead a different type of existence, that is, the modification was adaptive.

Within a given group, such as the insects, the many different modifications of legs and mouth parts resulted in a great variety of forms adapted to life in different habitats. Such a process is called *adaptive radiation* or *divergent evolution* and is found many times in the course of evolution in many different groups. Another source of evidence of evolution from comparative anatomy is found in *vestigial*, or *rudimentary*, structures.

These are reduced and generally useless structures that are found in many plants and animals, relatives of which often have the structures in a fully developed and functional condition. The snakes as a group are limbless vertebrates, but in the group to which the pythons and boas belong, the members have vestiges of a pelvic girdle and hind limbs.

Externally there is no sign of hind limbs in the whale, but embedded in the blubber are the much-reduced bones of the pelvic girdle and hind limbs. There are more than 100 vestigial structures in humans. Some of our vestigial structures are ear muscles, tail (*coccyx*), tail muscles, and possibly the appendix. In the study of comparative anatomy, structures are often found that have the same function and are *superficially* alike, such as the wing of a bird and the wing of a butterfly, yet are quite different in origin and in structural design. Such structures are said to be *analogous*.

They have arisen in the evolutionary process through adaptations of quite different organisms to similar modes of life. The flying adaptation was developed independently in three different groups of vertebrates: reptiles, birds, and bats.

The pterodactyl, an extinct flying reptile, had a wing formed by a fold of skin stretched between the body and the posterior surface of the forelimb and a greatly elongated outer digit. In birds the feathers are inserted on all three major segments of the forelimb.

The wing of the bat is composed of a membrane extending from the body to the forelimb, where its main support is formed by the four very elongated digits. When a comparison of the bones of the forelimbs of these three flying vertebrates is made, they are seen to be homologous.

However, as organs of flight, they are only analogous; different structures have been involved in adaptations for flight. There are many instances where different organisms that are not very closely related have developed similar adaptations for life in similar habitats.

This phenomenon is often referred to as *convergent evolution.* The development of the same fusiform type of body for life in the water by a shark (fish), the extinct *Ichthyosaurus* (reptile), and a dolphin (mammal) illustrates this very well.

EVIDENCE FROM DEVELOPMENT

The embryos of higher animals repeat many of the stages through which embryos of lower animals have passed. This has been referred to as *recapitulation.* This concept, as originally used by von Baer, indicated that some of the developmental stages of an organism are similar to some of the developmental stages of its ancestors.

Unfortunately, however, Haeckel modified the concept to mean that in its development, the individual passes through stages like the adult stages of its ancestors. Modern students of development insist that Haeckel's version is wrong.

As a matter of fact, our present knowledge of the heriditary mechanisms tends to support the views of von Baer. Several examples of recapitulation have been described in a previous section.

In the development of any mammalian embryo, the heart is a four-chambered in-series structure, as it is in fish embryos; then it develops partitions of the auricles (atria) similar to those of amphibian embryos, followed by ventricular division that is incomplete for a period, as it is in the embryos of reptiles.

The existence of a common trochophore larval stage in the development of many mollusks and many annelids is also typical of this process. There are many examples of recapitulation during embryonic development, but one of the best is afforded by a comparison of different vertebrate embryos at comparable stages in development.

In the first stage in the illustration all the embryos look very much alike. All have similar segmentally arranged *somites* and similar *pharyngeal arches* and *pharyngeal clefts*. In the second row the *limbbud* primordia are forming on all embryos in a similar way, and all of them have embryonic tails.

The embryos of the lizard, chick, pig, and human have strong resemblances, yet those of the fish and the salamander are beginning to assume recognizable forms. At this stage, gills have formed from the tissue lining the gill clefts of both the fish and the salamander.

Later each embryo has developed features that indicate fairly clearly its definitive nature. Why, it may be asked, do the embryos of reptiles, birds, and mammals develop similar pharyngeal modifications without ever having functional gills?

The best answer to this seems to be the same one that was given as an explanation of the presence of homologous bones in the appendages of adult vertebrates.

They have developed from a common ancestor and they possess a common heredity for the manifestation of these characteristics, and their persistence usually means they have adaptive value. For instance, although gills are not formed, the pharynx is a site of similar derivatives in all vertebrates.

EVIDENCE FROM PALEONTOLOGY

Paleontology is the study of the life of past geologic ages, and it is based on the fossil remains of ancient plants and animals. The evidence of evolution provided by fossils is the most forceful and direct evidence of evolution which we have. A *fossil* is some evidence of an animal or plant that lived a long time ago.

Kinds of Fossils

In the main, the hard parts of organisms (teeth, skeletal parts, and shells) are preserved as fossils. Occasionally animals are preserved with little or no change from the time of death. In 1929 a Russian worker described the finding of a frozen mammoth (an extinct form related to elephants) in Siberia. It was estimated that the animal had been preserved in the frozen state for approximately 25,000 years, yet the flesh was so well preserved that it could be, and was, eaten by dogs.

Numerous specimens of insects, spiders, and mites have been found preserved in amber in the Baltic region of Europe. During the Oligocene period, about 38 million years ago, northern Europe was covered with coniferous forests. The trees in these forests exuded a sticky resin that trapped the spiders, mites, and insects.

The resin ultimately hardened into amber, with the arthropods embedded in it. In some cases the preservation is so good that the colors do not seem to have changed.

Land animals occasionally have been covered with windblown sand or volcanic ash, or have been trapped in bogs, quicksand, or asphalt pits, and their hard parts have been preserved. Still other fossils are in the form of *molds*, or casts.

The shells, bones, and other parts of organisms may have became embedded in mud or silt that later became rock. In time the entire original specimen may have dissolved, leaving a cavity. The wall of this cavity contains an impression of the exterior of the original structure, and this constitutes a natural mold.

If some plastic substance is pressed into such a mold, the external replica of the original object can be obtained. Natural casts are formed in a slightly different way. If a clamshell, with its two valves closed, is buried in mud or sand, a natural mold may be formed, as has just been described, or a natural cast may be formed.

If, in the burial process, mineral matter fills the cavity and then the shell is completely dissolved, later leaving the mineral matter in the cavity in a hardened condition, a natural cast will be formed. The two most important conditions favoring fossilization are the possession of hard parts and immediate burial.

It should be clear that when a dead animal or plant is left exposed, it soon disappears as the result of the activity of scavengers and the bacteria and fungi of decay. Even the bones of horses and cattle that die on the plains soon disappear.

The chance of any exposed organism becoming fossilized is very slight indeed. Immediate burial is a prerequisite to the process; by far the most common kind of burial favorable for fossilization is that provided by waterborne sediments.

Sedimentary Rocks

To understand the nature of the formation of *sedimentary rocks,* one must take into account certain natural processes *that are occurring in* the world today and that have been occurring since the crust of the earth was formed.

By the process of *erosion,* through the action of wind and rain, and of freezing and thawing, rocks are gradually broken into the small particles that form soil. Through the action of rain the particles of the soil are carried into streams and rivers and ultimately into lakes or oceans.

This sedimentary material carries with it the bodies of many aquatic organisms and also the bodies of terrestrial forms that happen to be swept along by the streams and rivers. The hard parts of some of these organisms may be preserved, and in the course of time the sedimentary deposit, owing to the pressure of the water above it and also to chemical reactions, is converted into sedimentary rock. The nature of the sedimentary material determines the kind of sedimentary rock formed; limestone, sandstone, and shale are familiar kinds.

The method of formation of sedimentary rocks clearly distinguishes them from *igneous rocks*, which were formed by the solidification of molten material when the earth cooled, and are being formed by cooling of magma expelled from active volcanoes.

An understanding of the layers of sedimentary rock found M many places on the earth must take into account another natural process, the changes that have occurred in the past and that are still occurring between land and sea.

Slowand gradual changes in level between the land and the sea are now in process. For instance, it is now recognized that the land on the eastern coast of the United States is gradually sinking into the sea, whereas the land on the Pacific coast is gradually rising.

The sinking of land below the sea is called *submergence,* and the rising of land above the sea is called *emergence.* In the geologic past, many regions of the earth have undergone a series of submergences and emergences.

As a consequence, in many places a whole series of different layers of sedimentary rocks is found. A good place to see such a series of layers, or strata, is the Grand Canyon of the Colorado. Just as a person looks at a brick wall and realizes that the bottommost tier of brick was the first laid by the brick mason and the upper tiers were last in order, so must a person who views the mile-deep series of strata in the Grand Canyon realize that the deepest layers were deposited first and the other layers in succession at later periods of time.

This simple concept in geology is called the *law of superposition.* If each formed layer of rock were left undisturbed until another layer was deposited on top of it, one would have a perfect series for the study of fossil forms.

The rock record of the earth, however, is not so complete. Layers deposited under water can emerge as land and be partially or completely eroded away.

If a new submergence then occurs and a new layer of sedimentary rock is formed, there will be an unconformity between the two strata.

This lack of sequence between layers makes the study and identification of the strata difficult, but over 150 years ago in England, William Smith determined that each stratum is characterized by certain index fossils.

Thus it is possible to identify similar strata in different parts of the world. Another factor complicating the interpretation of the geologic record involves the numerous foldings and splittings that have occurred in the earth's crust.

Mountain ranges are formed by such foldings, and quite often a split in the fold occurs with a thrust of part of the fold over the rest. As a result of this, older strata are found to lie over younger ones. Also, fossils that were once formed may be destroyed in the formation of *metamorphic rock*.

As a result of great pressure and heat, deep layers may melt. When this material later solidifies again, the fossils originally present will usually be lost. Limestone isa form of sedimentary rock rich in fossils.

When limestone melts and crystallizes into metamorphic rock the result is marble. In spite of the paucity of fossil formation, the unconformities in the rocks, the overthrusts, the destruction of fossils by erosion and by the formation of metamorphic rocks, and other factors not mentioned here, the story of the rocks is a very convincing one with reference to evolution.

Determining the Age of Rocks

In the past, geologists and paleontologists were able to make fairly accurate estimations of the age of different rock strata by using the known rate of the accumulation of salt in the oceans. More recently the use of radioactive elements has provided a better method. The element uranium changes into an isotope of lead and helium through a long series of transformations.

The rate of this change is known, and the rate of change is independent of the conditions under which it occurs. This rate is such that 7,600,000 g of uranium yield 1 g of lead per year. Thus when a piece of igneous rock is found that contains both uranium and lead, its age can be determined.

If sedimentary rock containing fossils is associated with this igneous rock, its age is assumed to be the same. Only a few rocks have been dated by this method, but fortunately they are widely scattered in geologic time. The oldest rocks that have been dated by radioactive measurements are over3000 million years old.

Others are Cambrian deposits over 500 million years old, Permian deposits about 270 million years old, and Eocene deposits about 55 million years old. Recently the transformation of radioactive potassium to argon and rubidium to strontium has been used in a similar way for dating fossilbearing rocks. By the mid-1960s, rocks from a number of localities were dated at approximately 3500 million years.

There are indications that still older rocks exist. The exact age of the earth is still undetermined, but evidence from several sources suggests an age in the neighborhood of 4500 million years. For very recent fossils, 20,000 years old or less, the decay of carbon-14 has been very useful.

All organisms contain a relatively constant proportion of this isotope, and upon death no additional isotope is incorporated. All organisms are constantly incorporating

^{14}C in life in a balance equal to that in the atmosphere and at death ^{14}C starts to decay to ^{12}C with no new ^{14}C added. Measurement of the remaining isotope gives an estimate of the time since death.

The Geological Timetable

Geologists, as a result of their studies of the strata of sedimentary rocks in the different regions of the world, have classified geologic history into six eras. The oldest era with fossils is the *Archeozoic* (era of primitive life) and this is followed in turn by the *Proterozoic* (era of early life), the *Paleozoic* (era of ancient life), the *Mesozoic* (era of medieval life), and the *Cenozoic (era* of modern life).

The Paleozoic, *Mesozoic, and* Cenozoic eras are divided into *periods,* and the periods of the Cenozoic into epochs. There is evidence that between the different eras there were widespread geologic disturbances called *revolutions.*

In some of these revolutions a large part of the existing forms of life was destroyed. Table elsewhere in this chapter shows the eras and some of their subdivisions, the approximate duration of each era, some of the important geological features, and the characteristic animals and plants. Plants are added to make the period complete. It is not possible to describe the many interesting aspects of the fossil record here. However, a few of the outstanding things should be mentioned.

The Mesozoic era, often called the "Age of Reptiles," is interesting for a number of reasons. The largest animals that have lived on land, the dinosaurs, were dominant during this era. Many different orders of reptiles evolved and flourished, but only four kindslizards, snakes, crocodiles, and turtles-persisted into the Cenozoic.

It is clear that both the birds and mammals evolved from reptilian ancestors during this era. The earliest fossil bird, called *Archaeopteryx,* was found in the rocks of the Jurassic period. It was about the size of a crow and in certain respects quite like a reptile.

The tail, quite unlike that of modern birds, was long with a row of feathers on each side. The jaws were equipped with conical teeth. The wings were small relative to body size, and three of the digits on each forelimb persisted, armed with claws.

It is probable that the forelimbs were used for climbing as well as for flying. John Ostrom of Yale University has concluded that every bird in the world today is a lineal descendant of the coelurosaurs, an infraorder of small bipedal carnivorous saurischian dinosaurs that flourished from late Triassic times until the end of the *Cretaceous*.

Ostrom has examined the four existing fossils of *Archaeopteryx* and has concluded that were it not for the fact that clear imprints of feathers accompany the four skeletons, all four would probably have been identified as coelurosaurs.

It is his opinion that those forms which possessed feathers at that time in geologic history survived, while those that were bare-skinned did not, because the feathers gave them insulation from extreme heat and cold. The *mammals* of the *Mesozoic* were generally small and *inconspicuous* when compared with the large *reptiles*.

However, with the extinction of all the very large reptiles at the end of the Mesozoic, the Cenozoic era is marked by the great adaptive radiation of mammals, and it is often called the "Age of Mammals."

The rocks of the Cenozoic era furnish, in many instances, very detailed records of the evolution of different mammalian lines, including those leading to our modern horses, elephants, and camels.

Evolution of the Horse

Figure elsewhere in this chapter illustrates some of the stages in the evolution of the modern horse. The earliest known horse, *Eohippus*, lived in the Eocene epoch.

It was about the size of a fox terrier dog, but with a longer head. Its legs were short, with four toes on each front foot and three on each hind foot. The third digit was somewhat longer than the others. All the toes were placed on the ground and used in walking.

Eohippus was a forest *dweller*, subsisting on soft vegetation. The molar teeth were much like human molars. This animal lived in North America during the *Eocene* and *migrated* to Europe during the same epoch.

A number of different lines evolved from *Eohippus*, but only some of the stages in the direct line of evolution to the modern horse are shown in the figure. A number of changes or adaptations are seen in the evolution of the modern horse from its ancestor in the Eocene.

The most important of these changes are the following. The enlargement and elongation of the third digit, with a loss of the other digits; the elongation of the forepart of the skull; the development of the premolars and molars into high-crown, continuously growing grinders; and a general increase in body size.

All these changes were adaptations for life in open plains country where the primary source of food was grass. The enlargement of the third digit and the loss of the others, together with the general increase in body size, made possible greater speed in escaping from enemies on the *grassy plains*.

The *elongation* of the *forepart of* the skull and the elongation of the neck are adaptations for grazing. The changes in the teeth are associated with the grinding of the coarse siliceous grasses. The evolution of these grasses occurred simultaneously with the evolution of the horse and probably served as a selective force acting upon the horses.

Merychippus, a horse of the Miocene, was about the size of a small pony. It carried all its weight on the third digit of each foot with the other digits dangling at the sides. The first representative of the modern horse, *Equus*, appeared in late Pliocene times.

In the modern horse the side toes are reduced to the vestigial splint bones that are often fused to the metacarpal or metatarsal of the enlarged third digit. During the Pleistocene, the genus *Equus* achieved nearly worldwide distribution.

As mentioned before, many different kinds of genera of horses evolved during the Cenozoic, and only a part of them were in the direct line of evolution of *Equus*. *Eohippus* gave rise to several different lines, *Merychippus* gave rise to others, and so on. Some of them remained as browsers, others became grass feeders, but by the time of the appearance of the modern horse, all the other lines had become extinct.

It is interesting to note that although the continent of North America provided the place for the greater part of horse evolution, horses became extinct on this continent by the close of the Pleistocene.

The causes of this extinction are not fully understood. At any rate there were no horses in North America when the continent was discovered by the white man. The so-called "wild horses" in both North and South America are descendants of horses, brought over by the early explorers and colonists, that escaped or were allowed to run wild.

General Nature of the Fossil Record

The most important features of the fossil record can be summarized as follows.

1. The most primitive forms of life are found in the oldest rocks.
2. Moving up through the various strata, from older to more recent formations, there is a succession of higher and more complex forms of life.
3. In many instances a group arose in one period

or era and remained scarce, but in the next period or era it became dominant after undergoing adaptive radiation.

4. There have been many extinctions of large groups, but after the establishment of all *major* phyla, *some* species of each *phylum* have persisted down to the present.
5. None of the past forms of life are exactly like any of those now living.

EVIDENCE FROM GEOGRAPHICAL DISTRIBUTION

Other interesting evidences of evolution are found in studies of the present distribution of different kinds of animals and plants on the earth, especially when this distribution is considered in connection with the fossil record.

One might assume, on the theory of special creation, that the regions of the world with similar climates and similar environmental conditions would be inhabited by the same kinds of animals and plants. But this is not so generally.

The conditions for life in the African and American deserts are much the same, yet the flora and fauna of the two regions are quite different.

Tropical rainforests in different parts of the world afford the same conditions for existence, but the animals and plants in an African rainforest are not the same as those found in a South American rainforest. A very interesting aspect of the study of geographical distribution is the phenomenon of *discontinuous distribution.*

A few examples will illustrate. The only places where marsupials are native in the world today are Australia, the eastern United States, and South America. There are many kinds of marsupials found in Australia: kangaroos, koalas, wombats, and bandicoots, to mention a few.

The opossum is the only marsupial in the United States, and there are a few marsupials in South America. When the white man first appeared in Australia, there were no placental mammals on the entire continent except for some bats, the native human inhabitants, and some dogs and mice that were probably introduced when the first humans arrived there.

That Australia is suited for placental mammals has been demonstrated; all that have been introduced there have thrived.

This discontinuous distribution of marsupials can be accounted for by the geological record. There is evidence that Australia was connected with the other land masses during the Mesozoic, and at that time the-marsupials spread from South America to Antarctica and then to Australia.

After the land connections were broken, placental mammals, except for flying forms and humans, were unable to reach Australia.

In addition, the fossil record shows that marsupials were at one-time widely distributed over Europe, Asia, and North America.

In competition with placental mammals, the marsupials became extinct in most regions of the earth other than Australia. The distribution of the members of the camel family is another case.

Members of this family are found today in parts of Africa, Asia, and South America. The llama of the Andes is a member of the camel family. The fossil record shows that members of the camel group once existed over Asia, Europe, and North America.

During a part of the Cenozoic era, Asia and North America were connected in the Bering Strait region, and this served as a bridge for the spread of many different forms. But after the widespread distribution of the camel group, extinction occurred in most of the regions, leaving the present discontinuous distribution.

The flora and fauna of oceanic islands also provide evidence of evolution. Oceanic islands are of recent geological origin.

In the main, the species of animals and plants found on such islands are peculiar to them but are most like those forms found on the nearest mainland. As a young man, Charles Darwin became interested in the animals on the Galapagos Islands, 500 miles off the west coast of South America.

He found that 23 of the 26 species of land birds on the islands were peculiar to the archipelago, yet they were all obviously related to the birds of South America. He found 11 kinds of giant tortoise, each kind inhabiting a different island. They were all related, but those farthest apart were most unlike.

There were no land mammals on the islands and no amphibians, yet many habitats on the island were suitable for their existence. In considering the evidence of evolution from geographical distribution, one must keep in mind these things. Each type of organism had a place of *origin* in the beginning.

As the type increased in numbers, the members would tend to spread slowly or *disperse* from this region of origin into all suitable territory, and during this process evolutionary changes might occur.

Often *barriers* of some kind, such as oceans or high mountains, stopped the dispersal process. In the course of time, because of geological changes or action of enemies, *extinctions* over large areas might occur, and this would result in a discontinuous distribution.

Continental Drift

In the above discussion reference was made to a former' land bridge in the Bering Strait region. Other former land bridges are known. The Isthmus of Panama now constitutes a land bridge between North and South America.

However, this bridge has not always existed. Through

much of the geologic past the two Americas were not connected. That land bridges have played important roles in the past movements of plant and animals is a certainty.

In the past it has been assumed that the continents in general have been fixed masses, that there has been no lateral movement of continents. In explaining the distribution of fossils, where very similar forms are found in widely separated regions, such as the finding of very similar fossils of snails and earthworms in Africa and South America, hypothetical former land bridges between the two continents have been proposed.

The idea of continental drift was originally proposed by A. Wegener early in this century. According to his thinking, at one time the continents of Africa and South America were connected. (Anyone looking at the western coastline of Africa and the eastern coastline of South America on a map will see that they fit together like two pieces of a jig-saw puzzle.)

Wegener presented many evidences supporting his concept of continental drift, but geologists and geophysicists were not attracted of it. However, in the past decade evidence from a variety of measurements and observations by geophysicists has convinced most workers in this field that continental drift has occurred, and, for that matter, is still occurring.

This concept has been heralded as a revolution in the earth sciences that will rank in its effects on the earth sciences with organic evolution and its effect on biology. According to this concept, about 200 million years ago during the Mesozoic, the various land masses of the earth had moved together and formed one continuous land mass, called Pangaea.

Twenty million years later this single mass had separated into two masses *-Laurasia* and *Gondwana.* Laurasia contained North America, Greenland, and Eurasia. Gondwana contained South America, Africa,

India, Australia, and Antarctica. These two land masses broke up and the present continents moved apart through the rest of the Mesozoic and through the Cenozoic to give the positions found today. By the end of the Mesozoic the South Atlantic had widened into a major ocean.

Widening of the North Atlantic came later. With this concept of the history of the earth, it is no longer necessary to postulate hypothetical land bridges to explain the finding of very similar fossils on widely separated continents.

Colbert has recently described how the distribution of many land vertebrates and the fossils of many vertebrates can best be explained on the basis of continental drift. For example, the fossil remains of the reptile, *Lystrosaurus*, have been found in South Africa, Antarctica, and India.

This distribution can be easily understood on the assumption that continental drift has occurred. The idea of continental drift is now associated with the modern geological concept of plate tectonics.

According to this the surface of the earth is divided into a number of huge plates, each including not only a continental mass but some of the surrounding ocean basin as well, and these plates are and have been constantly moving in relation to each other.

The interested student should consult *Continents Adrift*, *The Dynamic Earth*, and *The Restless Earth*, listed at the end of the chapter. Associated with the movement and collision of these plates are earthquakes, volcanic action, and mountain formation. One of the most interesting movements, to this writer, was the movement of the Indian plate to join with Laurasia in the formation of the present Indian peninsula.

This was a long journey across the Tethys Sea, and it opened the Indian Ocean behind it. The collision occurred about 50 million years ago and resulted in the formation of the world's, greatest mountains, the Himalayas. You may ask, "What was the situation with respect to land masses before Pangaea?"

Much remains to be learned, but Palmer (1974), in his article "Search for the Cambrian World," indicates that there were probably four major continents in the north and Gondwanaland, as described above, in the south at that time in the earth's history.

EVIDENCE FROM BIOCHEMISTRY

Probably the first use of biochemical techniques in evolutionary studies was the use of the precipitation test developed by Nuttall early in this century. This test is based on the antigenantibody reaction already discussed. Nuttall prepared antihuman serum by injecting a rabbit with small amounts of human blood serum over a period of time.

When blood was then drawn from this rabbit and the serum was allowed to separate, this serum was used in making tests. By mixing a small amount of this rabbit serum with human blood, a heavy precipitate was formed. This indicated that the rabbit serum contained antibodies that precipitated certain proteins in human blood.

This was a good test for human blood, but it was not entirely species specific. When some of the serum from the immunized rabbit was added, in equal amounts, to five test tubes, and to these were then added sera from a human, an ape, an Old World monkey, a New World monkey, and a lemur, a precipitate formed in each tube, in decreasing amounts, however, from human to lemur.

This serological test then supported the theories of primate relationship that had been arrived at earlier from studies in comparative anatomy. Since the work of Nuttall, the precipitin tests have been used many times to verify or clarify other relationships.

For instance, it has been possible to show that the horseshoe crab is related to the Arachnida, that whales are most closely related to the even-toed ungulates like the hog, and that the rabbit, long placed with the rodents, is not very closely related to them.

Evolution of Hemoglobins

From what has been said in earlier discussions, it is fair to say that the DNA and protein molecules in every living organism are living documents of evolutio-nai'v history. A new discipline, *paleogenetics,* has emer-ged with the goal of determining how evolution proceeds at the molecular level.

Although only a little is known, as yet, about the linear sequence of nucleotides that carry the code for a single gene in a molecule of DNA, the sequence of amino acid residues in several polypeptide chains has been determined. Each amino acid in such chains was specified by a three-letter code in the DNA.

Emile Zuckerkandl states that enough is now known about the amino acid sequence in several polypeptides to enable a paleogeneticist to begin the study. Zuckerk-andl selected the hemoglobin molecule for his study, which involved the testing of three basic postulates.

(1) Polypeptide chains present in living organisms today have arisen by evolutionary divergence from similar polypeptide chains that existed in the past. The present and past chains would have many of the amino acids in the same places in the chains and would be homologous.

(2) A gene existing in some organism of the past might occasionally be duplicated, with the result that it is present at two or more sites in the genome of present-day organisms. Such an organism with two or more homologous genes would have two or more homologous polypeptide chains. Since these homologous genes could undergo mutations independently, their derived

polypeptide chains would not be identical in all their amino acids.

(3) The mutations most commonly selected in the evolutionary process are those that result in the replacement of a single amino acid in a polypeptide chain.

The study involved the protein *myoglobin* as well as various hemoglobins. Myoglobin serves as an oxygen repository in muscle, and an ancestral myoglobin apparently was the base molecule from which the hemoglobins were derived.

John Kendrew, in 1958, determined the three dimensional structure and the amino acid sequence in sperm whale myoglobin. This was the first complete determination of the structure of any protein molecule.

Since that time the structure of several hemoglobins has been determined; these include hemoglobin chains from humans, gorilla, pig, horse, cow, and rabbit. The three-dimensional structure of myoglobin and the various hemoglobin chains are very similar.

While the myoglobin molecule is a single chain associated with an iron-containing heme group, a hemoglobin molecule consists of four polypeptide chains, with each chain enfolding a heme group. In adult humans the principal kind of hemoglobin is composed of two a chains and two β chains, and it is assumed that they have a common ancestry. In people the β chains are sometimes replaced with other chains -γ, δ, and ε chains.

The ε chain is found for only a brief period in early development. The γ chain replaces the β chain during most of the embryonic development, and in adult life a small amount of the hemoglobin contains δ chains instead of β chains. The amino acid sequence is known for all the chains except the ε chain.

The α chain contains 141 amino acid residues, whereas the β, γ, and δ chains all contain 146. The differences could be explained by deletions or addition in the genetic material. When the α and β chains are compared, there are 77 sites different and 64 the same.

There are only 39 differences in amino acids between the β and γ chains, and only 10 between the β and δ chains. There are much greater differences between the whale myoglobin and the hemoglobin chains of humans.

There are 37 sites alike in the myoglobin and human a chains, and 35 alike in the myoglobin and human β chains. How can it be argued that all these chains are homologous when there are so many differences between some of them?

It seems quite improbable that different and unrelated polypeptide chains could evolve in such a way as to have the same function, the same three-dimensional configuration, and a substantial number of amino acids at corresponding sites.

The marked difference in amino acid sequence would seem to be an indication that a long time has elapsed since they diverged from a common ancestor. The number of differences in amino acid sequence between the α and β chains of the horse, the pig, the cow, and the rabbit and the corresponding human chains were determined.

The mean difference is 22 changes in the two chains. Assuming that the rate of mutations is the same in both chains, this would be an average of 11 changes per chain. From other evidence it is assumed that the common ancestor of presentday mammals lived about 80 million years ago.

This means that the average time to establish an amino acid substitution is about 7 million years. This information has been used to estimate roughly the time of the origin of the different human chains and the whale myoglobin chain from an ancestral chain through the process of gene duplications.

The rough estimates of the time of these divergences

are as follows: the β and δ chains, 35 million years ago; the γ chain, 150 million years ago; the a chain, 380 million years ago; and the myoglobin chain, 650 million years ago.

Zuckerkandl points out that techniques are now available for the determination of ancestral residues and for the construction of molecular phylogenetic trees. Such studies in the future, when many more polypeptide chains have been analyzed for their amino acid sequences, should provide additional evidence of evolution.

EVIDENCE FROM DOMESTICATION

Every state fair, every dog or cat show, and every horse show furnishes numerous examples of evolution through domestication. In a comparatively short period of time, with reference to the whole process of evolution, humans through their practices of selection and breeding, have developed a tremendous variety of domesticated animals and plants.

The different varieties of dogs, chickens, cattle, horses, and so forth, have been derived from original wild types. Darwin recognized this and made use of it in formulating his theory, to be discussed later. He realized that, in domestication, humans do the selecting in the evolutionary process, whereas in nature all the factors of the environment act in the process.

EVIDENCE FROM TAXONOMY AND GENETICS

The fact that living organisms can be fitted into a scheme of classification, involving species, genera, famili-es, orders, classes, and phyla, is best interpreted as indicating evolutionary relationship. Also the fact that the genetic material in nearly all species is found as variations of DNA makes evolution in all of its ramific-ations more readily comprehensible.

Chapter 16 HUMAN EVOLUTION

The preceding chapter presented abundant evidence that animals have evolved. What about humans? This chapter considers this question. Although there are, at the present time, a few gaps in the fossil record and a few places where the relationships of some of the fossils are not clear, the general picture is clear— humans have evolved like all other living things.

In earlier discussions the relation of humans to other vertebrates has been indicated. A comparison of the different organ systems in humans and any other vertebrate shows a similarity of structure throughout. Humans, like all other mammals, possess hair and mammary glands.

As a primate, the human being shares with the other members of the order such characteristics as one pair of mammary glands, nails instead of claws, hands with opposable thumbs for grasping and handling objects, and eyes directed anteriorly instead of laterally.

Another pharacteristic of primates, when compared with other mammals, is the proportionately greater brain development that seems to have originated as an adaptation or specialization for life in trees.

ORIGIN OF PRIMATES

In the late Mesozoic the two main groups of mammals, the marsupials and placentals, were in existence. Placental mammals of this period were small insect eaters belonging to the order Insectivora and, at present, are known only from fossils collected in Mongolia.

They were generalized in nature, and it is believed that they gave rise to the other orders of placental mammals, including the primates. The tree shrews of the early Eocene, descendants of the insectivores, were probably the first primates and the ancestors of higher primates.

EVOLUTION OF PRIMATE

During the Eocene several lines developed from this ancestral stock of primates. One line gave rise to the *lemurs.* They are small treeliving animals and at present are found mainly on the Island of Madagascar. They resemble monkeys in many ways, having nails instead of claws and a long tail.

However, their faces are characterized by a prominent snout much like that of a dog. Another line developed into the tarsiers that are found today on some of the islands of the East Indies. They were also small with long tails, but the snout was greatly reducedand they had very large eyes and stereoscopic vision.

The lemurs and tarsiers and a few other forms are placed in the suborder Prosimii. Some of the Eocene prosimians were the ancestors of the higher primates. There is some evidence that the line that gave rise to the living tarsiers might have been ancestral to the higher groups. The higher primates—monkeys, apes, and humans-are placed in the suborder Anthropoidea.

The New World monkeys (family Cebidae) diverged from the ancestral stock late in the Eocene or in early Oligocene. These monkeys are flat-nosed with widely spaced nostrils in contrast to the other higher primates in which the nostrils are close together and point downward.

A striking trait of the New World monkeys is their

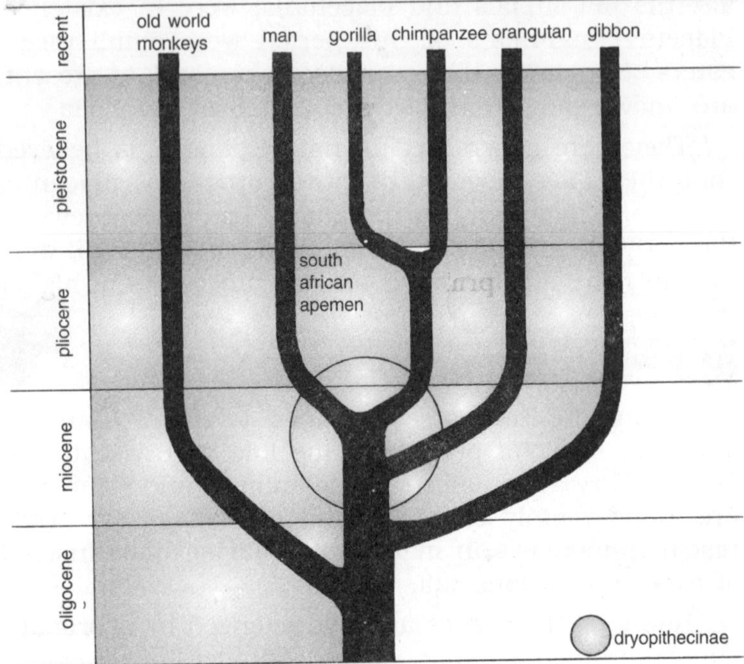

Figure 16.1: Family tree of humans and higher primates.

prehensile tail by which most of them can hang or swing from branches or which they can use like a hand. The New World monkeys have no direct bearing on the ancestry of the other primates. Figure elsewhere in this chapter shows suggested relationships among the other primates.

The Old World monkeys (family Cercopithecidae) probably arose from the ancestral line in the early Oligocene. They lack prehensile tails and some, like the baboon, have become terrestrial, living in rocky open country.

The other higher primates are placed in the superfamily Hominoidea-the apes in family Pongidae and humans in the family Hominidae. There are four groups of living apes—the gibbons, the orangutans, the gorillas, and the chimpanzees. The gibbon is indicated as having originated from the ancestral line late in the Oligocene. These forms, which are found today in Southeastern Asia and the East Indies, are most unlike the other three types of great apes. They have slender bodies and are highly specialized for swinging through the trees by their long arms.

The encircled region on Figure elsewhere in this chapter, labeled Proconsul, represents a group of fossil apes of the Miocene from Africa, Europe, and India. One genus of these, *Dryopithecus* (formerly called *Proconsul*), is among the less specialized and seems to be close to the ancestral forms of the other higher apes and of humans.

They did not have the very long arms which modern brachiators have by which they move hand over hand from one tree branch to another. Also they did not have the "simian shelf" on their jaws, which supports the strong muscles used in tearing and chewing the bark of trees; nor did they have the very large canine teeth characteristic of the higher apes.

The orangutan of Sumatra and Borneo is considered to have been derived from this ancestral group, whereas the chimpanzee and gorilla of Africa are believed to have diverged from a common ancestor later. With the exception of the gorilla, all the living great apes spend most of their lives in trees.

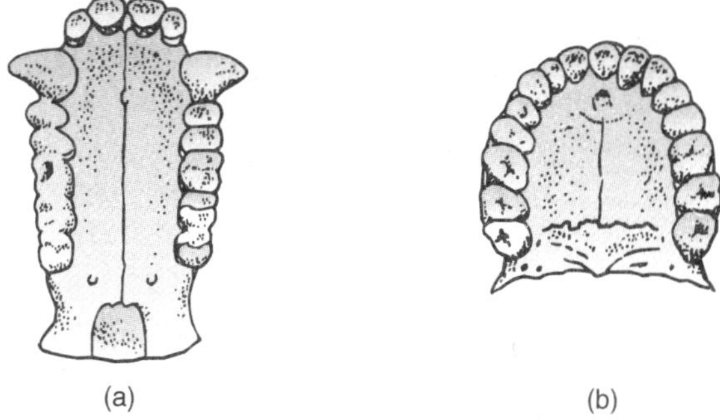

Figure 16.2: Dentition pattern in upper jaws. (a) ape. (b) Human.

Although a few of the monkeys lack tails, all of the apes do. In general the apes have relatively larger brains than the monkeys and are more intelligent.

FOSSIL HOMINDS

Although the number of human and subhuman fossils is not large, the record is extensive enough to reveal the evolutionary trends. It would take us too far afield to describe all the hominid fossils that have been found; only a few of the well authenticated ones are considered.

One of the problems in this area of study is to determine what distinguishes a true human from a manlike ape. Several criteria are used and the following are among the important ones.

1. A true human has upright posture, that is, he is bipedal. An expert anthropologist can tell by examining the femur and certain other bones whether the specimen walked upright or on all fours. Upright posture is an adaptation associated with life on the ground in contrast to life in trees.
2. A true human will have a brain distinctly larger than the brain of apes. It is customary to give the capacity of the skull in cubic centimeters in referring to brain size.
3. The teeth of humans generally are smaller than the teeth of apes and the canine teeth are also small. The changes in the teeth were associated with a change in diet from a vegetarian to one of at least some meat.
4. The teeth in the jaws of apes are arranged in a U shape, while in humans they form a curved row.
5. A true human is a tool maker. In studying fossil remains tools must be present with the fossil remains, or be found nearby, if toolmaking is to be associated with the specimen.

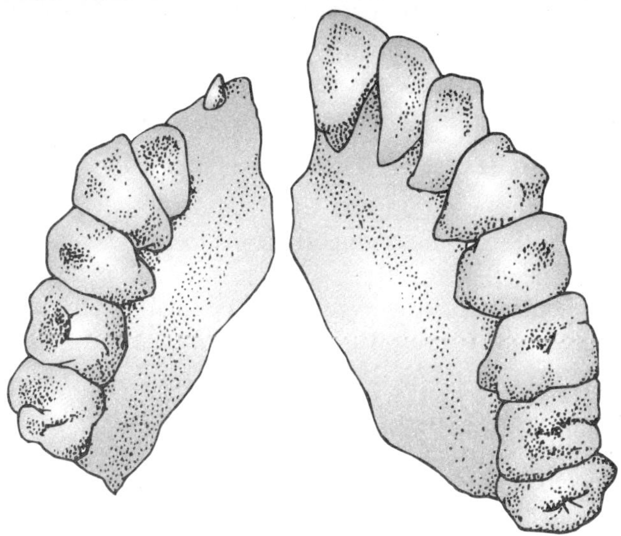

Figure 16.3: Part of the upper jaw of Ramapithecus. The shape is more humanlike than apelike.

One of the most distinguishing characteristics of humans is the use of language. Ordinarily it is not possible to tell whether a fossil specimen used language, although Alan Walker believes that he has detected in the underside of skull 1470 (to be discussed later) an area similar to Broca's area in modern man, the part of the brain that makes speech possible.

Three genera of the Hominidae are recognized: *Ramapithecus, Australopithecus,* and Homo.

Ramapithecus

Two species of *Ramapithecus* are recognized; one from East Africa and the other from the India-Pakistan border. They were found in late Miocene deposits and are dated from 9 to 14 million years ago. Parts of jaws and several teeth were found in each case.

At the present these fossils are considered to be the oldest known fossils in the family Hominidae, and they were probably derived from the dryopithecines. Their teeth were more humanlike than apelike.

The molar teeth were broad, shortened, flat, and compressed and of about equal size to those in humans, and the canine teeth were apelike in shape but about the size of human canines.

Australopithecus

There is a long gap in the human fossil record from 14 to 9 million years ago (the period of *Ramapithecus)* to the time of the oldest known Australopithecine, 5.5 million years ago. However, an ancestral strain or strains leading from *Ramapithecus* to *Australopithecus* must have existed during the Pliocene.

Australopithecus africanus was first found by R. Dart in 1924 in South Africa and was recognized as a possible missing link in the ancestry of humans. Since then parts of over 300 specimens have been unearthed.

They have been found not only in South Africa but also in East Africa (Tanzania, Kenya, Ethiopia) and Java. Fossils of A. *africanus* are dated from 5.5 to 1.5 millions years ago, while those of the related species, A. boisei, are dated from 3 to 1.2 million years ago. The evidence indicates that A. *africanus* was adapted for bipedal locomotion with essentially human dentition.

Estimates of height based on single leg bones range from 1.30 m to 1.68 m (4 feet, 3 inches to 5 feet, 6 inches). They were taller generally than *Ramapithecus,* but shorter generally than their successor Homo.

The cranial capacity ranges from 435 to 724 cubic centimeters ($crrr^3$). The face was rather massive, the jaws were large, the brow ridges were well developed, and there was no chin. In general it can be stated that the earlier specimens of *Australopithecus* were more like *Ramapithecus*, while the later specimens were more like *Homo.*

There was great variation in their structure during the 4½ million years of their existence. In recent years many of the fossil specimens of this genus were discovered by a man and wife team, Louis and Mary

Leakey, working in Olduvai Gorge, located in Tanzania, East Africa.

In 1959 Mary Leakey unearthed some primitive stone tools and an almost complete skull, which, to their amazement, turned out to be 1¾ million years old. This was almost a million years older than the oldest specimen of *Homo* known at that time. L. Leakey created a new genus for this specimen, *Zinjanthropus*, and stated that this represented the connecting link between the australopithicines and modern humans.

However, in 1961 the Leakeys made an even more striking find in the same deposits. They found another skull that looked much more similar to modern humans than *Zinjanthropus*. The teeth were more like those of modern humans, the cranium was much larger than that of *Zinjanthropus*, and it lacked the gorillalike crest at the top of the head.

Leakey called this creature *Homo habilis* and said that he was the true ancestor of humans. Leakey decided that *Zinjanthropus* was an australopithecine that lived alongside of *Homo habilis* for a long period before becoming extinct. There is now fairly general agreement on this, and *Zinjanthropus boisei* is now called *Australopithecus boisei*.

This species was more massive than A. *africanus*, was a herbivore with large grinding molars and reduced front teeth, and with a cranial capacity of about 530 cm^3.

By 1972 many workers were of the opinion that what Leakey has described as *Homo habilis* was just an advanced *Australopithecus africanus* and that *Homo erectus* evolved from this strain.

Recent Finds

Two discoveries, one in 1972 and one in 1974, have cast some doubt on the correctness of the human lineage as expressed in the preceding paragraph. In 1972 Richard Leakey, son of Louis and Mary Leakey,

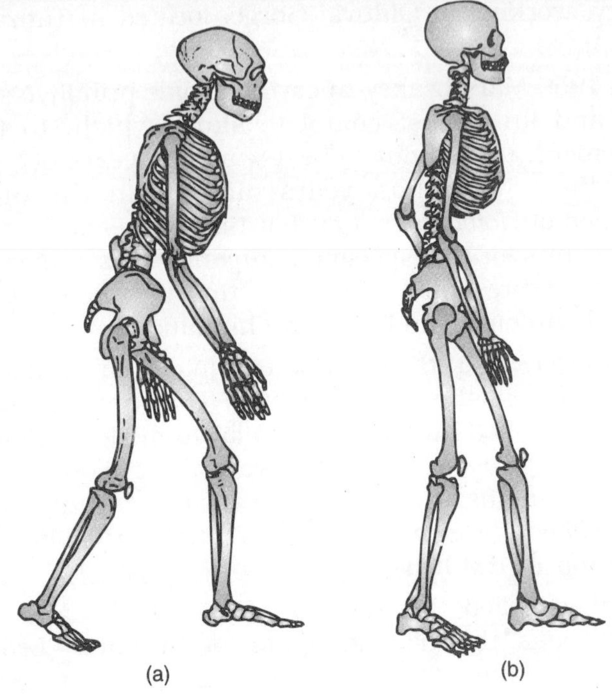

Figure 16.4: (a) Skeleton of Neanderthal man. (b) Skeleton of modern human.

and his party, working at Lake Rudolf in Kenya, found a human skull with a cranial capacity of about 800 cm^3.

This is about one third larger than the *Homo habilis* skull. And even more important is the fact that it was dated as almost 3 million years old, at least a million years older than *Homo habilis.* If the dating is correct, it means that a member of the genus *Homo* existed alongside the australopithecines for a long period of time. Richard Leakey has not named this specimen but refers to it as Skull no. 1470.

If other studies bear out the authenticity of this dating, this would be further evidence for discarding *Homo habilis* as a direct ancestor of modern humans. According to Richard Leakey, this may mean that there was a common ancestor of both the *Homo* line and the *Australopithecus* line in the period between 4 aRd 5 million years ago.

The *Australopithecus* line divided into the two species (already described) and the *Homo* line, of which skull no. 1470 is a part, gave rise to *Homo erectus* about a million years ago.

The latest finds, those of 1974, were made in Hadar river in north-central Ethiopia by Alemeyu Asfew of the four-nation Afar research expedition. He was working with D. Carl Johanson of Case Western Reserve University.

The finds here included a complete upper jaw, half of another upper jaw, and half of a lower jaw, all with teeth. The dating of these finds places them back as far as 4 million years ago. According to Johansen the small size of the teeth in these jawbones may well mean that genus *Homo* was walking, eating meat, and using tools as much as 4 million.years ago.

This latest find could fit right into the concept of Richard Leakey as given in the preceding paragraph.

Homo Erectus

Fossils of this species have been found in Africa (Olduvai), Java, Algeria, Germany, Hungary, and China. The oldest specimens were found in Africa and Java and are about 1 million years old. Outside of their skulls, the skeletons were much like that of modern humans.

The face was larger and the jaws were more powerful than those of modern humans. The skull was thick and heavily built. There was no chin. The cranial capacity was larger than any australopithecine, ranging from about 900 to almost 1100 cm^3.

Compared to modern humans it was a muscular, stocky, thickset creature with perhaps slightly longer arms and shorter legs. This human mastered fire, often lived in caves, and survived the northern winters. The earliest specimen of this species was unearthed at Trinil in Java in 1891 by Eugene Dubois.

He called it *Pithecanthropus erectus*, and it is often referred to as the "Java ape man." The first findings there consisted of a skull cap, a jaw fragment, and a femur bone. Later a numof other fossils were discovered there. Davidson Black discovered a number of fossils in a cave near Peking, China.

These humans lived at about the same time as the Java men and had the same characteristics. They left their hearths, their tools, their food remains, and many of their own bones in the cave. Black named this human *Sirianthropus pekinensis*, but it is now placed in the species *Homo erectus*, along with the Java man and others.

Homo erectus existed in the period from about 1 million years ago to about 300,000 years ago. After that time our ancestors become almost indistinguishable from modern humans.

Homo Sapiens

The fossil record is extremely sparse in the period between 300,000 and 100,000 years ago. There have been only eight finds in this period, four substantial ones and four fragmentary ones. There is enough evidence, however, to say the following about the humans of this period:

1. Their brain size was well within the range of modern humans.
2. Their bodies were indistinguishable from modern humans.
3. They had long skulls and heavily built faces and jaws.

Neanderthal Man

This man, originally called *Homo neanderthalensis*, lived in Europe from over 100,000 to about 35,000 years ago. The skeletal remains, some of them quite complete, of over 100 individuals have been studied. They have been found in deposits in Asia Minor, Africa, and Siberia, as well as in widely separated parts of Europe.

Neanderthal man was about 1.50 m (5 feet) tall and powerfully built. He walked with a slight stoop. His hands and feet were large. The cranial capacity was about 1400 cm^3, about the same as modern humans.

However, the shape of the skull was different; the forehead was low and slanting, there were heavy ridges projecting over the eyes, and there was no chin. This man lived primarily in caves, used fire, and made flint tools.

There is evidence that the Neanderthal man buried his dead with ornaments and flint tools, which has been interpreted as an indication that he had some form of belief in immortality of the spirit. Between 50,000 and 35,000 years ago the Neanderthal people were replaced by people like ourselves.

At this time it is not possible to say just what happened. In part of its range (western Europe) Neanderthal man showed little variability, and his replacement was rather sudden. In another part of his range (southern Africa) the two forms overlapped in time.

In still another part of his range (western Asia) intermediate specimens have been found. A number of skeletons of Upper Pleistocene age were found at Mount Carmel in Israel that show an odd mixture of Neanderthal and Cro-Magnon characteristics.

Some were tall, some had chins, and others did not. Some had high foreheads, some had low foreheads, and some had an intermediate condition.

Because of his rather abrupt disappearance in western Europe, some students have proposed the extermination of the Neanderthal type there by the more modern form who came in from the east.

Today more and more workers are suggesting that the Neanderthal race in western Europe just evolved into their successors or that they were genetically swamped by the invaders in crossbreeding.

Cro-Magnon Man (Homo Sapiens Sapiens)

This is one of the first modern humans. Fossils of this type have been found that date back at least 40,000 years. Although specimens have been found in several parts of Europe, western Asia and Africa, Cro-Magnon man is primarily known from numerous specimens found in a French cave.

The males averaged over 1.80 m (6 feet) in height, whereas the females were about 1.65 m (5 feet, 5 inches). The skull was of the modern type with a high forehead, no heavy ridges over the eyes, and a distinct chin. In addition to using stone for tools and weapons, this man also used bone.

Numerous bone needles have been found which they apparently used in making clothing. The CroMagnons are best known for their excellent drawings of contemporary animals on the walls of caves in France and Spain. The origin of the Cro-Magnons is not known, but one theory holds that they developed in Asia and then invaded Europe.

They were contemporaries of the Neanderthal man for many years and ultimately replaced him. The age of the Cro-Magnons was from about 40,000 to 10,000 years ago. They were expert hunters but did not develop agriculture or domesticate animals. These cultural activities came later, as did the use of metals in tool making.

Possible Relationships of Prehistoric Men

In the past it was customary to describe each new fossil and then represent it as a separate branch of the evolving human line. As a consequence none of the fossil men were ever indicated as being ancestral to any other type of man.

The present tendency among students of the field is

to move away from this view and to consider that all the prehistoric men, beginning at least with *Homo erectus*, belonged to the same genus, *Homo*. This concept assumes that throughout human evolution hominids living at any one time, although members of different races, have been capable of exchanging genes through interbreeding.

If the recent discoveries of fossil men dating back 3-4 million years turn out to be authentic, we have the following line of descent in human evolution starting in the Miocene: dryopithicines, *Ramapithecus*, unknown direct ancestor of both the *Homo* and the *Australopithecus* lines, *Homo sp.*, *Homo erectus*, and *Homo sapiens*.

If these recent discoveries turn out to be other australopithicines, then the line of descent is as follows: dryopithicines, *Ramapithecus*, *Australopithecus*, *Homo erectus*, and *Homo sapiens*. It appears that the transition from an apelike form to modern humans was a gradual process.

CULTURAL EVOLUTION

Most of the above discussion has been concerned with the biological evolution of humans changes in posture, brain size, dentition, and so forth-changes that involve gene changes and the selection processes. With respect to their biological evolution humans have changed little in the past 35 million years. But with human biological evolution there has come into existence another kind of evolution-cultural *evolution*.

This new evolution is a product of biological evolution, but different from it. Our ancient ancestors lived in the tropics; later ancestors became adapted to live in temperate climates, and still later ones to cold climates.

Some of our apelike ancestors used tools, but only humans and our humanlike ancestors made tools. There has been an evolution of stone tools. Early humans began hunting in groups, then they developed fire and started living in caves.

By Cro-Magnon times they were making clothing and practicing art. All these activities are a part of human culture and its evolution. Culture involves learning and instruction, and for instruction to occur there must be means of communication, that is, language.

So although the fossil record does not tell us when language began, it can be assumed that, when our ancestors began making tools and hunting in groups and sharing food, some kind of language existed. Culture is fhe learned part of behavior. It involves ideas, laws, customs, traditions, inventions, and all the other learned responses that regulate human societies.

Culture is transmitted, not by specific genes, but by conditioning, training, and learning. The study of culture and cultural evolution unites the fields of biology, anthropology, psychology, and sociology. Humans, through their language, are able to transmit the knowledge learned in each generation to the next.

Humans, of all the products of organic evolution, are the one kind of organism able to exercise control over their environment. They have already done much in this direction, and the possibilities for the future are great.

This means that in this new cultural evolution humans can slowly determine the future course of their evolution, both biological and cultural, by instituting human purpose and will in its direction. But humans also have the power for self-destruction. The responsibility for what happens belongs to everyone.

RACES OF MODERN HUMANS

If the same taxonomic criteria are applied to humans as are applied to other species, there is but one human species living at the present time. The entire human population shows great variability, and it is divided into a number of races, but it is one species because members of the different races can and do interbreed.

David Merrell states that probably the only racial cross that has not occurred is between Eskimos and African bushmen. It is not possible to draw sharp lines of distinction between racial groups because one race blends with another in the region of contact.

Humans have always been wanderers, and the present rapid movement of people, throughout the world is tending to break down further the distinction between the races. There is no such thing as a pure race of humans.

The human races differ from each other in the incidence of certain of their genes; this constitutes the basic distinction between races. There is no general agreement on the number of distinct human races; more than 30 have been recognized.

Three rather distinct racial groups are described below: the Negroid, the Caucasoid, and the Mongoloid. In terms of numbers and widespread distribution, these three are major human races. Prior to the settling of the Americas, members of the Negroid race were found in tropical Africa and in the islands of the western Pacific from New Guinea to Fiji.

The Negroids are usually dark-skinned with black woolly hair, sparse body and facial hair, broad flat noses, and thick lips. The Caucasoid race was native to Europe and western Asia, southeast into the tropics of India and to North Africa.

Caucasoids generally have rather light skin, long narrow noses, relatively straight hair, fairly abundant facial and body hair, and medium to thin lips. However this so-called "white" race varies all the way from the blond blue-eyed Scandinavian to the darkeyed dark-skinned native of India.

The Cauca soid race is quite variable, and a number of subgroups are recognized, such as the Mediterranean, the Nordic, and the Alpine. The Mongoloid race is native to North and East Asia. Members of the Mongoloid race generally have straight black hair, sparse facial and body hair, yellow to brown skin, brown eyes, an eye fold, and a flattened face with high cheekbones.

This race includes not only the yellow-skinned Asians and Eskimos, but also, in many classifications, the American Indian. Certainly the American Indians had Mongoloid ancestors. The characteristics of each race stated above are only general ones. Individuals within each race exhibit great variation.

In recent years a more precise method of differentiating between human races has been undertaken using the differences in the frequencies of the different blood group genes. William Boyd has thus proposed a fivefold race classification: Caucasoid, Negroid, Mongoloid, American Indian, and Australoid (the aboriginal population of Australia).

There is no evidence that any race is inherently better than another. So far all attempts to demonstrate hereditary differences in intelligence between races have failed. Of course, what is measured as intelligence is strongly influenced by learning opportunities.

THE MECHANISM OF EVOLUTION AND THE ORIGIN OF LIFE

Two explanations have been offered for the origin of the different forms of life-special creation and evolution. Many evidences have been presented in previous chapters to support the concept of *evolution*, and almost without exception modern biologists are convinced of *evolution*. But now we must ask the question: What are the factors responsible forthe process?

Although a vague idea of evolution was held by some of the early Greek *philosophers*, no important theory to explain it appeared until the nineteenth century. One of the first of these theories, which is now only of *historical* importance, was that of Jean Baptiste de Lamarck.

LAMARCK

Lamarck spent the early part of his life as a botanist. Then, at the age of 50, he turned his attention to zoology, particularly to the study of invertebrates. (We are indebted to Lamarck for the terms "*invertebrate*" and "*biology*.")

As a result of his *systematic* studies he became convinced that species were not constant but rather were derived from preexisting species. This idea was in *conflict* with the view of the period-that of fixity of species.

As a result Lamarck's views were challenged by most of the biologists of that time, particularly by Georges

Cuvier, and Lamarck's influence was not great. In 1809 Lamarck published *Philosophie Zoologique*, which included his theory explaining the changes that occur in the formation of new types.

Lamarck believed that environmental influences are the chief causes of evolutionary change. According to him, when an animal's environment changes, its needs change, and this leads to special demands on certain organs. Organs used more *extensively* would enlarge and become more efficient.

Conversely, an organ, or organs, no longer used would degenerate and atrophy. He postulated that such changed characteristics would be transmitted to the offspring. Lamarck's theory, then, was based on the ideas of use *and disuse* and the *inheritance of acquired traits*. He visualized the evolution of the giraffe as follows.

An original deerlike animal, finding the supply of grass and herbs inadequate, started to feed on the leaves of trees. It needed greater height to reach the higher leaves, and in the process of reaching, its neck became longer and longer.

In the course of generations the long neck became a more accentuated feature, and our modern giraffe was the result. His theory was simple, and it had some appeal. Everyone knows that exercise results in larger muscles. The theory also afforded a means of *explaining* reduced or vestigial structures.

Through disuse the eyes of a cave animal, for example, might become functionless and might even disappear. The great deficiency in the Lamarckian theory was the *assumption* of the hereditary transmission of acquired traits.

It must be recalled that at this time in history all notions of inheritance were vague and fanciful. No one tried to test this part of Lamarck's thesis until late in the century, when the Germanworker August Weismann tried cutting the tails off mice for many successive generations. At the end of his experiment the mice in the last generation grew tails as long as their ancestors. Since Weismann's time, many workers have devised experiments to test this *hypothesis*, and the net result has been the same, acquired traits or modifications are not inherited.

In this connection it can be pointed out that mutilation experiments, such as Weismann performed, were not necessary. The Chinese bound the feet of their women for many generations, yet this has not resulted in any modification of the feet of present-day Chinese women.

Also, Jewish boys have been circumcised for thousands of years, but this has not resulted in a tendency toward reduction of the prepuce in this group.

DARWIN

The most impressive study of evolution made by any single man was that of Charles Darwin. His principal publication, *The Origin of* Species *by Means of Natural Selection or the Preservation of Favoured Races in the Struggle for Life*, which appeared in 1859, contained not only a masterful assemblage of evidence for evolution, but also his theory which, with certain modifications, is still accepted today.

Charles Darwin was born in Shrewsbury, England, in 1809, the son of a physician. He spent three years at Edinburgh studying *medicine* and another three years at *Cambridge* studying *theology*.

Although his university record was creditable, his heart was not in either medicine or the ministry. As a boy he became interested in natural *history* and collecting natural objects of all kinds. He spent much of his time at the universities *finding* out more about *botany*, *zoology*, and *geology*.

When, following his graduation from Cambridge, he was offered the opportunity to travel around the world as a naturalist on H.M.S. *Beagle*, his father agreed to let him go. So at the age of 22 Darwin set out on a voyage that lasted five years and affected profoundly his own life and *ultimately* the thinking of much of *mankind*.

When he eh barked on this voyage, he believed, as did most people at the time, in the fixity of species-of special creation. When he returned, the concept of evolution was firmly fixed in his mind. He made numerous observations during the five-year period that led him to this view.

He was especially impressed with the striking adaptations found in the animals and plants that he collected and with the progressive changes in the different species of a given genus as the expedition moved along the South American coast.

In the Galapagos Islands he found many species of a given genus confined to a single island, yet resembling other species on other islands and the mainland. Such facts, Darwin reasoned, could be explained only by the supposition that species may become modified.

After his return home he began to gather all the information he could on this idea of the modification of species. For over 20 years he collected data, performed experiments, read extensively, and thought about a possible *mechanism* that would explain the modification of species. During this long period in which he amassed his evidence and developed his theory, many things affected his thinking, of which three in particular deserve mention here.

He had taken with him on the voyage of the Beagle a copy of Charles Lyell's *Principles of Geology*, which had been published only a short time before. This book attempted to explain the past changes in the earth's surface on the basis of processes now in operation.

It extended greatly the older ideas about the age of the earth, and it gave Darwin a basis for *appreciating* some of the tossil material that he found. In addition, Lyell's insistence on explaining the past history of the earth in terms of processes still operating affected Darwin's thinking about the causes of evolution.

Darwin was aware of the similarities of many *domesticated* animals and plants to wild forms and realized that members of our society, for centuries, selected individual plants and animals with desirable traits for breeding.

In this way the various lines of domesticated forms have been developed. He found himself asking the question: Might not some sort of selection operate in nature to produce the various highly adapted forms found on the earth? While Darwin was thinking about this possibility, he happened to read the famous Essay on *Population by* T. Malthus.

From this he obtained a suggestion that was to serve as the basis for his explanation of evolution. Malthus, who was a *mathematician* and an economist as well as a minister, was concerned with problems of the increasing human population.

He pointed out that human population, as well as plant and animal populations, tends to increase at such rates that its numbers *outstrip* its resources, and because there is not food or space enough for all, there is a struggle for existence.

Malthus argued that in time the human population would outstrip the possible food supply and therefore that steps should be taken to control human reproduction. He proposed late marriage and *sexual* restraint as means of doing this and stated that unless steps were taken by humans to limit their population, checks apparently beyond their control-in the form of famine, disease, and war-would limit it instead.

Darwin was familiar with the struggle for existence that occurs everywhere in nature. He reasoned that in such situations, favourable *variations* would be preserved and unfavourable ones *destroyed*, and the result would be the formation of new species.

Darwin conceived this theory of evolution when he was 29 years old, but he did not publish his ideas until many years later. Meanwhile he continued to collect data bearing on the question of evolution. It was not until 1842 that he wrote out a first brief abstract of his theory.

By 1844 he had expanded this to a document of 230 pages. In 1858 before the final manuscript of *The Origin* of Species was completed, Darwin received a manuscript from Alfred Wallace, who had been studying the natural history of the Malay Archipelago, with the request that Darwin read it, and if he found it worthy, to forward it to Lyell for publication.

When Darwin read the manuscript, he found that Wallace had proposed a theory of natural selection similar to his own. He forwarded the manuscript to Lyell for publication, but Lyell, who had become acquainted with Darwin's work over the years, arranged to have Darwin submit an abstract of his own work, to be presented *simultaneously* with Wallace's paper.

In the following year Darwin's complete work was published. It is interesting that two great naturalists developed the idea of natural selection independently.

But Darwin, who spent much of his life in the study of this theory and who organized such an overwhelming mass of evidence in support of the concept of natural selection, made the greater contribution.

Darwin's Theory of Natural Selection

Darwin's theory is based on three observable facts and two deductions drawn from these facts.

First Observable Fact

Every species, in the absence of environmental checks, tends to increase in a *geometric* manner. If a population of a given species doubles in one year and if there are no checks on its increase, it will *quadruple* the next year, and so on.

The great reproductive potential of different species may be easily observed in nature. It has been estimated that a common Atlantic coast oyster may shed as many as 80 million eggs in one season.

A single pair of English sparrows would be the ancestors of over 275 billion individuals in 10 years if they and their descendants could reproduce at their natural rate without any checks.

Darwin calculated that even a pair of elephants which are about the slowest breeding animals known, could, in the *absence* of any checks, have 29 million *descendants* at the end of 800 years.

Second Observable Fact

This *tremendous* reproductive potential is not realized in nature; the size of the population of each species remains relatively constant over long periods of time. This is not to say that given species will not vary some from year to year. This relative constancy in the numbers of each species is discussed again in other chapter of this book in connection with the concept of a balance in nature.

First Deduction

Because the great *reproductive* potential of different organisms is not realized in nature (that is, because not all individuals that are produced do *survive*), there must be a struggle for existence.

Third Observable Fact

Within every species there is individual variation. For instance, no two human beings are exactly alike, and so on.

Second Deduction

In the struggle for existence those individuals that have favourable variations will survive in *proportionately* greater numbers and will produce a proportionately greater percent of the next generation. This is natural selection.

Great Controversy

With the appearance of Darwin's book in 1859 a veritable storm of controversy broke out. Many people became interested in his presentation; the arguments for and against that developed were often heated. The concept was opposed primarily on ethical and religious grounds.

But the sheer weight of evidence and the logic of Darwin's presentation finally convinced a majority of the educated people. The concept of evolution affected many aspects of our thinking and it will continue to do so. The impact of *Darwinism* on social and economic thinking has been *unfortunate* in certain respects.

The idea of "the survival of the fittest" has been erroneously interpreted by many to mean survival only by "tooth and claw," an interpretation that has led in many cases to rationalizations for the attitude of "every man for himself" in social and economic affairs.

But this view of Darwin's theory and of its present-day modification is a *misinterpretation*. The process of evolution is not all "tooth and claw." Plants have evolved, too, and there is no bloody competition between them. In all forms, plants and animals alike, a part of the selective process involves the action of inanimate nature, factors such as drought, storm, moisture, temperature, and others that are considered in more detail in other chapter of this book. Active *competition* between organisms is a part of the process, but as Warder Allee and others have pointed out, *cooperation* has in many cases been involved in survival.

Natural selection results in the survival of those forms that are best integrated with the various factors of the environment in which they live. *Survival* of the fittest merely indicates those whose offspring survive to reproduce. Darwin's theory had one great weakness; it did not explain the origin and transmission of variations. Although Darwin criticized many aspects of *Lamarck's theory*, he did not deny that acquired characteristics can be transmitted.

He realized that the nature of inheritance was unknown, but he devised a working hypothesis to explain how acquired variations may be transmitted. According to his hypothesis the parts of the body give off tiny particles, which he called *pangenes*, into the body fluids, and these are collected in the eggs or sperms.

Later, when a fertilized egg undergoes development, according to the concept, the pangenes present are responsible for the particular features of the new individual.

This hypothesis, of course, has been proved untenable. However, it should be remembered that Darwin (and Lamarck, too) did as well as they could with the information they had.

Mendel published his paper on the mechanism of inheritance seven years after Darwin published the theory of evolution, but it was 1900 before these laws of inheritance became generally known to the scientific world and helped in bringing *rationality* to the theory of evolution.

MODERN VIEWS OF EVOLUTION

Many studies have been made during the past 75 years to explain further the mechanism of evolution. As a result it can be said that the general thesis of Darwin, except his ideas about the origin and transmission of variations, has been upheld.

There are many different aspects of the mechanism of evolution, and no one is willing to say that we understand the entire process by any means. What is presented here is only an outline of some of the major features.

Mutations

Darwin made no distinction between environmentally induced variations (which we now know are not inherited) and inheritable variations. It is now recognized that mutations are the raw materials for evolution by natural selection.

These changes in genes and in chromosome configurations, together with the recombinations that result in sexual reproduction, are the only known *inheritable* changes that occur in organisms.

Natural selection does not cause these changes, but it plays an important role in determining which of them survive. Hugo de Vries, a Dutch botanist and one of the discoverers of Mendel's paper, first focused attention on the importance of mutations.

In his studies on the evening primrose he found several individual plants that differed markedly from the rest, and these new types bred true. He regarded some of these new types as elementary species, and as a result of his studies he *announced* his "*mutation theory*" of evolution.

He considered that new species arise by sudden changes or steps rather than by *gradual processes*. According to de Vries it was mutations and not selection that should be considered as the primary factor in evolution.

Later studies on the same material showed that some of the new types described by de Vries were not true mutations but were recombinations.

Though some mutations may cause major changes, most of the ones that have been studied produce relatively slight changes. The great importance of de Vries' contribution was in directing attention to the study of mutations.

Selection of Mutations

When a mutation occurs that is beneficial (that gives

some survival advantages to its *possessor*), it will probably appear with increasing frequency in subsequent *generations*.

The rate at which the new gene replaces the original one in the population will be determined by a number of factors: whether the new mutation is *dominant* or *recessive*, the intensity of the selection, the rate at which the mutation occurs in the population, the rate of reverse mutation, the *breeding* structure of the population, and the size of the population.

On the basis of the studies that have been made it must be assumed that many, many generations are needed for the incorporation of an ordinary mutation into the majority of the individuals of a large population.

In the earlier discussion of mutations it was pointed out that most mutations are deleterious in their effects and thus are not of survival value.

How does this fit into our present *concept*? At first glance it might seem to mean that mutations cannot be the source of new materials for the evolutionary process.

However, a little thought will show the following fact. All organisms now living in the world are the products of hundreds of thousands of years of this process of selecting *favourable* mutations, and they are well adapted for the particular environment in which they live.

During this process of evolving, when the environmental conditions have remained relatively constant for a long period of time, most of the mutations that could give *survival* value have occurred and have been selected.

Thus it would be surprising if beneficial mutations occurred with very great frequency. Also, in the discussion of mutations it was pointed out that the rate of mutations is low and that most mutations produce only slight effects.

Is it possible, then, to explain the results of the process of evolution on the basis of mutations as a part of the process? George Simpson, in his study of horse evolution, has estimated that something over 5 million years was required for the formation of each of the genera in the evolution of the horse.

Assuming that about 45 million years were involved, and making certain assumptions about the size of the population involved, it has been possible to show that if a very conservative estimate of the rate of mutation is assumed, mutations producing very slight effects could have produced the changes in the size of the teeth of the horse, the modifications in the legs, and other characteristics.

The discussion so far has implied that selection deals with single mutations, without reference to the whole gene complex. In general this is not so. Modern genetic studies have shown that many, if not most, genes produce manifold effects in the developmental process.

Thus the selective forces will act on different gene combinations or complexes. In the discussion on heredity we have already considered how, as a result of sexual reproduction, many, many re*combinations* of genes are produced through independent assortment and crossing over.

It is from this great range of variation that the best combinations are selected. One of the weak points of the original theory of natural selection-one recognized by Darwin as such-was that it did not adequately explain the existence of the many apparently nonadaptive characteristics found in organisms.

Every student of taxonomy and natural history knows that quite often some of the more obvious characteristics that distinguish two related species apparently have no survival value. This is now *understa-n-dable* on the basis of our knowledge of heredity.

Some genes that give no survival value may become fixed in a population by chance (see the subsequent discussion of genetic drift); others may be carried in the *gene pool* of the population for generations in the *heterozygous* state.

Thus it is not necessary to assume that all genes of an organism are beneficial or that all characters of an organism have survival value. As one worker has expressed it, all that is necessary for survival is that the gene pool of the species provide in excess of 50 percent overall adaptation for the members of the species.

This reservoir of nonadaptive genes in the gene complex of each species appears to be an important feature in the process of evolution. The size of this reservoir, or the degree of adaptation, will vary from species to species. It is at the time of great environmental changes that this reservoir of genes becomes important.

A species that is very highly specialized for a particular environment may be unable to survive a radical change in the environment. On the other hand, a species that is not so specialized and that has a larger reservoir of *nonadaptive genes* (for the original environment) may survive in a very different environment because some of the originally nonadaptive genes now have survival value. Many workers call this *preadaptation.*

The Population as the Unit in Evolution

An individual organism does not evolve; only a population does. Great strides have been made in recent years in the study of population genetics as related to the process of evolution. A population, as discussed here, is a group of organisms of the same species that *interbreed* with one another in a particular *geographical* area.

As a result of the interbreeding in the population, there is a free flow of genes within it. All genes within the population are often referred to as the *gene pool* of the population.

What happens within a population when random mating occurs in successive generations? This was first answered in 1908, independently, by G. H. Hardy and by Wilhelm Weinberg, and we now refer to their findings as the Hardy Weinberg law.

Before discussing this law, a review of simple genetics is in order. Suppose a cross of two rabbits, homozygous black with *homozygous* brown, is made. In this case the gene for black *(B)* is dominant over the gene for brown (b). Such a cross would result in all *heterozygous (Bb)* black offspring in the F_1 generation. Now if one or several matings of F_1 individuals are made to obtain many F_2 offspring, the theoretical results can be represented on a Punnett square as follows:

		Eggs	
		B	*b*
Sperm	B	BB	Bb
	b	Bb	bb

According to the Punnett square, one would expect that three fourths of the F_2 generation would be black (¼*BB*, ½*Bb*) and one fourth would be brown (bb). If large numbers were obtained, this ratio would be approximated in the actual results.

Now assume that 1000 of these F_2 rabbits are distributed as follows: *250 BB, 500 Bb,* and *250 bb.* These are placed on an island where the conditions for their existence are quite favourable. What would the next generation be like? Assume the following conditions:

(1) *mating* is purely *random*;

(2) there is no selection acting, that is, all the rabbits are equally viable and all are *capable* of producing the same number of *offspring*;

(3) no mutation occurs; and

(4) no rabbits are added from the outside and none are lost.

It would be a long and tedious process to set up all possible matings within the population of 1000 rabbits. This, however, is not necessary. A look at the original F_2 cross that created the F_2 generation in the first example above shows *Bb* × *Bb*.

Here one has the same number of *B* genes and *b* genes. One can represent the frequency of *B* as *0.5* and the frequency of *b* as *0.5*. Now if the F_2 generation is examined, it be comes obvious that the same frequency of these alleles (or *0.58* and *0.5b)* exists.

To determine the frequency of the genes, of the genotypes, and of the phenotypes of the next generation that the 1000 rabbits on the island would produce, one can thus represent not the cross of two individuals, as was done above, but what would happen when the whole population reproduces, assuming the conditions outlined above.

Because there are as many *B* genes as *b* genes in both the males and females of the population, the gametes can be shown as follows:

		Eggs	
		0.5B	*0.5b*
Sperm	0.5B	0.25BB	0.25Bb
	0.5b	0.25Bb	0.25bb

This generation of rabbits on the island, which would total several thousand, will have the same frequency of genes *(0.5B, 0.5b)*, of genotypes *(0.2588, 0.5Bb, 0.25bb)*, and of phenotypes (¾ black, ¼ brown) that the simple F_2 laboratory cross had.

This population is in equilibrium, and this is the type of relationship discovered by Hardy and Weinberg. According to their law, in the absence of forces that change gene frequencies, the relative frequencies of alleles in a population tend to remain constant from generation to generation.

This relationship can be expressed in the form of an expanded binomial. The proportion of *B* alleles in a population can be represented by *p*, and the proportion of *b* alleles by *q*, and $p + q = 1$. In the expanded binomial $(p + q)2$, $p2$ will represent the proportion of *BB* individuals in the population; $2pq$, the proportion of *Bb* individuals; and q^2, the proportion of *bb* individuals.

A very simple situation has been used to illustrate this, a situation in which the frequency of each of the alleles was the same, *0.5*. However, this is not the type of situation usually found in nature. When two alleles are present, their frequencies may vary from almost 0 to almost 1.

Another hypothetical population where the alleles are not equal in frequency is now examined. Consider a population of rabbits on an isolated island in which the brown rabbits constitute 64 percent of the population and the black rabbits, 36 percent. What is the gene frequency here, and what percent of the black rabbits are homozygous and what percent are heterozygous?

One of the handy things about the Hardy-Weinberg formula is that if the percentage of the recessive genotype (the brown rabbits in this case) is known, one can determine the answers to these questions. Consider the expression, $p^2 + 2pq + q^2$. In this case q^2 stands for the proportion of brown rabbits, and the frequency of the *b* gene can be determined by taking the square root of 0.64. This is 0.8, or 80 percent. The frequency of *p* (black gene) must be 0.2, or 20 percent, because $p + q = 1$.

The term p^2, which represents the proportion of the homozygous *(BB)* rabbits, would be $0.2 \times 0.2 = 0.04$, or 4 percent. The proportion of the heterozygous *(Bb)* black rabbits is represented by $2pq$, and this would be $2 \times 0.8 \times 0.2 = 0.32$, or 32 percent.

So the black rabbits in the population, which constitute 36 percent, would be composed of 4 percent homozygous individuals and 32 percent heterozygous individuals. What would be the situation in the next generation?

Again this can be represented as before:

		Eggs	
		0.2B	0.8b
Sperm	0.2B	0.04BB	0.16Bb
	0.8b	0.168b	0.64bb

The results are the same, and this would then continue generation after generation in the absence of forces that change gene frequencies. This type of situation-in which the alleles of a given pair are not present with equal frequencies is the most common type found in natural populations.

People who have an *acquaintance* with only the most elementary concepts of genetics sometimes assume that all dominant genes are expressed in three fourths of the population and that all recessive genes are expressed in one fourth of the population, but this is not the case.

The populations that have been discussed so far were in equilibrium. What happens in a population not in equilibrium? One can illustrate this with another hypothetical case. Assume that 1000 black rabbits are placed on an island free of other rabbits and that half of them have the *BB* genotype and half the *Bb* genotype.

What will their offspring be like? Assume the same conditions as before. All the genes contributed by the *BB* individuals will be *B*(0.5) and, in addition, half the genes furnished by the *Bb* individuals will be 8(0.25). Hence the frequency of the *B* genes is 0.75. The frequency of the *b* genes is 0.25. Then $p = 0.75$ and $q = 0.25$.

$$(p + q)^2 = p^2 + 2pq + q^2$$

$$= (0.75)^2 + 2 \times (0.75) \times (0.25) + (0.25)^2$$

$$= 0.5625 + 0.375 + 0.0625$$

Thus there will be 56.25 percent 88, 37.5 percent *Bb*, and 6.25 percent *bb*, or a total of 93.75 percent black and 6.25 percent brown individuals. The parental population was composed of only black rabbits, but this one has some brown rabbits. Is this population now in equilibrium? This can be answered by determining the frequencies of genes *B* and *b*.

The percent of individuals having only *B* genes is 56.25, so they will contribute that percentage to the gene pool; 37.5 percent are heterozygous, so they will contribute 18.75 percent *B* genes to the pool and 18.75 percent *b* genes to the pool; 6.25 percent of the individuals have only *b* genes and they will contribute that percentage to the pool. Thus

$$p = 56.25 + 18.75 = 75 \text{ percent}$$

$$q = 6.25 + 18.75 = 25 \text{ percent}$$

This result is the same as that at the start, and so the population is now in equilibrium and the same frequencies of genes, of genotypes, and of phenotypes will recur in generation after generation under the conditions outlined.

This example demonstrates that when a population is not in equilibrium, it tends to attain equlibrium in one generation. In this discussion very simple *hypothetical* populations were used in order to keep the mathematical analysis simple.

However, it can be stated that the Hardy-Weinberg principle applies to natural populations wherever it has been tested. Snyder has studied the frequencies of the genes that determine the *M*, *MN*, and *N* blood groups in several different human populations.

In this case gene *M* in the homozygous state determines the *M* group, gene *N* in the homozygous state determines the *N* group, and genes *M* and N together determine the *MN* group. All three of these blood groups can be detected *serologically*.

In a sample of 1200 Swedes the distribution was as follows: 0.361 *MM*, 0.470 *MN*, and 0.169 *NN*. Using the HardyWeinberg formula, the frequency of *M* \/*0.361* is approximately 0.60, while the frequency of *N* /0.169 is approximately 0.40. The estimated frequency of *MN* [2 × (0.60) × (0.40)] would be approximately 0.480.

This corresponds very closely to the observed 0.470. The same type of agreement was found in the samples of other human populations studied. The Hardy-Weinbbrg law states that the relative frcquency of alleles in a population tends to remain constant from generation to generation when (1) the population is large enough so that accidents of sampling may be ignored; (2) mating occurs at random; (3) mutation does not occur or, if it does, the rate is the same in both directions; (4) all members of the population are viable and have equal reproductive rates; and (5) there is no emigration or *immigration* involved. This is a very important principle in population genetics, but it *describes* a situation in *equilibrium*.

This is a static condition, and evolution does not occur under these conditions. For evolution to occur there must be some disturbance in the gene frequencies of the population. The four primary factors that disturb genetic equilibrium are mutation, selection, genetic drift, and differential migration. The first three of these are discussed below.

Mutations in Populations

Different genes mutate at different rates. Assume gene A, which mutates at such a rate that one gene a is found in every 100,000 gametes formed. Assume also that the organisms that have gene a are as fit to survive and reproduce their kind as those with gene A.

In this situation the frequency of gene A will decrease and that of gene a will increase in each succeeding generation. Gene A might mutate itself out of existence, but this is not likely because of the process of *backmutation.*

Gene a will probably mutate to A with its own rate of mutation. In many cases studied the rate of backmutation (from the recessive to the dominant gene) is usually lower. At any rate, under these conditions an equilibrium will be established in the population when the number of changes of A to a is the same as the number of changes of a to A in each generation.

It is possible that such a tendency to reach an equilibrium of opposing mutation rates may be the basis for the persistence of many alternative traits found in human and other populations. The situation described above is not the usual one.

As mentioned before, most mutations have a harmful effect, which varies from lethal, as when the particular mutation is present in the homozygous recessive state, to very slight.

Suppose that we have a recessive mutation a which, when present in the homozygous state (aa), results in the production of only 99 offspring that are viable and capable of reproduction, in comparison with every 100 offspring that the AA and Aa individuals produce.

In this situation the frequency of gene A increases with each generation. Although the *selection pressure* in this case is low, the results over a long period of time would be definite; gene a would be eliminated from the population unless other factors intervened.

In most situations one cannot assume that only mutation or only selection is operating. Selection works against the spread of deleterious mutations in a population, but a certain number of such mutations of various kinds are introduced into the gene pool of a population in each generation.

What is the general nature of the results of the action of these two opposing forces? When more mutations are produced than eliminated, the frequency of the mutant allele will increase; when more mutations are eliminated than formed, the mutant allele will become less frequent; and when the number of mutant genes produced equals the number of such genes eliminated, an equilibrium will be established.

Theodosius Dobzhansky (see Suggestions for Further Reading) has described an interesting situation in fruit flies, where the equilibrium reached is affected by the survival qualities of the heterozygote.

In this situation the *heterozygotes* have greater survival value than either *homozygous* type under certain conditions. The *sickle-cell* condition in humans is another example.

Selection

One of the difficult concepts in population genetics involves the rates of selection. In most cases complete selection against a dominant (lethal) mutation will occur in one generation; complete selection against the homozygous recessive is slower; and partial selection against the homozygous recessive is much slower.

Assume a population in which the mutation a represents almost 100 percent of the genes at that locus in the population.

It can be shown, by methods developed by population geneticists, that with complete selection operating on the homozygous recessives, their frequency will be reduced from almost 100 percent to 10 percent in about two generations.

However, it will take 7 generations to reduce it from 10 percent to 1 percent, 22 generations to reduce it from 1 percent to 0.1 percent, and 68 generations to reduce it from 0.1 percent to 0.01 percent. Thus the rarer any trait becomes, the less effective is any further selection against it.

This is something that should be kept in mind when eugenic sterilization programs are considered. In such programs the traits involved are usually rare ones, and there is no possibility at present of approaching complete selection against them.

Genetic Drift

The concept of *genetic drift*, developed by S. Wright, is concerned with changes in gene frequencies in small populations. A gene may be fixed purely by chance in a small population in the course of a few generations.

In the discussion on genetics it was emphasized that whether one obtains actual genetic ratios that correspond with the *theoretically* expected ratios is dependent upon having large numbers of offspring. This is because the *assortment* of genes into gametes and the *combination* of gametes to form *zygotes* are *random* processes.

In small breeding populations where only a few offspring are produced, great *fluctuations* from expected ratios may occur by chance. Thus in a very small population consisting of two mating pairs, if one individual contains a new mutation a, its *genotype* would be Aa and that of the other three would be AA.

It is entirely possible, purely on the basis of chance, that if this individual with the new mutation and its mate produce six offspring that live to maturity, and the other pair produces four that live to maturity, five of the offspring of the first pair will have the mutant gene a.

Thus out of 10 individuals to produce the next generation half of them would contain the *mutant gene*. Assuming that there is no selection against this gene, it would have very good possibilities of spreading further in subsequent generations.

On the other hand, the opposite might occur in the same situation. None of the offspring of the first pair, purely by chance, might receive the gene a, and it would be lost immediately.

This chance fixation of genes is called *genetic drift*, and there seems to be little doubt that it plays a role in the evolutionary process. Conditions that favour genetic drift occur in nature. One such situation is that of a very small group completely isolated on an island.

Another situation favouring the operation of this chance fixation of genes occurs at times when large populations are reduced to very small size as the result of epidemics or weather.

It may be that many of the so-called nonadaptive characters that distinguish one species from related ones may have arisen as mutations that eventually became established by genetic drift.

The ideal situations for rapid evolution are found in populations of medium size that are broken up into a number of smaller populations, each of which is almost completely isolated from the others.

In these relatively small populations, mutant genes may become established either through selection or through drift. After a gene that has survival value has become established in the small population, if the isolation is only partial and if individuals in this one small subpopulation migrate and mate with individuals in other subpopulations, the stage is set for the modification of the whole species.

It should be pointed out also that species that are divided into a number of small subpopulations, because they have several partly differentiated groups, are better able to survive major environmental changes than are single large species lacking this differentiation.

Survival of the Fittest

From the studies on population genetics a more plausible interpretation of "the survival of the fittest" has emerged. In Darwin's day in the minds of many the "fittest" meant literally the strongest in a physical sense.

This was the origin of the "tooth and claw" concept, a concept that unfortunately was taken over in other areas and was used to justify exploitation of the weak.

On the basis of the knowledge today, it is apparent that *the fittest are merely those in a population that produce the most offspring in the next generation.*

This is the modern concept of the survival of the fittest, and it is more in line with what is seen in nature. As has been mentioned, the old idea of tooth and claw never did fit the evolution of plants, and they are certainly an integral part of the whole process.

From this modern point of view natural selection, then, is the differential reproduction of certain genotypes.

The population geneticist describes the evolutionary process in terms of changes in the frequency of genes in a population.

Indeed, the expression "survival of the fittest" can be applied with more accuracy to the behaviour of genes over many generations than to that of individual organisms in one generation.

Role of Isolation in Speciation

The process of evolution involves more than just change in the characteristics of a species; it involves the formation of new species, or *speciation.* Beyond this it involves the differentiations that are of genus significance, family significance, order significance, and so on.

Speciation may occur in two ways: by replacement and by branching. Speciation by replacement may occur in the following way. A freely interbreeding population exists in a given area. Over a long period of time, the descendants of this population remain as one freely interbreeding group.

Mutation and selection operate over the years, and after many generations the population has so changed in some of its characteristics that a taxonomist would call the later group a new species. There is, of course, no way of testing whether the later group would be able to interbreed with the original group. However, it has been assumed by many biologists that this may have occurred in the past, and if so, it would be speciation by replacement.

How can one species give rise to another or to several other species? According to one definition, a species is a group of similar organisms that freely interbreed and produce viable and fertile offspring. In such a group, when a beneficial mutation arises, it will ultimately be incorporated in the gene pool of the species. What causes a division?

There is general agreement that speciation, in the sense under discussion now, involves some kind or kinds of *reproductive isolation.* Mechanisms that prevent successful reproduction between members of two or more populations that have descended from the same original population are called *isolating mechanisms.* A number of such mechanisms have been identified, and several of them are discussed later.

It is further recognized that for these reproductive isolating mechanisms to evolve, the separated populations of an original single group must be separated spatially or geographically for a long period of time. The only clearcut exception to this, speciation by polyploidy, is considered in a later section.

Geographical isolation for long periods of time, however, does not necessarily produce reproductive isolation and thus speciation.

The catalpa trees of eastern North America and eastern Asia are fully fertile, yet they have been separated for a few million years. In many instances, however, such spatial separation does lead to reproductive isolation and speciation.

Darwin was impressed with his findings of distinct, but closely related, species on many of the different islands of the Galapagos archipelago, and it is this kind of phenomenon that many modern biologists have studied.

When an original population is divided into two or more groups by geographical barriers that prevent interbreeding between them, in the course of time different mutations may become incorporated in the gene pools of the different groups. Often these differences are of such a nature that the separated groups, when they come in contact again, do not interbreed; thus species have been formed.

Over the long haul, geographic isolation is seldom permanent. Changes in geography, migrations resulting from great population pressure, or chance dispersal during storms may bring separated groups in contact again.

If they then interbreed and have fertile offspring, speciation has not occurred; but if they do not interbreed, or if they interbreed and have sterile offspring, new species have been produced; reproductive isolation has occurred.

This does not take into account speciation in asexually reproducing organisms. Oceans and mountain ranges with deep valleys between provide this type of spatial isolating mechanism. It is well established that there are more different species of the same genus in mountainous country than in plains regions.

For instance in the eastern part of this country, there are eight species of cottontail rabbits, whereas in the mountainous regions of the west there are 23 species of these rabbits.

Often in mountainous country many of the plants and animals found in deep valleys, which are separated by high peaks but which may be only a few miles apart, are peculiar to those valleys.

Darwin found similar situations in the Galapagos Islands. David Lack, in his recent studies of "Darwin's finches" in the Galapagos Islands, believes that only through geographical isolation combined with ecological specialization could the great variety of finches have been produced.

Finches belong to one of the largest families of birds, which include sparrows, cardinals, goldfinches, and canaries, among others. The more typical forms possess stout conical bills adapted to crush seeds. In Darwin's finches the different species are differentiated morphologically, primarily by the nature of their bills.

Some feed on seeds, some on leaves and fruit, some on insects in the manner of the woodpecker, and others in the manner of the warbler, also on insects.

These finches are all clearly related, and they are quite different from any of those on the mainland of South America; yet everything points to their origin from the South American group.

Several of these different types are now found inhabiting the same island. Lack's explanation of this evolution is, briefly, as follows. Some of the South American finches originally reached one of the Galapagos Islands.

They were seed eaters and in time population pressure caused some to migrate to another island. The conditions there were such that this group, through mutations and selection, gradually became modified morphologically for food-getting and life in a different habitat.

In time, some of this group migrated back to the original island. Now the members of the two groups could inhabit the same island because they had different ecological requirements and they were reproductively isolated.

As time went on, the other differences were added to the original ones, while the groups were occupying the same general region. Lack believes that several such separations, leading to specialization along different lines in the different islands and subsequent remeetings of the groups, would explain the adaptive radiation that has occurred in this group of birds.

Lack supports his argument by pointing out that on Cocos Island, a single island located north of the Galapagos Islands in the Pacific and hundreds of miles from any other land mass, where the conditions for life are quite similar to those on the Galapagos Islands, only one kind of finch is found, and it is placed in a different genus from any of the finches on the Galapagos.

Apparently such adaptation leading to speciation can occur on an archipelago but not on a single small island. A number of different kinds of isolating mechanisms have been identified, and they can be placed in two categories: those that prevent fertilization and zygote formation, and those that prevent development after fertilization occurs or that cause weak or sterile hybrids.

In the first category difference in habitat may be the effective mechanism. Two populations may live in the same general area but because of differences in specific habitats they do not meet to cross-fertilize. This situation is found between many closely related species of trees.

In other cases mating between two closely related species does not occur because their gametes are produced at different seasons of the year. In many instances in animals small differences in behaviour patterns in courtship, such as calls and songs, between two closely related species prevent mating.

An interesting example of this type in *Drosophila* is described in other chapter of this book. In many of the flowering plants differences in the structure of the flower are a very effective way of preventing cross-pollination between two closely related species because of the close adaptation of each insect pollinator.

In the second category all the effects are due to genic disharmony, that is, the genes brought in from the two lines do not work in harmony in the cells of the hybrid, or of its progeny. Death may occur at any stage in development or a very weak hybrid may result. A vigorous hybrid may be formed, but it is sterile.

This may be due to the abnormal development of the gonads or it may be due to the failure to produce normal gametes in the process of meiosis. In some cases viable hybrids are formed that are at least partly fertile, but the F_2 generation is weak, abnormal, or sterile.

There is much interest in the genetic basis of these isolating mechanisms. Several experimental studies indicate that all isolating mechanisms are controlled by several genes in multiple-factor inheritance.

An illustration of this is found in Dobzhansky's studies of backcross progeny between two species of *Drosophila, D. pseudoobscura* and *D. persimilis.* He found the male F_1 hybrids to be completely sterile because of much reduced abnormal testes, while the females were partly fertile.

When the females were 'backcrossed to either parent, the males of such crosses showed a wide range of testis sizes. All of the chromosomes in the cultures used of the parental species could be identified by means of recessive genes which they bore, and Dobzhansky was able to determine that the degree of abnormality of the testes of a fly was directly proportional to the number of his autosomes which were derived from a different species from that which contributed his single X chromosome.

This means that genes tending to reduce testis size in the hybrids are present on every autosome of the parental species.

Also, related species are usually separated from each other, not by one, but by several different isolating mechanisms. All this means that the process of speciation usually involves the incorporation of many mutations over a long period of time.

EVOLUTION IN PROGRESS

In the preceding discussion evolution has been described as a process that has been going on for many millions of years and is still going on. How much of the process, if any, are we able to observe? The importance of the time factor in the process has been emphasized, and with this in mind perhaps one should not expect to be able to observe many significant changes in the course of a lifetime.

In the course of several lifetimes one could expect a little more-and still more in the course of many generations. It has been pointed out that there is a difference between just the modification of species and the formation of new ones.

Several things can be pointed out about the observed modification of species. Reference has already been made to the great number of different varieties of domesticated plants and animals that were developed in historical time.

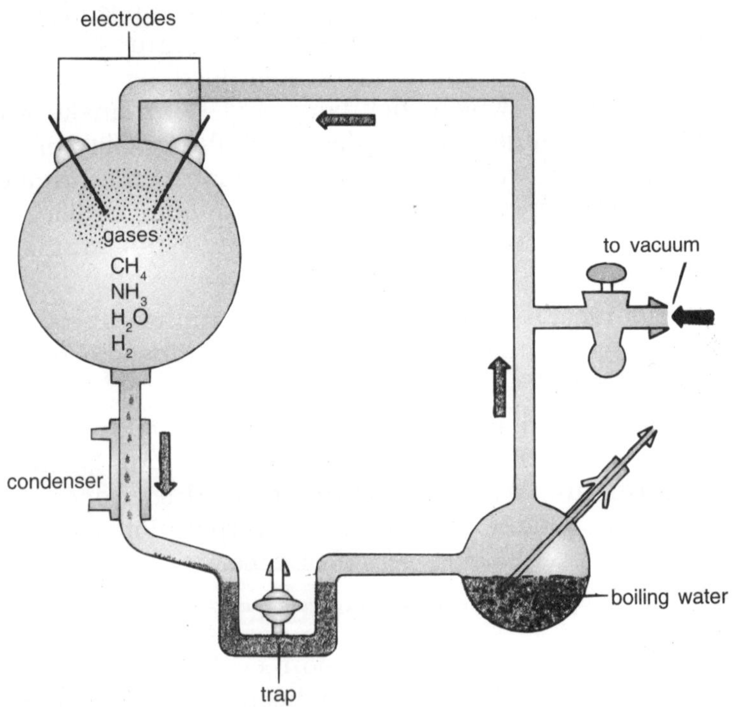

Figure 17.1: Spark discharge apparatus used in Miller's experiment simulating conditions assumed to exist early in earth's history.

In these cases we have done the selecting, and although this differs from what happens in nature, it shows the modifiability of species under selection and thus has a bearing on the problem. There are, in addition, a number of cases where species have been observed to change in nature, and a few of these cases are mentioned.

Records show that populations of certain species of insects have, in recent times, changed from predominantly light-coloured forms to darkcoloured forms. These changes have occurred in industrial regions characterized by large amounts of smoke and soot.

Originally the lightcoloured forms blended well with their background. When black mutants appeared, they were easy prey for birds. But now, with a darker background in many regions the dark-coloured forms have become the prevailing types.

Kettlewell, who furnished the photographs for Figure elsewhere in this chapter, has studied this phenomenon *(industrial melanism)* in England. His chief study was on the light and dark forms of *Biston betularia.* The black form was first reported from Manchester, England, in 1848.

The black form is caused by a dominant mutation. Collections made in 1958 showed that 90 percent were black and only 10 percent light. Kettlewell released marked moths (both the dark and the light varieties) in a polluted woods near Manchester and also in an unpolluted woods. He recorded their captures on film.

The results were quite definite: more of the light moths were captured in the polluted woods and more of the black moths were captured in the unpolluted woods. In recent years there has been a drive on in England to cut down on the smoke in industrial regions.

It is interesting that a count in 1974 on the frequency of the two forms of *Biston betularia* in the Manchester region showed an increase in the light forms over the

1958 count. In society's attempts to control various insects that are injurious to crops or that are household pests, a number of new chemicals have been developed.

In many cases a specific chemical has been found that would effectively control a given pest for a few seasons, but which seemed later to lose its effectiveness. A good example is resistance to DDT.

A study of some of these cases has revealed that resistant strains have developed. There seems to be little doubt that in some cases the resistance was a product of mutated genes and was inherited.

A similar situation has been observed in the fungus that causes wheat rust. As mentioned earlier, plant breeders have been able to develop rustresistant strains of wheat. Such a strain may work well in a given locality for a few years, after which it may become susceptible to rust.

It now appears that this happens because anew strain of fungus has developed. In this situation the fungus must either become adapted to the new strain of wheat or die out.

So just as the plant breeder practices artificial selection on the wheat, natural selection operates on mutations in the fungus and new strains appear.

With regard to the observation of the formation of new species, there is less to say. By and large, the first steps in speciation seem to require spatial isolation.

An exception to this, however, is found in the phenomenon of polyploidy a phenomenon rather common in the plant kingdom.

As a result of irregularities during cell division, a plant may come to have more than two haploid sets of chromosomes in each of its cells. The increase in number of chromosomes by multiples of haploid sets is called *polyploidy*.

Such a condition may arise in various ways from

diploid ancestors. One way this dan happen is by the formation of diploid germ cells. If a diploid egg is fertilized by a diploid sperm nucleus, the result is a zygote with the 4n condition, called *a tetraploid.* Many tetraploids are entirely fertile among themselves or are self-fertile.

But there is a high degree of sterility between the tetraploid and its ancestral diploid type. In such cases reproductive isolation has occurred without spatial isolation. Studies of the chromosomes of plants indicate that polyploidy has been a rather common method of speciation in plants.

This has not been true, however, with animals. It was stated in an earlier chapter that in the past most organisms have been classified primarily on the basis of morphological features.

In the discussion in this chapter the statement was made that separated populations of a species must remain apart spatially a long time in order for isolating mechanisms to become established, if they are to develop into separate species.

If this is so, then it should be possible to find related separated groups that are in the process of becoming completely reproductively isolated. In other chapter of this book reference was made to John Moore's studies on the frog, *Rana pipiens,* which has a distribution from Minnesota to Texas.

When specimens from Minnesota and Texas were crossed no viable offspring were produced, yet matings from closely adjacent regions between Minnesota and Texas always gave viable offspring.

Jens Clausen has described another interesting situation in a group of plants of the genus *Layia* of the daisy family (often called "tidy tips") in California.

These species differ in morphology, geographical distribution, and habitat preferences. Six species have been recognized. Figure elsewhere in this chapter shows their distribution. Geographically they fall into three groups.

One consists of two species: (C) in the region around San Francisco Bay and (F) directly east of the first in the foothills of the Sierras. The second group consists of three species.

These are located about 250 miles south of San Francisco: one (J) on the coast, another (M) about 50 miles inland, and the third (L) about 100 miles inland.

The third group consists of one species (P), and is located along the coast from southern California to north of San Francisco Bay. For part of its distribution it overlaps the distribution of members of the first two groups.

Clausen has made matings between all the species, and in all cases vigorous hybrids resuited. Hybrids between the two species in the first group showed 25 to 30 percent of normal fertility.

The same was true for the hybrids between the three species in the second group.

This might be taken to indicate that these species are really on the borderline between subspecies and species.

Hybrids between populations of the first group and those in the second group were much more often sterile.

Their chromosomes do not pair normally in meiosis. This would indicate that these *two groups* have certainly reached the stage of separate species. Hybrids involving the third group are almost completely sterile.

Furthermore, where members of this species overlap other species in their distribution, they occupy quite different habitats and there are no signs of gene exchanges between them and the members of the other groups.

This study provides an example of evolution in progress; for example, not all these species have developed complete isolating mechanisms.

ORIGIN OF HIGHER TAXONOMIC CATEGORIES

In our taxonomic system species, genera, families, orders, classes, and phyla are recognized. An account has been given above of the processes involved in the formation of new species. Have these same processes been involved in the formation of the higher categories, or have other factors been involved?

G. Ledyard Stebbins has given an interesting discussion of this problem. He says that the answer to the above question depends on the answer to the following questions: "Are the categories of the systematic hierarchy intrinsic entities which the naturalist merely discovers, or are they groups which naturalists themselves have established in order to understand better the complex patterns of living beings in nature?"

Stebbins goes on to say that if the categories are intrinsic entities, it would be predicted that the more intensively a group was studied by different workers, the more easily could they agree on the limits of the categories.

On the other hand, if the categories are created by investigators, it might be predicted that they would have difficulty in agreement on the limits of the categories because each .worker would have somewhat different ideas as to which characteristics are more important.

When the different groups of organisms are considered it is found that the first prediction holds for many of them. For example, the orders of mammals have been recognized as such for over a hundred years, and modern knowledge

has, with only few exceptions, confirmed the system. Within many of the orders of mammals modern families are also widely agreed upon. A similar situation exists in higher plants. In the pines and other conifers, genera are well defined and agreed upon.

However in some of the flowering plants, such as grasses, which are flourishing and evolving, genera are often hard to define. In a similar way among the mammals, the rodents, which are still flourishing, are often difficult to delineate.

This seems to indicate that groups that originated a very long time ago show clearcut characteristics that can be agreed upon easily, whereas groups that originated late in the evolutionary process may provide difficulties for the student of classification.

What does this mean? According to Stebbins we can only understand the origin of higher categories by taking into account extinctions-extinctions of intermediate forms. When many extinctions have occurred, gaps between groups are formed. This applies to the gaps between genera, families, orders, classes, and even phyla.

When intermediate groups are still living, there are no gaps and the student of classification has trouble. The factors or processes described above (mutation, recombination, natural selection, chromosomal change, and reproductive isolation) operate at all times in the process of evolution and result in the production of new species.

But to understand the origin of the higher taxonomic categories, the factors of extinction and time expanses of millions and millions of years must also be taken into account.

THE ORIGIN OF LIFE—A HYPOTHESIS

The discussion of evolution has been based on the assumption that a very simple form of life arose in the dim and distant past and that from this simple beginning, with the operation of the various causal factors of evolution that have been described, has resulted the great variety of living forms that have lived in the past and those that are now living.

In this study quite a bit has been said about the results of evolution and about the mechanisms operating, but practically nothing has been said about the origin of life.

Louis Pasteur provided the final proof that spontaneous generation of life does not occur under present conditions. Darwin and his successors have discredited the old idea of the special creation of living things just as we find them in the world today.

As a result of these two findings, biologists for many years had no real anchor as far as the origin of life was concerned. It was not until 1936, with the publication of Alexander Oparin's *The Origin of Life* that a reasonable working hypothesis appeared.

Although we may never be able to prove that life first arose in a specific way, it is now possible, with the information available, to formulate a working hypothesis concerning the conditions and circumstances under which life might have arisen.

This working hypothesis or modifications of it may make it ultimately possible for biochemists to simulate in the test tube the conditions under which the first living entities arose on the earth many millions of years ago and thus demonstrate how the first living things might have started.

The hypothesis involves spontaneous generation of a sort, but not the appearance of life all in one stroke and not under the same conditions that are found on the earth at present.

Rather what one may think of as the first living thing arose gradually, through many steps and in a changing environment quite different from that of today. Actually, to envisage the origin of life one must broaden the meaning of the term "evolution."

Students must consider an evolution of chemical elements, an evolution of inorganic chemical compounds, and an evolution of organic compounds before they consider living matter first arising. From the data of astronomy and chemistry there is evidence that our universe began between five and six billion years ago, possibly in an explosion.

Matter was in the form of elementary particles, such as electrons, protons, and neutrons. Soon these particles combined to form the elements helium and hydrogen, and later the other elements were formed. In time compounds formed, first inorganic and later organic.

It is estimated that our sun and its planets were formed a billion years later, which would make our earth about four and a half billion years old. Proof that spontaneous generation does not occur now is not proof that it could not have occurred under other environmental conditions.

What were the conditions of the earth and its atmosphere during the first two billion years of its existence? As the mass that made our earth cooled, atoms of the various elements combined to form simple compounds. In the surface gas of the earth mass were atoms of hydrogen, nitrogen, oxygen, and carbon, and these combined to form water vapor (H_2O), ammonia (NH_3), and methane (CH_4).

According to Harold Urey the primitive atmosphere of the earth contained water vapor, ammonia, methane, and hydrogen gas; there was no free oxygen and little, if any, carbon dioxide. Upon further cooling, a crust formed on the earth, vapors and gases condensed, and rain started to fall.

In time the seas were formed, in which were dissolved ammonia and methane, in addition to salts and minerals washed in by the rains. Much highenergy radiation in the form of ultraviolet light came in from the sun. The atmosphere was characterized by violent thunderstorms and much lightning. Such was the stage, according to the hypothesis upon which the first signs of life were ultimately to appear.

It was stated in other chapter of this book that, in addition to much water and minerals, living material is composed of the four basic kinds of organic compounds: carbohydrates, fats, proteins, and nucleic acids. We also know that even though many different organic compounds have been synthesized by chemists in the laboratory, organic compounds in nature are only formed by living organisms in cellular syntheses. Is it possible that organic compounds were formed in nature before the origin of life?

In the present working hypothesis it is assumed that formation of organic compounds did indeed precede the first living things and that during the first two billion years of the earth's history many kinds of organic molecules were formed and accumulated.

Some writers have referred to the contents of the seas of this period as "*organic soup*." There was energy available for such syntheses in the form of ultraviolet light and of lightning; raw materials were present; although no enzymes were present, there were millions and millions of years available in which these possible reactions could occur; and the compounds could have accumulated, once formed, because there were no decay bacteria around and there was no free oxygen to attack them.

Is there any evidence that organic compounds will form under conditions that simulate those assumed to exist in the early history of the earth? The now famous experiments of Stanley Miller in 1953 provide such evidence. Miller's experiments involved circulating a mixture of water vapor, methane, ammonia, and hydrogen gas in a closed system continuously for a week and over an electric spark.

The circulation was maintained by boiling water in one limb of the apparatus and condensing it in the other. When the liquid was analyzed, using paper chromatography, sizable amounts of the amino acids glycine and alanine were detected along with traces of a few other amino acids and some unidentified organic compounds. In a later experiment Miller was able to identify several other amino acids. The source of the energy for the syntheses in Miller's experiment was an electric spark, which simulated the lightning in the primeval skies.

Other investigators have used ultraviolet and high temperatures as energy sources for similar syntheses. In 1970 a husband and wife team, Akibs and Nurit Bar-Nun, working at Cornell University, were able to show that shock waves, such as might have been produced by thunderclaps or by meteors plunging into the atmosphere, could have been involved in such syntheses.

They filled one end of a tube with a mixture of ammonia, methane, ethane, and water vapor. This mixture was separated by a thin plastic membrane from the other end of the tube containing the relatively chemically inert gas, helium. These experimenters increased the helium pressure until the membrane broke. This produced a shock wave, and the temperature increased momentarily several thousand degrees.

In several different experiments they found that at least four different amino acids had been formed. They also found a relatively high yield, with 36 percent of the ammonia present converted into amino acids. Thus another possible mechanism for such syntheses has been demonstrated.

It has been shown that many kinds of organic molecules have a natural tendency to form large aggregates, and that in some of these the molecules orient in a specific way to provide a certain organization or structure. The organization of collagen is a good example.

Aggregates of various kinds may interact, forming larger and more complex entities. It has been suggested that growing aggregates, when they reach a certain size, may break up, with each particle able to grow.

It may have been, as Oparin suggests, that selection started to operate in the ancient seas, favouring those aggregates that could most readily capture from the environments the molecules necessary for their growth.

The question of the nature of the first particles that exhibited precise replication is still to be solved, but from what we know about genes and viruses, the assumption is made that this must have started when something like DNA was'present.

Since the original work of Miller, many other experiments have been performed. It has been shown that a number of important compounds, including *organic acids*, *purines*, *pyrimidines*, and many of the amino acids, may be synthesized from methane, *ammonia*, *hydrogen*, and water under *prebiological* conditions.

It is assumed that, in time, the changing conditions on the earth prevented the further formation of organic compounds. The original replicating particles, which may have been viruslike, presumably gave rise to cellular forms.

But just how the first cells came into existence we do not know. For a long period these simple forms lived upon the organic compounds in their environment. It should be noted here that these first forms of life were *heterotrophs*, not *autotrophs*, as the older theories assumed.

According to the resent hypothesis, these first living organisms utilized the organic material around them, in a form of fermentation, for theirenergy sources.

As has been seen in other chapter of this book, fermentation or anaerobic respiration is the first stage in the respiration of most living forms today and is the only form of respiration used by some organisms. It is not a very efficient process, but it does suffice for simple organisms.

In this next long period of the evolution these

primitive anaerobic forms were adding carbon dioxide to the atmosphere, but they were also depleting the supply of organic compounds that had formed and accumulated.

The production of carbon dioxide was important because this, as we know now, had to be present before any simple form of photosynthesis could appear. It is assumed that in this period, and before the store of organic compounds had become exhausted, one series of mutations (of the many that must have occurred in these simple forms) provided the mechanism for photosynthesis.

This made possible the great diversity of life found today. The first simple photosynthetic organisms were the first autotrophic organisms in the process of evolution. They, of course, began adding oxygen to the atmosphere. The addition of free oxygen to the atmosphere was important for two reasons: (1) with free oxygen present, organisms could evolve the mechanisms for aerobic respiration, a much more efficient form of respiration; and (2) with free oxygen present, a layer of ozone (03) formed high in the atmosphere and filtered out ultraviolet radiations so that life was possible on land and in the air below the protective layer.

We assume that from these first autotrophs evolved all other living things-the long succession of photosynthetic plants and the many kinds of heterotrophs, both plant and animal.

It was stated above that we do not know just how the first cells came into existence. However, it must be inferred that they were of the procaryote type. The oldest known fossils (3.1 billion years old) from South Africa were bacterialike.

Furthermore many of the fossils from the Gunflint formation in Canada (1.9 billion years old) resemble blue-green algae. The oldest known eucaryotic fossils are of green algae in the Bitter Springs deposits in

Australia, which are 1 billion years old. How did eucaryotic cells develop from procaryotic cells?

Again we really do not know. However, some biologists have suggested that many of the organelles that characterize eucaryotic cells were once independent organisms that somehow came to live symbiotically in larger host cells.

In a recent article Margulis describes how such a transformation might have taken place.

Not long ago there was no basis for a reasonable working hypothesis about the origin of life on this earth. Now that we have one, and with astronomers telling us that there are other planets like the earth scattered throughout the vast reaches of the universe, many predict that life has probably evolved on some of those other planets.

INDEX

A

B

C

D

E

F

G

H

I

K

L

M

N

T

U

V